Urban Transportation
Innovations Worldwide

Urban Transportation Innovations Worldwide

A Handbook of Best Practices Outside the United States

Edited by ROGER L. KEMP *and*
CARL J. STEPHANI

McFarland & Company, Inc., Publishers
Jefferson, North Carolina

LIBRARY OF CONGRESS CATALOGUING-IN-PUBLICATION DATA

Urban transportation innovations worldwide : a handbook of best practices outside the United States / edited by Roger L. Kemp and Carl J. Stephani.
p.   cm.
Includes bibliographical references and index.

ISBN 978-0-7864-7075-4 (softcover : acid free paper) ∞
ISBN 978-1-4766-1827-2 (ebook)

1. Urban transportation.   2. Urban transportation—Planning.
I. Kemp, Roger L.   II. Stephani, Carl J.

HE305.U6965 2015   388.4—dc23   2014045133

BRITISH LIBRARY CATALOGUING DATA ARE AVAILABLE

Cover image: high speed rail, Kaohsiung Station,
Taiwan (Chih-chang Chou/Dreamstime)

Printed in the United States of America

*McFarland & Company, Inc., Publishers
Box 611, Jefferson, North Carolina 28640
www.mcfarlandpub.com*

Roger and Carl
dedicate this book to
their grandchildren:

Roger to Anika, and
Carl to Megan, Kate, Paige, Joshua,
Nathan, Claire, Clayton, and Skye.

Acknowledgments

Grateful acknowledgment is made to the following organizations
and publishers for granting permission to reprint the material in this volume.

Center for Design Excellence
Center for New Urbanism
City of New York
City of Paris
ICLEI—Local Governments for Sustainability
International City/County Management Association
National Research Council
OpenPlans
Project for Public Spaces
The Next American City, Inc.
United Nations
Urban Land Institute
The Walkable and Livable Communities Institute (WALC)
World Future Society

Table of Contents

Preface

Introduction

Citizens throughout the world for years have considered the automobile as an instrument of freedom providing individuals with immediate transportation. People can now live in rural areas, or suburbia, and work in the city. Conversely, they can live in the city and have a workplace in the country. Because of housing costs in urban areas, many younger families are now forced to purchase their homes many miles away from the city in which they work. Suburbia and shopping malls throughout the world were made possible by the widespread use of the automobile. None of this would have been possible over the decades if not for the legal and financial commitments made by all levels of government throughout the world to construct freeways, regional highways, expressways, arterials, commercial avenues, and residential street systems.

Countries, states, regions, and cities throughout the world have experienced a number of significant diseconomies associated with the individual use of the automobile over the years. Traffic congestion and pollution in inner-city areas have led to a new wave of policies and practices to improve these conditions. Cities in countries throughout the world now commonly provide bicycle ridership options—bikeways and walkways—and public mass transportation options such as trains, light-rail systems, and the increased use of buses and bus rapid transit. Traffic

management practices, and the redesigning of public rights-of-ways for streets and sidewalks have been commonly undertaken to improve the environment of cities.

Local public officials, citizens, and nonprofit organizations throughout the world in increasing numbers, are investing in transportation demand management programs to facilitate positive planning practices in their downtowns, as well as enhanced general planning practices within their respective communities. The goal of these efforts is to improve our natural and man-made environments.

Public officials, especially in cities outside the United States, are learning that they have the municipal power, typically granted by their respective state and national governments, to shape their environments, both in their respective urban downtowns and their adjoining suburbs, to enhance the quality-of-life of their citizens. No single country has the best transportation planning practices, but cities in various countries have adopted the best state-of-the-art practices, and other countries, like the United States, can learn from all aspects of these adopted urban development transportation planning best practices.

Not only can those public officials and citizens involved in local government processes renew their respective downtowns and neighborhoods, they can also have a profound influence on new growth patterns within their jurisdictions. The implementation of the best contemporary urban planning growth management practices to decrease the use of automobiles, manage their usage, and come up with other transportation options for citizens, is quickly becoming a way of life in communities throughout the world.

The types of modern urban planning and development practices that regulate the personal use of automobiles, and provide other public transportation options, have been evolving. These options involve measures that promote planning practices to restore our natural environment. Such options are exemplified by trends in the facilitation of public transportation systems, pollution reduction practices, and the promotion of walking and the use of bicycles as desirable transportation alternatives, especially in urban centers. Many communities throughout the world have implemented such initiatives, and public officials and citizens in the United States can learn from them.

This reference work assembles, for the first time in a single volume, materials based on an international literature search and makes this information available to citizens, nonprofit organizations, and public officials in cities and countries throughout the world. The goal is to help educate citizens, as well as their public officials, about the latest and best use of these new urban city planning and development practices that can be used to improve the quality of life within their respective communities. The goal of such efforts is typically to reduce the use of vehicles, and to develop and promote other transportation options such as the use of bicycles and walking, and reasonably priced public transportation.

This volume is divided into three sections for ease of reference. The first section introduces the reader to the rapidly evolving and dynamic field of urban planning practices related to private and public transportation options. The second section, and by design the longest, includes numerous case studies, or best practices, about how cities

throughout the world, as well as their public officials and nonprofit organizations, are initiating measures to adopt these best urban planning practices which are essential to maintaining urban quality-of-life. The third section focuses on the future of cities and new trends in the urban planning movement that will improve our communities during the coming decades.

Also, several appendices have been assembled to promote a greater understanding of this dynamic and evolving field, as well as to provide resources for those citizens and public officials interested in obtaining additional information on the best international urban planning practices and major trends taking place in this field.

Based on the general conceptual schema outlined above, the three sections of this volume are examined in greater detail below under the headings of *International Transportation Planning, The Best Practices,* and the *The Future.* The *Appendices,* and *About the Editors and Contributors* portions, located at the end of this volume, are also highlighted.

I. International Transportation Planning

This section includes descriptions of some of the latest and most innovative trends in cities throughout the world in the dynamic and evolving field of urban planning as it relates to transportation. The state-of-the-art policies described include the best development and redevelopment practices throughout the world that decrease citizen reliance on the use of personal automobiles. More roads and wider roads are not the answer to increased traffic congestion. These introductory chapters provide an overview of this subject, and set the foundation for the various best practices that are presented in the following section of this volume.

Briefly, these chapters focus on the evolution of sustainable communities, the need to restore and improve various aspects of our natural environment, and the need to decrease our reliance on automobiles and to promote and provide other public transportation options. The types of modern urban planning and development practices evolving in cities throughout the world include measures that relate to the creation, protection, preservation, restoration, and enhancement of not only our natural environment, but also our built environment. Cities, and the colleges and universities that are located within them, are working together in this regard. Topics related to managing local governments in an era of world-wide information sharing, sometimes called managing in a *global era*, are also examined.

These chapters provide the framework and background against which the best international urban planning, development, and redevelopment practices, that have emerged in recent years, are examined. Cars are changing, and other transportation options are being provided, with the goal of restoring our neighborhoods and their natural environments.

II. The Best Practices

The various cities examined in this section, including the nations, states and provinces in which they are located, are listed in alphabetical order, along with highlights of the evolving best practices in the new discipline of international urban transportation planning, development, and redevelopment.

These best practice case studies provide an important and significant research foundation upon which to build a body of knowledge in the field of international planning, development, and redevelopment at the municipal levels of government. The best international practices section includes about 40

best practice case studies that involve 33 states and provinces, and 19 countries on six continents.

Terms vary from country to country when it comes to the names used for cities, states, and countries. Some nations use the term "cities" for all of their municipal governments, while others use the terms towns, villages, boroughs, and townships, to name a few. Other countries also use other terms like local authorities and federal districts. When it comes to states, some nation's use the terms prefectures and provinces, among others. Two fairly common international terms are countries and nations. So for the purpose of identifying the best practices in this volume the terms cities, states, nations, and continents are used.

A *Municipal Resource Directory (MRD)*, is included at the end of each chapter in Part II—to make it easier for the reader to obtain additional information from the municipality/city of interest. The following information is provided in each MRD to facilitate future research: the name of the municipality, its population, the region, the province/state, and country/nation in which it is located, and the municipality's website.

The various best practices described in this volume involve the following city governments as well as the states in which they are located (including special regions, emirates, prefectures, and provinces) and, lastly, the nations in which they are located (primarily kingdoms, republics, and united territories). The continents in which these nations are located are also noted. They are listed below under the categories of cities, states, nations, and continents to facilitate reference to different geographic areas of the world.

CITIES

Abu Dhabi	Beijing
Addis Ababa	Berlin
Amsterdam	Bogotá
Barcelona	Bolognia

Bremen
Changwon
Copenhagen
Dar-es-Salaam
Dubai
Egedal
Freiburg
Groningen
Halifax
Hangzhou
Hilden
Hong Kong
Istanbul
London
Lund

Manchester
Mexico City
Monrovia
Montreal
Münster
Nagano
Paris
Rome
Songdo City
Strasbourg
Tokyo
Toronto
Vancouver
Victoria

STATES

Abu Dhabi
Addis Ababa
Alsace
Baden-Wurttemberg
Balognia
Berlin
Bogotá
Bremen
British Columbia
Catalonia
Copenhagen
Dar-es-Salaam
Dubai
Egedal
England
Gyeonggi
Groningen

Hebei
Hong Kong
Istanbul
Monrovia
Nagano
North Holland
North Rhine-
    Westphalia
Nova Scotia
Ontario
Paris
Rome
Scania
Seoul
Tokyo
Quebec
Zhejiang

NATIONS

Canada
Federal Democratic Republic of Ethiopia
Federal Republic of Germany
French Republic
Italian Republic
Kingdom of Denmark
Kingdom of Spain
Kingdom of Sweden
Kingdom of the Netherlands
People's Republic of China
Republic of Colombia
Republic of Korea
Republic of Liberia
Republic of Turkey
State of Japan
United Arab Emirates

United Kingdom of Great Britain and Northern
    Ireland
United Mexican States
United Republic of Tanzania

BEST PRACTICES

Implementation and use of sustainable transportation options

Use of light-rail transportations systems

Encouragement of citizens to use bicycles for health reasons

Redesigning cars from primarily rural suburban uses to inner-city urban uses

Changing the national focus from cars to railway transportation systems

Utilization of mixed-use railroad station provides a valuable transportation hub

Development and implementation of a plan to use non-motorized transportation systems

Vehicular restrictions, and bicycle and pedestrian infrastructure, reduce traffic in city center

Growth and use of intermodal transportation EcoMobility systems

Using a public bicycle system to create an eco-friendly urban environment

Designing inner-city places for the comfort and enjoyment of pedestrians, rather than vehicles

Development of transportation networks based on sustainable urban mobility options

Using transportation systems capable of sustaining future inner-city urban growth patterns

Building bicycle lanes to connect the inner-city with its suburban communities

Developing affordable and convenient alternatives to the use of vehicles for transportation

Using the right tools for planning public street systems

Construction and strengthening of walkable communities

Development of the world's largest bike sharing transportation network

Strategies to reduce traffic on streets to allow for pedestrian-oriented uses

Developing public transit options for both commercial and residential communities

Development of transportation systems that mitigate climate change

Redesigning public spaces for people rather than vehicles

Innovations that reduce car travel and increase walking, cycling, and public transport.

Conversion of some streets into pedestrian walkways

New transportation and mobility strategies for a municipal Green Plan

Development and promotion of non-motorized transportation options

World's finest streets being redesigned for people rather than vehicles

Cities develop, improve, and promote bicycling and public transportation facilities and options

Cities implement Intelligent Transportations Systems (ITS) to reduce traffic congestion, as well as improve their environment

Bicycle sharing systems being used to reduce vehicular traffic, congestion, and pollution

Green transportation options reduce congestion, dependence on cars, and increase safety

Cities are creating transit-oriented waterfront developments

Public electric street rail lines are used to reduce the use of vehicles and eliminate traffic congestion in inner-city areas

Manufacturing of gasoline free cars, pollution free vehicles, is on the increase world-wide

Many public roadways are being re-examined and redesigned to enhance public safety

Cities are reducing the use of cars, and the number of parking spaces used to accommodate them, freeing up downtown space for other public uses

New transportation policies include traffic reduction, right-of-way and parking savings, and environmental protection.

III. The Future

The final section of this volume examines future transportation planning practices and development trends. The changing societal and environmental standards that are facilitating these trends are also examined. Regardless of the city, state/province, country, or continent, citizens throughout the world now have an interest in improving the quality-of-life where they live, and in protecting, restoring, and enhancing all aspects of their community's natural environment. These goals include regulating the use of personal vehicles, providing public transit options, improving the built environment, and redesigning existing roadways to serve people as well as vehicles. These appear to be generic goals, regardless of where a citizen lives, their race, ancestry, or their country of origin.

The various topics covered in this section include the planting of street trees on public rights-of-way, alternative forms of public transportation, such as the use of bicycles, the increased use of mass transit systems, redesigning the use of street rights-of-way for public use (the complete "streets movement," and "road diets"), the use of streets for different transit uses by citizens, public infrastructure financing options, and redesigning and creating successful public places.

All these subjects relate to the major trends that have been implemented and are evolving in the fields of international urban planning practices focusing on the future planning, development, and redevelopment of environmentally friendly neighborhoods in cities, states and provinces, and nations throughout the world.

Modern planning, development, and redevelopment, practices that achieve these goals are being implemented with greater frequency over the past few years in cities, states and provinces, and nations. The various diseconomies associated with past planning, development, and redevelopment practices dealing with public transportation systems which have resulted in the deterioration of our natural environments, and have engendered these positive planning practices.

Appendices

This is the first edited reference volume of its type on this topic that offers options for public officials and citizens in nations, and their states/provinces, to consider when implementing state-of-the-art best international public transportation practices for urban planning, development, and redevelopment. To help achieve that objective, several important reference resources are included as appendices. Their respective titles, and details about each of them, are briefly described in the following paragraphs.

Periodicals Bibliography. A listing of major U.S. periodicals focusing on contemporary urban planning and development transportation issues, as well as disciplines related to the various related issues and problems that are facing municipal governments today. The website for each publisher is listed to provide immediate access to these periodicals, as well as the information on how to acquire them. These periodicals may also be available in the reader's local public library free of charge.

Glossary. Because the dynamic and evolving field of international urban transportation planning and development relates to existing local government planning and development laws, regulations, and planning practices, a list of commonly used terms is included for the reader's information and reference. These terms are commonly used in the international planning field by public officials, government professionals, and citizens of cities in countries throughout the world.

Acronyms and Abbreviations. For the reasons mentioned above, the various acronyms and abbreviations that are increasingly commonly used in the field of international urban transportation planning and development are listed for the reader's reference. While seasoned municipal planners, and other professionals in this field, may have a working knowledge of these letters, other individuals reading this volume, such as public officials and citizens, may find the definitions of these commonly used acronyms and abbreviations helpful.

State Municipal League Directory. Most states in the U.S. have a professional municipal government association, which serves as a valuable source of information about their state's city governments. State leagues typically have copies of important municipal laws and policies, as well as model practices, available for public officials and cit-

izens in their respective states to review. The website for each state's municipal league is listed to provide the reader with access to these valuable documents and related sources of online information about urban transportation planning, development, and redevelopment practices, in cities in states throughout America.

National Planning and Development Resource Directory. This list includes all major national professional, membership, and research organizations serving public officials, professionals, and concerned citizens, in the United States. Many of these organizations focus on various issues related to cities, zoning, land-use practices, as well as major issues and subjects related to transportation planning, development, and redevelopment topics. The websites are identified for each of these U.S. organizations and associations.

International Planning and Development Resource Directory. This list includes all major international professional, membership, and research organizations that serve public officials, professionals, and concerned citizens, in nations throughout the world. Many of these organizations focus on various issues and subjects related to transportation planning and development, zoning and land-use practices, as well as other practices in these areas. The websites are listed for each of these international associations and organizations.

International Local Government Resource Directory. Most nations throughout the world have national professional associations that provide services to those employees that work in their local governments. This resource serves as a valuable source of information about each country's municipal governments. These national professional associations typically have copies of their nation's municipal laws and policies, as well as model transportation planning practices available for public officials to review for their nation. The name and the website for each of these international local government professional organizations are listed to facilitate future research in the area of desired state-of-the-art urban transportation planning, development, and redevelopment practices.

State Library Resource Directory. Each state in the U.S. has a central state library, and each one typically includes in its collection copies of their respective state laws, proposed and adopted, in an online database. This would include state laws and policies relating to transportation planning, development, and redevelopment. A city's local laws, policies, and practices, in every state, typically must be consistent with the laws and policies adopted by the public officials of the state in which they are located. Many state libraries also have copies of the various laws adopted by public officials in those cities and towns within their jurisdiction. These public libraries serve as excellent information resources. The website for each of these state libraries is listed to provide the reader with direct access to this valuable online information.

The last section of this volume, titled *About the Editors and Contributors*, briefly describes the backgrounds of the two editors of this volume, Roger L. Kemp and Carl J. Stephani, and highlights the titles and affiliations of the author(s) of each chapter. The affiliations of the contributors are as of the time the various articles selected to be included in this volume were written. Each contributor's affiliation also includes the name of the organization with which they are affiliated, as well as the city, state, and nation in which their organization is located.

The editors hope that the information contained in this volume will assist local public officials, government employees, and citizens, as well as leaders of municipal organizations, as they attempt to make sense out of, and try to adopt, evolving and emerging environmental and sustainability planning policies in their communities that relate to personal and public transportation systems. The best evolving practices from cities in countries around the world have been assembled to help achieve this goal. The future of America's municipalities depends upon the proper planning and management of our urban inner-city areas, as well as the neighborhoods and suburbs that surround them, especially when it comes to transportation options for citizens. Bad transportation planning practices have facilitated the deterioration of our natural environment over the years.

The transportation planning, development, and redevelopment field is evolving in such a dynamic fashion that it hard for public officials, government employees, and citizens, to keep up with best practices in the field. Citizens now expect the use of state-of-the-art international urban transportation planning practices by their public officials.

Citizens of cities in the United States, as well as in other cities throughout the world, not only expect, but demand, that prudent measures be adopted and implemented by their respective public officials to ensure that future growth will enhance the built environment and not negatively impact what's left of our natural environment. Positive transportation options help achieve these goals. Citizens throughout the world, including the United States, desire such transportation planning, development, and redevelopment policies and practices that will not negatively impact, but help create, protect, preserve, restore, and positively impact their natural environments.

The best practice case studies presented in this volume are typically applied in a piecemeal and incremental fashion. For the most part, public officials in government agencies, are busy doing their own thing within their own communities. They do not have the time to find out what their counterparts in other neighboring areas are doing, let alone what public officials are doing in other states and provinces, and other countries. For this reason, the case studies selected for this volume represent an important codification of knowledge on successful ways to improve the conditions of the urban transportation systems available to citizens, and to enhance their environments.

Lastly, and most importantly, the editors would like to thank representatives from numerous national and international professional and not-for-profit organizations for granting permission to reprint the chapters contained in this volume. If it were not for their contributions to this research effort, this volume would not have been possible. Now, with their respective permissions, this information can be used to inform citizens and public officials in cities, states and provinces, and countries throughout the world.

PART I. INTERNATIONAL TRANSPORTATION PLANNING

Chapter 1

Vehicles and Sustainable Communities

Center for New Urbanism

The Problem

MANAGING GROWTH, reducing traffic, creating sustainable development, and making smart transportation investments; these are all challenges we face today. New Urbanism is a development strategy that addresses these issues and more by creating communities that are livable, walkable, & sustainable, while raising the quality of life.

OUR CURRENT FORM of growth is unsustainable: a continuous outward expansion of development and the ever increasing need for more transportation capacity, despite the fact that regional population and employment are fairly stable. These trends threaten both the quality of life, as motorists spend more and more time in their cars and auto-dependency increases, and the quality of the environment, as green space continues to vanish while air quality and other environmental problems persist. The problem of constant traffic congestion is quite serious, and is reaching dangerous, epic proportions as our mobility is rapidly decreasing along with our quality of life.

1. 42,000+ Americans are killed every year in auto accidents. The Insurance Institute for Highway Safety reports that motor-vehicle ac-

cidents in the United States cause one death every 11 minutes, and an injury every 18 seconds. According to environmentalist Andrew Kimbrell, 90 million Americans have sustained disabling injuries in auto accidents, while more than 2.5 million Americans have died violent deaths on our highways.

This represents more than four times the 641,691 Americans killed in World War I, World War II, Korea and Vietnam combined. This is the equivalent of a fully loaded 747 crashing every 3 days and killing every passenger, week after week, year after year! If this many planes did crash, the airline industry would be shut down (as it was on September 11), but little is done about the deadly automobile situation.

WORLDWIDE, there are more than 2,500 fatalities and 50,000 injuries each day from traffic accidents. According to the World Health Organization, over 1 million people die each year in motor vehicle accidents. In the year 2000, 1.26 million people died worldwide as a result of road traffic injuries.

2. The road system is unable to efficiently move the overwhelming number of cars that clog it daily, resulting in constant congestion for thousands of miles across the country.

Originally published as "Sustainability: The Problem, the Solution," *Creating Livable Sustainable Communities* (July 2013), by the Center for New Urbanism, Alexandria, Virginia. Reprinted with permission of the publisher.

Since 1982, while the U.S. population has grown nearly 20 percent, the time Americans spend in traffic has jumped an amazing 236 percent! In major American cities, the length of the combined morning-evening rush hour has doubled, from under three hours in 1982 to almost six hours today.

3. Hundreds of billions of dollars are spent continuously expanding our road system in an attempt to keep up with the rising congestion. Despite the fact that the national interstate highway system is fully built, governments spend $200 million EVERY DAY constructing, fixing and improving roads in the U.S. This represents a large portion of our tax dollars directed towards constant road expansion, which actually furthers the problem rather than solves it.

According to a study issued recently by the Surface Transportation Policy Project, residents of the 23 American metro areas that added the most new road capacity per person in the 1990s saw the annual number of hours spent stuck in traffic increase by 70.4 percent.

4. The National Transportation Board predicts that delays caused by congestion will increase by 5.6 billion hours in the period between 1995 and 2015, wasting an unnecessary 7.3 billion gallons of fuel. 70 percent of all daily peak-hour travel on interstates now occurs under stop-and-go conditions. This peak "hour" has expanded to more than half of every day, and into the weekends as well.

5. The money and time spent in this congestion adds up to over $78 billion per year in unnecessary waste and inefficiency, up 39 percent since 1990. Time magazine has said that the average American motorist will spend 6 months of their life waiting for red lights to change, and over 5 years of life just stuck in traffic.

6. Cars are extremely expensive to own and operate, and collectively adds up to hundreds of billions of dollars spent annually by Americans. A third of all household expenses go to-

ward transportation: owning and operating a single vehicle cost between $8,000—$15,000 per year (large SUVs are at the top of this range). Since the average suburban family owns at least 2 vehicles, they are spending at a minimum, $16,000—$30,000 per year on transportation, not including children's cars.

7. Cars are highly polluting, and are the single largest source of poisonous exhausts that treat the air as an open sewer. Cars produce numerous air pollutants including carbon monoxide, nitrogen oxides, hydrocarbons, sulfur oxides, carbon dioxide, methane, and particulate matter, as well as toxic dust from tires and brake pads. The sum total of the 600 million cars driving daily around the planet causes a tremendous amount of permanent environmental damage in the form of toxic air, acid rain, forest damage, habitat destruction, crop damage, ocean pollution, fish contamination, climate change, and global warming.

8. According to the American Lung Association, air pollution from motor vehicles causes $40 billion to $50 billion in annual health-care expenditures, and as many as 120,000 unnecessary or premature deaths.

9. Other environmental concerns associated with automobile dependence include noise pollution, premature loss of farmland, wetlands, and open space (from auto-induced sprawl), soil pollution and contamination, water pollution from drilling, processing, and shipping of petroleum as well as from runoff of automobile fluids and road salts, and the scarring of natural landscapes.

10. Cars are the most expensive, most inefficient, most polluting form of mass transportation known to humankind, and when used in mass quantities, fail to provide even reasonable mobility.

Cars are totally dependent on oil, which is a finite resource that has reached its limit globally. Senior geologists and investment bankers for the oil industry say we have now reached world "peak oil" production and will begin to experience an irreversible decline in supply each year, until it runs out, or becomes too expensive to recover.

"We cannot fool ourselves—or the public—any longer: we can no longer build our way out of our highway congestion problems. It is not an environmentally or financially feasible solution."—Parris Glendening, former Maryland governor.

"There's never been an urban center in America with the magnitude of Northern Virginia that has ever road-built their way out of a traffic jam. God knows Los Angeles tried."—Sen. Richard L. Saslaw (Springfield) on whether it was time the state changes its way of developing and building roads.

"Traffic congestion is the #1 quality of life complaint of Americans."

Most traffic engineers now agree that we cannot build enough new road capacity to significantly reduce congestion. This means that doing so is a waste of hundreds of billions of dollars which could be more wisely spent building a network of new clean electric train systems.

"We need to look down the road and decide which forms of transportation will give us the convenience, reliability, comfort, speed, and safety we need. We can build a national passenger rail network and achieve all these goals. We can build more highways and airports and probably achieve none of these goals. Or we can do nothing and watch the whole U.S. become a congested, choked freeway. We can continue to insist on profitability and privatization, and then we won't have any transportation system at all."—Mark Hemphill, Editor, *Trains Magazine*

"Since the end of World War II, government policy has funded and encouraged the suburban lifestyle, subsidizing highways while starving mass transit and keeping gas taxes much lower than in some other countries."—Washington Post, August 2008

"The long-standing preoccupation with automobiles has degraded our communities to such a degree—physically and otherwise—that our destinations are no longer places worth reaching."—World Watch Institute

The Solution

The solution is in rebuilding our existing cities, and densifying our suburbs into compact, walkable towns and cities connected by extensive train systems. This form of development is known as a Transit Village, or *Transit Oriented Development* (TOD), and provides a higher quality, sustainable living environment. This gives us the choice of getting around by a number of different means including trains, bicycles, walking, rollerblading, and scooters.

TRAINS have the potential to solve many serious problems facing society, from reducing traffic congestion & airport congestion, to saving lives and the environment. They are the smart transportation solution for our society today and well into the future.

A good train system is a long-term, community-building investment that benefits many. The more new trains that get built, the better the entire system becomes. This is the finest example of smart transportation.

EDITORS' NOTE

The Center for New Urbanism's website (http://newurbanism.org/) has additional information on international transportation initiatives being undertaken in cities throughout the world.

Chapter 2

Transportation in the United States

Project for Public Spaces

I started at the New Jersey Department of Transportation in 1973 right out of college as a civil engineer trainee. For the first twenty years of my career as a transportation planner, I bought into the prevailing belief of the profession that the solution to congestion was to build more and bigger roads. We felt we were not doing our jobs properly unless enough lanes were added to ensure free flowing traffic 24/7, 365 days a year.

I was part of a profession that for five decades viewed its mission as simply accommodating the demands of traffic, whether on local streets or on state and national highways. The quality of life in communities and the condition of the environment were someone else's business; our job was to move cars and trucks as smoothly and rapidly as possible.

Gradually my faith in this "wider, straighter, faster" paradigm of traffic planning began to change. This occurred while I was in charge of a new unit at the New Jersey Department of Transportation (NJDOT) that had been created to meet with communities, business owners, public agencies and other community stakeholders to seek their support for various road projects. We were supposed to reduce community resistance, which was beginning to delay and even cancel projects. But as time went on, it became clear

to me that the real point of transportation projects should be building successful communities and fostering economic prosperity.

How Did We Get into this Jam?

Prior to the introduction of the automobile, Americans' concept of what constituted a good road had a vastly different meaning from today. Serving the community and creating an efficient and livable pattern of development were essential values at the center of street design. In short, transportation was fully integrated into land use planning.

The growing popularity of automobiles after 1910 created pressure for the federal government to become more directly involved in financing roads. Spurred on by cries of "Get farmers out of the mud," Congress passed the Federal Aid Road Act of 1916, which made continuous funding available for states to make road improvements. Motorists and other organized interests began to apply intense pressure to build more highways. In the 1930s many American officials visited the German Autobahn network and returned with a sense of urgency that we must create a national system of high-speed highways. This ultimately led to federal legislation in 1944 to establish the Interstate System and

Originally published as "Transportation in the U.S.: A Look Back, and Forward," *Back to Basics in Transportation* (December 2013), by the Project for Public Spaces, New York, New York. Reprinted with permission of the publisher.

in 1956 to fund it, which ignited the great road-building era of the 1950s, '60s and '70s.

Today, it is fashionable to vilify the transportation profession for ignoring the negative effects of large-scale road building on our communities. However, two men at the top of the transportation field during the years the Interstate highway system was shaped—Thomas H. MacDonald, chief of the federal Bureau of Public Roads (BPR), and his top aide, Herbert S. Fairbank— warned that thoughtless planning and improperly placed roads: "will become more and more of an encumbrance to the city's functions and an all too durable reminder of planning that was bad." They recognized that a shift of population to the suburbs was beginning to take a toll on cities.

Unfortunately, the federal government ignored MacDonald and Fairbank's vision of connecting highway development to a broader regional planning approach. As late as 1947, at the annual meeting of the American Association of State Highway Officials (now AASHTO), MacDonald urged his colleagues to do whatever they could to reverse politicians' refusal to subsidize mass transportation. Repeatedly, however, Presidents Roosevelt, Truman and Eisenhower along with Congress ignored these sensible recommendations for an integrated and balanced transportation network in the various federal highway acts that were enacted.

Starting in the 1950s, the transportation industry mobilized in an unprecedented way to deliver a mandate for a new generation of highways that would eliminate hassles and obstacles to the rapid flow of traffic. Planning in the U.S. became dominated by transportation engineers, while citizens, advocacy groups and planners in other fields saw their influence decline. The transportation profession was remarkably successful in convincing two generations of politicians, developers, construction industries, special interest groups, and the public about how things should be done.

With blinders firmly attached, the transportation planners and the nation at large ignored mounting evidence of the unintended consequences of this huge road-building campaign.

The Transportation Profession "Hits the Wall"

By the early 1990s, when the Interstate Highway System—one of the biggest construction projects in human history—was essentially completed, congestion in urban areas was still growing worse and community opposition was stronger than ever to new road projects. Within the transportation profession, there was a dawning recognition that something was innately wrong with the way we think about and design highways.

Yet not knowing any other way to operate, the transportation profession continued to plan new road projects in the same old way: attempting to meet peak demand according to a formula based on maintaining the free flow of traffic at the thirtieth busiest hour of the entire year.

When the inevitable resistance from affected communities arose, state DOTs found that invoking the "national interest," which worked so well during the Interstate era to override community objections, was no longer effective in pushing through the projects. By the 1990s, citizen opposition was able to bring many projects to a standstill.

Meanwhile, evidence was mounting that the wider, straighter, and faster approach was not solving the problem. The Texas Transportation Institute (TTI), in their 2005 Urban Mobility Report, revealed that over the last two decades of the 20th century, congestion indicators had spiraled out of control. The hours each year a motorist spends in congestion had quadrupled.

This was occurring because of the way street and road networks were being planned.

Spread out development made possible by the new highway capacity was creating congestion faster than transportation agencies could widen or replace failing highways. Furthermore, mass transit could not serve the new sprawling suburbs and street design made biking and walking all but impossible. This all caused vehicle trips and vehicle miles to explode at a rate many times faster than population growth. Transportation professionals and state DOTs watched these problems worsen but stood aside and did nothing in the belief that their job was building roads and that land use planning was someone else's responsibility.

Now it has become clear with each new fiscal year that construction costs for adding new capacity to roads is escalating sharply at exactly the same time our aging transportation infrastructure demands more and more attention. And in most states, revenue sources have been flat for almost a decade. State legislatures are afraid to mention the "T" word—taxes. Many roads and bridges built in the highway boom years between the 1940s and 1960's have aged to the point of needing major repairs or replacement, creating a towering backlog of Fix-It-First projects. All of these factors make it far less likely that even the most determined DOTs can build their way out of congestion.

As congestion has worsened in a transportation system focused on high-speed travel, so have other social problems. The skyrocketing vehicle miles traveled (VMT) in the U.S. is a major factor in oil consumption and CO_2 emissions that spur global warming. Our nation's public health indicators are also taking a nosedive. The National Center for Disease Control (CDC) reports that 25 years ago, only two states had obesity rates above 10 percent, and none had rates above 15 percent. Today, in a startling turnaround, no state has less than a 10 percent obesity rate, and only one is below 15 percent. Twenty-eight states—more than half the union—are above 20 percent, and one is above 25 percent.

The CDC classifies this rapid deterioration of public health as an "Inactivity Epidemic," and warns us that our increasing lack of fitness brings major health problems in addition to obesity: diabetes, cardiovascular disease, increased symptoms of depression and anxiety, as well as poorer development and maintenance of bones and muscles. While some still dispute our transportation system's role in this widening health crisis, new studies linking sprawl and obesity are accumulating.

How Can We Get Out of this Jam?

1. Target the "right" capital improvement projects first: The first step is to recognize that transportation decisions make a huge impact on land use and community planning—and vice versa. Major investments in roads should be pursued only in communities and regions with effective land use plans in place, which will protect the public investment in new highway capacity. With funds for expanding our road system now at a premium, we can no longer afford to invest in areas whose inadequate land use practices will mean the new roads are soon overburdened. Taxpayers deserve to know that their money will be spent in ways that solve our transportation problems—not in creating new problems. The transportation profession itself needs to accept that road projects carry significant social and environmental consequences. Transportation professionals need to heed Thomas MacDonald's and Herbert Fairbank's advice from the 1930s: "Freeway location should be coordinated with housing and city planning authorities; railroad, bus, and truck interests; air transportation and airport officials; and any other agencies, groups, and interests that may affect the future shape of the city." (Quote from THE GENIE IN THE BOTTLE: The Interstate System and Urban Problems, 1939–1957 by Richard F. Weingroff)

2. Make Placemaking and vision-based land-use planning central to transportation decisions: Traffic planners and public officials need to foster land use planning at the community level, which supports instead of overloads a state's transportation network. This includes creating more attractive places that people will want to visit in both existing developments and new ones. A strong sense of place benefits the overall transportation system. Great Places—popular spots with a good mix of people and activities, which can be comfortably reached by foot, bike and perhaps transit as well as cars—put little strain on the transportation system. Poor land-use planning, by contrast, generates thousands of unnecessary vehicle-trips, creating dysfunctional roads, which further worsens the quality of the places. Transportation professionals can no longer pretend that land use is not our business. Road projects that were not integrated into land use planning have created too many negative impacts to ignore.

3. Re-envision single-use zoning: We also must shift planning regulations that treat schools, grocery stores, affordable housing and shops as undesirable neighbors. The misguided logic of current zoning codes calls for locating these amenities as far away from residential areas as possible. Locating these essential services along busy state and local highways creates needless traffic and gangs local traffic atop of commuting and regional traffic, thus choking the capacity of the road system. It also makes walking or bicycling to these destinations nearly impossible in many communities.

4. Get more mileage out of our roads: The 19th and early 20th century practice of creating connected road networks, still found in many beloved older neighborhoods, can help us beat 21st century congestion. Mile for mile, a finely-woven dense grid of connected streets has much more carrying capacity than a sparse, curvilinear tangle of unconnected cul-de-sacs, which forces all traffic out to the major highways. Unconnected street networks, endemic to post–World War II suburbs, do almost nothing to promote mobility.

5. View streets as places: Streets take up as much as a third of a community's land. Yet, under planning policies of the past 70 years, people have given up their rights to this public property. While streets were once a place where we stopped for conversation and children played, they are now the exclusive domain of cars. Even the sidewalks along highways and high-speed local streets feel inhospitable. But there is a new movement to look at streets in the broader context of communities (see the Federal Highway Administration's website on Context-Sensitive Solutions.) It's really a rather simple idea: streets need to be designed in a way that fosters desired activities, whether that is local shopping on a Main Street, recreation on a street adjacent to a waterfront or park, or high speed vehicle travel on a freeway. A street's design, management, the traffic speeds fostered, and the modes accommodated should all reflect the specific purpose for that street.

6. Think outside the lane: Last but not least, the huge costs of eliminating traffic jams at hundreds of locations throughout a state will allow for only a few congestion hot spots to be fixed by big engineering projects each year. That means that most communities must wait decades or even a century for a solution to their problems unless we adopt a new approach that incorporates land use planning, community planning and alternative modes of transportation to address ever increasing volumes of traffic.

A New Approach to Transportation for a New Century

The transportation profession responded to a mandate from government officials in the post–World War II era to build a new generation of highways for public mobility and national defense. They should be commended for a job well done. A new generation of solutions is needed for the 21st Century, however, and this well-organized and well-trained profession should apply its talents to help us adapt to these new realities. We need a new vision of transportation that truly improves our mobility, sustains our communities, protects our environment and helps restore our physical fitness and health.

The transportation profession can no longer respond to mounting levels of congestion, as well as community and environmental dilemmas, by simply trying to widen existing roads or build new ones. New highways are now packed with cars almost as soon as they open. And today there is just not the money available for that kind of large-scale road building. Most states can't even keep up with the backlog of repair projects.

When I was at NJDOT, we came to realize the 1950's were long past and that we needed a new approach to meet the needs of our citizens. So we began collaborating with the public on solutions that took into account the whole context of communities being served by a particular road—the approach known as Context Sensitive Solutions. Like most people we initially believed that Americans were in love with the automobile and would demand we continue to provide them with bigger, faster roads separated from shopping and neighborhoods. While we did find this response in some communities, we were surprised by how many more communities firmly supported better land-use and community planning.

Americans may always love their automobiles, but that does not mean we want to spend all day stuck inside them. Transportation systems that afford Americans the choice of getting to places without using their cars actually offer more freedom than those where people are solely dependent on the auto to get everywhere. People easily understand this, and can see that a transportation network catering exclusively to cars has harmed our communities, compromised our health, fueled the environmental crisis and made us dependent on foreign oil.

There is nothing un–American about planning communities as a whole, and acknowledging that roads are just one of the elements that create a livable place. This was the common sense that guided our communities until at least 1920. While pre–20th century community planners were by no means perfect, they did create places where transportation was integrated into broader public hopes. The roads and bridges in these areas were built to foster economic development and quality of life in the community, not to hamper it.

If we are to really embrace the concept of healthy, livable communities that serve a diverse population and that make choices for mobility a priority, then we must integrate our transportation planning with other goals and we must design our roads for all users. In short, we must capitalize on the wisdom of our roots.

Editors' Note

The Project for Public Spaces' website (http://www.pps.org/) has additional information concerning the best practices for placemaking being used to improve neighborhoods in cities throughout the world.

This article was written by Gary Toth, Senior Director, Transportation Initiatives, for the Project for Public Spaces. The author thanks Ian Lockwood, Senior Transportation Engineer, at Gladdng, Jackson, Kercher, Anglin, Inc., Orlando, Florida for his contributions to this piece.

Chapter 3

Land Use Planning and Cars

Troy Russ

The road to creating livable communities is full of detours—many of which can be attributed to the transportation industry. Often times, transportation planners and engineers are blamed for being inflexible in roadway capacity requirements, access requirements, and street design, preventing the creation of livable communities. But transportation issues are not the only culprits.

Looking at the big picture, everyone in the land development community—architects, planners, and urban designers—should examine their own practice and ask themselves, "Are we partially responsible for the transportation profession's seeming inflexibility toward livable community design?"

For far too long, the land development community—either deliberately or through land development regulations—has created communities that are very burdensome to the transportation system. As a result, there is little flexibility in how infrastructure can be built, in turn limiting a community's livability and a region's sustainability.

Going forward, the "rules of the road" need to change, and both the land development community and the transportation industry need to change their approach as fuel costs, climate change, and the cost of public infrastructure affect the economics of community design.

It is time for the land development community to retool its design approach, embrace some well-understood transportation principles, and develop (or redevelop) communities from a transportation perspective. The result would be a stronger relationship with the transportation industry and a more solid framework for building livable, long-lasting, and successful communities.

The form, function, and character of transportation infrastructure and adjoining land uses are intrinsically linked, starting with the first crossroads, rail stations, or interstate interchanges. In fact, transportation infrastructure is the foundation of city building. It provides the means for circulation, establishes the block structure, organizes land uses, and influences the architectural qualities of buildings. It is also a city's most immediate and accessible public space.

What is the most significant barrier to creating livable, walkable communities? Incomplete street networks. Disjointed networks burden traffic operations, causing roadways to increase in size, limiting travel options, and restricting land development opportunities. A disconnected street network causes less-efficient, larger streets to be built.

Basic transportation planning principles suggest that a traditional network of con-

Originally published as "Land Writes: Rules of the Road," *Urban Land*, Vol. 66, No. 8 (August 2007), by the Urban Land Institute, Washington, D.C. Copyright, the Urban Land Institute, all rights reserved. Reprinted with permission.

nected streets has more capacity than a conventional suburban pattern. Well-connected street networks distribute traffic, enable more transportation choices, and increase land use opportunities. Properly designed networks provide transportation planners with alternative routing options, relieving the pressure to accommodate all traffic movements along a single corridor. Smaller, more efficient streets outperform conventional patterns. When it comes to roadway efficiency—measured by the number of cars per hour per lane–size *does* matter, according to the Institute of Transportation Engineers (ITE) *Highway Capacity Manual.*

For example, as a roadway increases from a two-lane roadway, which can handle 600 cars per hour per lane, to a three-lane roadway (which can handle nearly 900 cars per hour per lane), its efficiency increases by nearly 300 cars. The reason? In two-lane roadways, left-turning vehicles block through-traffic. The three-land street is the most efficient street size.

However, increasing street size beyond three lands will not increase efficiency. A five-lane roads, which can handle 500 cars per hour per lane, is less efficient than a three-land road, which can accommodate up to 900 cars per hour per lane. A seven-lane road is even less efficient, handling only 450 cars per hour per lane. The primary reason why roadways lose efficiency as they increase in size is intersection capacity and signalization. As roadways increase in size, protected left-turn signals are needed to allow left turns, robbing the through movement of "green-time" and reducing the efficiency of the roadway.

In addition to efficiency issues, five- and seven-lane streets impede the creation of livable, walkable communities. In places with such oversized streets, large parking lots often are constructed to buffer the buildings from the street. Meanwhile, the development community opts to erect a wall separating residential neighborhoods from the oversized

streets. As a result, land use options are limited and the walking environment is damaged. In addition five- and seven-lane roads reduce the viability of public transit as a transportation alternative.

The efficiency statistics do not mean that a three-lane road carries more cars than a five-lane road. But they do indicate that two two-lane roads handle more cars than a single four-lane road. This is noteworthy because two-lane roads enable land to be used for a variety of purposes while promoting community design principles such as allowing buildings to address the street, and creating walking and cycling environments.

In transportation planning, a common misconception is the belief that higher speeds allow for greater capacity than lower speeds, according to ITE's *Highway Capacity Manual*. The ITE has found that a free-flowing roadway will carry more cars per lane traveling 25 to 30 miles per hour (mph) (40 to 48 km per hour [kph]) than any other speed. That is because when speeds top 30 mph (48 kph), motorists allow for larger gaps between cars; yet speeds below 25 mph (40 kph) compromise the roadway's efficiency. The quality of the street influences the quality of the built environment. Likewise, the speed of the street influences the quality of the street and its roadside amenities. Therefore, the speed of the street affects the quality of the built environment.

In addition to increased vehicular capacity, speeds of 25 to 30 mph (40 to 48 kph) are more conducive to the creation of livable communities. This speed encourages a variety of successful streetfront land uses while enabling pedestrians and bicyclists to share the corridor. As such, urban roadway design solutions should limit corridor speeds to a reasonable 30 to 35 mph (48 to 56 kph). Higher speeds do not increase street capacity and often compromise the pedestrian-friendliness and land use compatibility of a corridor.

While well-connected street networks

and slower streets translate into increased efficiency and livability, roadway safety is perhaps the most important objective of the transportation industry. According to Eric Dumbaugh, assistant professor of landscape architecture and urban planning at Texas A&M University, when engineers design a roadway corridor transportation, they attempt to avoid two types of errors:

• Random error, which occurs naturally as a result of human fallibility. Random error assumes error is constant and fixed, and strives for a single, "fail-safe" design solution that is "forgiving" when human error is made.

• Systematic error, which is a design problem that results from mismatches in the interaction between people and their environment. Systematic error recognizes that designs may *produce* error, and occurs when a roadway encourages inappropriate expectations regarding safe operating behavior. Systematic error also focuses on understanding and addressing unsafe driver behavior, rather than attempting to engineer "fail-safe" designs.

A safe street design eliminates systematic error while simultaneously reducing the consequences of random error.

Two different approaches to roadway safety are implemented in the United States. The first approach resolves safety issues by increasing sight distances—flattening curves, eliminating conflicts, and removing obstacles, for example. These actions, however, increase design speeds, which compromise the quality of the pedestrian environment and adjoining land uses in urban areas.

The second approach focuses on lowering design speed so that motorists can adequately react to existing curves, sight limitations, and conflicts. Often referred to as traffic calming, this approach—coupled with lower design speeds—can increase the quality of the surrounding environment for pedestrian cyclists and adjoining land uses in urban areas.

Since the 1940s, conventional city-building practices throughout the United States have separated disciplines, rather than integrated expertise. As a result, many professionals in the land use planning community have lost sight of basic transportation planning principles necessary to build high-quality communities.

The land use planning community can no longer allow its land development codes and subdivision regulations to be created without basic transportation responsibilities, and can no longer allow private development initiatives to continue to burden the transportation system, which is alienating the transportation industry.

Instead, land use planners need to position community design so that transportation planners can design corridors that accommodate the needs of all roadway users and adjacent land uses—not just the needs of automobiles. This inclusive process will increase corridor livability, directly benefiting other modes of travel and adjoining land uses, without compromising vehicular travel patterns.

As the development community begins to adopt a more holistic process and implement basic transportation principles, the transportation industry will be able to provide the flexibility needed to build livable, sustainable, successful communities.

Chapter 4

Smart Growth Controls Urban Sprawl

Center for New Urbanism

"We are witnessing in essence the genesis of a set of rich, diverse and varied coalitions—each member bringing to the whole their own unique interests and views."— Bruce Katz, Director of the Center on Urban and Metropolitan Policy at the Brookings Institution, who foresaw the rapid increase of the forces of Smart Growth.

Sprawling land development has been consuming our nation's countryside at an alarming rate. Sprawl is defined as development that is dispersed, auto-dependent, single use, and impossible to walk to your daily needs. It is usually located along highways and in rural areas outside urban and village centers. There is a growing general awareness that low-density residential development threatens farmland and open space, raises public service costs, encourages people and wealth to leave central cities, creates serious traffic congestion, and degrades the environment and our quality of life. In the words of James Howard Kunstler, author of *The Geography of Nowhere* and *Home from Nowhere*, "The living arrangements Americans now think of as normal are bankrupting us economically, socially, ecologically and spiritually." In response to these trends, public interest groups, citizens and even government at all levels have begun to develop solutions for curbing sprawl, preserving open space, and rebuilding our cities and older suburbs. Smart growth initiatives identify the relationship between development patterns and quality of life by implementing new policies and practices promoting better housing, transportation, economic development and preservation of environmental quality.

Smart Growth on the Rise

Smart Growth promotes a shift in the conventional development patterns, and reaches out across disciplines. It is surprising the extent to which a wide variety of professionals, elected officials and individuals recognize that the ability to address development challenges and serious contemporary problems is dependent on a new vision of metropolitan and regional cooperation and an interdisciplinary process.

As a response to the increasing popularity of smart growth, several organizations have emerged across the nation. In the mid–1990s The American Planning Association joined 60 public interest groups across the United States to form Smart Growth America, a nationwide coalition that coordinates efforts to promote smart growth. After its debut in October 2000, it rapidly became the focal point for advocacy on a series of issues confronting communities nationwide. Today,

Originally published as "Smart Growth Advances Nationally," *Smart Growth Resources* (December 2013), by the Center for New Urbanism, Alexandria, Virginia. Reprinted with permission of the publisher.

it advocates better growth policies and practices at local, state and federal levels to promote farmland and open space protection, neighborhood revitalization, affordable housing, and the creation of livable communities. The University of Maryland, in cooperation with former governor Paris Glendening and the State of Maryland, created the National Center for Smart Growth. It endeavors to lead the nation in research-based knowledge and education by tackling a wide range of growth, preservation and development issues.

In November last year the U.S. Environmental Protection Agency gave out the first annual National Smart Growth Awards to encourage anti-sprawl planning. This event is significant in that it signals recognition by the U.S. Government that land use and transportation policies directly influence smart growth, energy conservation, and environmental protection. According to the Environmental Protection Agency (EPA), "Smart growth development practices support national environmental goals by preserving open spaces and parkland and protecting critical habitat; improving transportation choices, including walking, bicycling, and transit, which reduces emissions from automobiles; promoting brown field redevelopment; and reducing impervious cover, which improves water quality." The award recognizes outstanding achievement in smart growth by state, local or regional governments in four categories: Built Projects, Policies and Regulation, Community Outreach and Education, and Overall Excellence in Smart Growth.

EPA's 10 guidelines for smart growth are:

1. Mix land uses
2. Take advantage of compact building design
3. Create housing opportunities and choices for a range of household types, family size and incomes
4. Create walkable neighborhoods

5. Foster distinctive, attractive communities with a strong sense of place
6. Preserve open space, farmland, natural beauty, and critical environmental areas
7. Reinvest in and strengthen existing communities & achieve more balanced regional development
8. Provide a variety of transportation choices
9. Make development decisions predictable, fair and cost-effective
10. Encourage citizen and stakeholder participation in development decisions

In what signals a major victory for the Smart Growth and New Urbanism movement, a new funders' network has been formed. With the backing of some of the country's most influential foundations, this new network pools resources to help fund smart growth activities and projects around the country. "It now operates in every region of the country—indeed it's performed a dozen regional assessments of smart growth goals, strengths and strategies, involving 31 states, some 500 leaders and 40 foundations" according to Neal Peirce in his recent article Committed Foundations: Smart Growth's Ace In The Hole. "The network has sought to give smart growth a firm intellectual base through 10 papers on topics ranging from smart growth's role in transportation reform to its implications for biodiversity and environments for America's aging."

This is just a glimpse at the broad number of organizations attempting to educate by advocating smart growth principles as an alternative framework to build communities and help create and preserve a sense of place. The Smart Growth America's website states in their mission "We're not the only ones calling for smart growth. Increasingly, citizens across the nation are demanding it—in polls, in the market, and at the ballot box. Americans want fewer hours in traffic and more opportunities to enjoy green space; housing that is both affordable and close to jobs and activities; healthy cities, towns and suburbs; air and water of the highest quality; and a landscape our children can be proud to inherit." For all these reasons Smart Growth continues to move forward across America with the increasing participation of the general public. In a recent case last April, for example, more than 1,000 citizens from across Michigan attended a series of public hearings. Michigan's hearings revealed overwhelming support for controlling sprawl and reflected an influential public consensus for state action.

In response this popularity, more and more local governments are turning to the policies of smart growth to solve their problems. Over the past few years a number of reforms have been enacted across America according to the American Planning Association: 17 governors issued 19 executive orders on planning, smart growth, and related topics during the past two years compared to 12 orders during the previous eight years combined; Eight states issued legislative task force reports on smart growth between 1999 and 2001, compared to 10 reports between 1990 and 1998; 27 governors—15 republicans, 10 democrats, and 2 independents—made specific planning and smart growth proposals in 2001. During the same time periods, voters passed numerous measures nationwide to limit sprawl, halt road-building projects, and to get new train systems built.

"New Governors are taking the Smart Growth Mantle" headlines a Smart Growth America press release in February this year as it introduced former Maryland Governor, Parris Glendening as head of SGA's Smart Growth Leadership Institute. "We are trying to work with elected officials by sharing our experience" says Glendening in a live interview, whose interest in Smart Growth began at least 35 years ago. Today, he is recognized for creating the nation's premier Smart Growth program as governor of Maryland. "We understand there is no exact model

to follow since every state is different and needs a different approach, but we provide examples of things that have worked." Since Glendening left office he has continued to make a significant contribution in the fight against sprawl. At the same time, several new governors in other states are on a course to continue his legacy.

Governor McGreevey of New Jersey recently signed a sweeping new anti-sprawl executive order. Environmental and other groups battling sprawl were quick to praise the order and deem it the most comprehensive attack on over development ever initiated by a governor. Pennsylvania's new governor, Ed Rendell, made smart growth policies a priority and hired Roy Kienitz, who helped implement Maryland's Smart Growth Initiative as that state's planning director. In Massachusetts, Mitt Romney promised to implement smart growth principles in addressing the state's critical issues of housing affordability, environmental protection and transportation investment. South Carolina's governor, Mark Sanford, made the issue of "school sprawl" a central theme of his state of the state address. Utah's governor Mike Leavitt helped found the Utah Quality Growth commission and has negotiated an agreement to finance the development of commuter and light rail systems. Smart growth America serves as a major resource to any of these administrations by providing them with a range of tools to follow in an effort to halt sprawl. "There is such a range of tools," says Glendening, "but the feeling is that what seems to work best across the country is a series of incentives."

There are a number of specific tools governments can use to help stop sprawl. In most cases it is easier and cheaper to build on virgin land than to reuse urban areas. "Any builder would tell you it is easier to buy a farm, change the zoning and build out there somewhere than to take an old and beautiful building, restore it and convert it into condominiums," says Glendening. "Generally the laws are stacked against that type of reuse," he adds. He goes on to say that there is a need for a change in the regulations. According to Glendening the government should not use its resources to subsidize sprawl, instead, it should stop building schools, roads, and sewer lines in order to stop encouraging sprawling developments. "On the other hand if a developer or investor wants to use the road to improve smart growth, the government should participate as a partner and help with the construction," states Glendening. He feels everyone benefits economically, from the government to the homebuyer. "The net effect there is to create a dramatic impact on the bottom line," he adds.

Solutions

Current government policies favor an increase rather than a decrease in the use of cars. There is a need for a shift in government investment towards transit-oriented development, which currently has a number of barriers to overcome. "The government policies are generally anti-transit and pro sprawl," says Glendening. "In terms of governmental policy, roads are generally free but transit is increasingly expensive. So in federal and local policy we [have to be] really committed to transit and a transit-oriented budget for transportation." According to Glendening, about 80 percent of the budget is spent building roads and 20 percent for mass transit. "There needs to be a redirection towards 50 percent investment in highway and 50 percent mass transit," he adds. "What we need are two things: one is a change in land use

so we won't continue to go forward [in the same direction] and be in need of more transportation, and the second is a much better balance between transit and road building," suggests Glendening. The fact is that we need to greatly reduce road building in America, and transfer the majority of the money into building state-of-the-art train systems like in Europe. "A rational well-used mass transit system is key to our strategy," says Glendening. "It is going to involve several decades, but step by step we can get there. I am encouraged by things that are going on," he adds.

Smart Growth advocates provide a valuable source of information and a significant contribution to the future of our communities. "More than anything else we want to raise the general public's awareness of the issue of sprawl," says Glendening. "An educational campaign would help the average voter understand the issues," he adds.

We now acknowledge that sprawl and high car dependence is bad for us and the planet, and that together we have the tools and energy to face the tremendous challenge ahead in changing the way we build our communities. In the words of Bruce Katz, "Perhaps the most important glue holding these coalitions together is the simple notion that our current growth and development patterns are reversible."

Editors' Note

The Center for New Urbanism's website (http://newurbanism.org/) has additional information on international planning initiatives being undertaken in cities throughout the world.

This article was written by Jessica Tirado, a contributing author to the Center for New Urbanism.

Chapter 5

Electric Cars Replace
Gas-Powered Ones

Michael Horn

By the middle of this century, the United States may have completely transitioned from gasoline to electric vehicles, or EVs. Its economy will then enjoy an EV-energy bonus, somewhat like the peace bonus at the end of the Cold War, but this one will result from saving half of the money that U.S. consumers previously spent on oil imports to make gasoline for all their cars.

By then, the bankruptcies of GM and Chrysler will be a long-forgotten anomaly in the history of the auto industry, because once the auto companies replace the 254.4 million gasoline-powered cars in the United States with electric ones by mid-century, they will create a manufacturing boom that completely wipes out the losses that they sustained during the 2008 recession.

These electric cars will have come a long way from the twentieth-century electric prototypes that required drivers to stop frequently to recharge the batteries, making highway driving nearly impossible. In the coming decades, highways might be outfitted with guardrails that emit harmless radio-frequency charging waves. Special coils inside each car will receive the waves and harness them to recharge the battery continuously while the car is driving. The human passengers will have the luxury of never having to stop for a refueling.

The chore of pumping gas will seem akin to shoveling coal, and the ignominy of driving out of a gas station with the smell of gasoline on your hands from the pump handle will be memories only older folks might recall. The electric car, emitting no fumes and being virtually silent in operation, will make the gasoline-powered cars of the past seem utterly primordial by comparison.

Late in the century, historians may even debate why it took so long to make the transition from oil to electricity, when oil was so inefficient, involved so much peril, and all the elements necessary for transition to electric were well in hand by the end of the twentieth century.

Gasoline's Problems

But back to the present, where for the last 100 years, the U.S. economy has continued to depend on the gasoline-fueled, internal-combustion engine for powering cars and trucks. This engine is only a small technological step above the steam engine. The fact that it's primitive is not the problem; it's

Originally published as "Roadmap to the Electric Car Economy," *The Futurist*, Vol. 44, No. 2 (March–April 2010), by the World Future Society, Bethesda, Maryland. Reprinted with permission of the publisher.

that it is so inefficient. For every $1 that we spend on gas, 85¢ is wasted in heating the engine block and the surrounding air (the reason it needs both an oil and water pump to cool it); only 15¢ goes into moving the car down the road.

Obtaining the gasoline is fraught with serious environmental and political perils. We are facing many questions concerning global warming, not the least of which is how much automobile exhaust contributes. Then there's the question of what happens to our frail economy if our oil supplies are disrupted. But our societal attitude is curiously sanguine concerning how imperiled we make ourselves when we rely so heavily upon the gasoline-powered engine. We seriously need to reconsider our options.

Continued Dependence On Oil

Over the last 30 years, each American president has vowed to reduce the nation's consumption and dependence on oil (i.e., gasoline) by increasing gas mileage of all cars and light trucks through a program called CAFE (Corporate Average Fuel Economy). After 30 years, however, the United States is still locked into an oil economy, and CAFE, which has done little to alleviate the situation, continues to be its only option for reducing oil imports.

President Obama has continued to follow the course of previous presidents and recently raised the CAFE standards from 27 mpg to 35 mpg. He also enacted a $3 billion cash-for-clunkers program in an effort to get gas-guzzlers off the road. At the same time, billions are being spent on alternative-fuel cars, with research money still being spent on getting fuel out of corn. America is desperately trying to wean itself off oil imports from unstable sources around the world, but has yet to come up with a winning formula for doing so. When the CAFE was intro-

duced in the 1970s, the average fuel economy mandated was 18 mpg. Now more than three decades later the fuel standards have gotten to 35 miles per gallon.

At that rate of development, it would take about 350 years for the internal-combustion engine cars to reach the more than 200-mpg efficiency already realized by battery-powered cars today! So why not put all available resources into making the electric car the successful replacement to the gasoline-powered car? It's been tried before, and we see the result all around us: Electric cars are far from becoming mainstream.

The problems were not so much with the cars, but with the environment into which the cars were cast. Back in 1990, the California Air Resources Board (CARB) introduced new regulations mandating that progressively larger shares of auto manufacturers' fleets of cars must produce zero emissions: By 1998, according to the CARB mandate, 2 percent of all the vehicles on California's roadways would have to be zero-emissions vehicles (ZEVs); by 2003, 10 percent. The only ZEVs circa 1990 were battery-powered cars. So, somewhat reluctantly, the auto industry began projects to develop battery-powered cars. GM and Toyota produced very impressive electric cars (based on relatively primitive battery technology compared to today) that eventually attained ranges of over 100 miles.

After huge investments and low sales, however, General Motors and Chrysler filed a lawsuit against CARB in 2002 to reverse the ZEV regulations. The auto companies got their way, and CARB was forced to repeal its mandates for 2003 and 2004. The program resumed in 2005, but with vastly lowered expectations. Today, of the more than 28 million cars registered in California, only 30,400 of them—less than a tenth of one percent—run on batteries.

Regardless of the reasons, the electric cars were doomed from the start because there were few places to recharge them, recharging them was time consuming, and the vehicles have limited range.

The electric car still faces the obstacle of having places to recharge, and now the Obama administration is putting money into electric car technology research without, once again, providing for an infrastructure to support it. It's like planning an aquarium and buying the fish before you build the tanks for the fish to swim in. Right now the electric car is like a fish out of water.

The other side of this issue is the auto industry, which has been burned by the hundreds of millions of dollars lost in the last round of electrics that failed to capture the imagination of all but a small sector of the car-buying public. Auto manufacturers realize the issues and limitations of the electric car and don't want to invest millions or maybe billions more in a car that might not sell. So the bottom line becomes this: Above and beyond getting society away from dependence on oil, what makes the electric car worth all the trouble?

Benefits of the Electric Car

The thing that makes the electric car worth all the trouble is its efficiency. Money and energy are interchangeable. When we waste energy, we waste money, and we waste a tremendous amount of money on oil. Half of all the oil that the United States imports goes into making gasoline. Switching to electric cars would eliminate about half of U.S. oil consumption and dependency.

According to the Energy Information Administration, America used about 137.8 billion gallons of gasoline in 2008. With an average price of $3.55 per gallon that year, the nation spent nearly half a trillion dollars on gasoline! But the worst part is that, since the gasoline engine is only 15 percent efficient, 85 percent of the money spent went up

in smoke. That's $400 billion that was simply wasted. Any economy that has to contend with that degree of wasted resources is going to be in trouble, sooner or later.

In EVs' favor, most of the extra electricity needed to charge up the new swarm of electric cars wouldn't be coming from burning oil, because it's not the fuel of choice for the electric power industry. Moreover, most of the cost to charge up a battery powered electric car actually goes into moving the car and is not wasted. That's what I mean by efficiency. Even the charging process is pretty efficient, at better than 85 percent, according to a study by Sandia Labs.

Along with all the efficiency there's also the immediate and complete cessation of direct air pollution. Despite what detractors of the electric car say, there is no pollution coming out of an electric car itself. There may be pollution created at the point where fossil fuels are burned to make electricity, but at least there are not engines pumping out fumes on every street corner of your city. And besides, there are ways to cap pollution from power plants and keep it from escaping into the atmosphere.

Making the EV Future Viable

Despite public perception of electric vehicles as slow, ugly "golf carts," they can be made to accelerate as fast as any gasoline-powered cars. In fact, an electric motor can accelerate a car faster than any gas engine, and it has done so many times—just check out the YouTube video, "unveiling of the Tesla." The electric car is also virtually silent and very clean, with no oil drips on the driveway or fumes filling up the garage while you warm up the engine in the winter—their motors don't even need to be warmed up!

Electric cars only expend energy when they're moving, so if you're stuck in a traffic jam, at least you can take comfort in knowing that your electric isn't using any energy at all.

Also, it's nearly as efficient going 50 mph as it is going 5 mph. Electric cars can be made large or small, and can carry as many people and look as cool or sophisticated as any gas powered car. They can be made in two-wheel or four-wheel drive. Electric motors are small enough to be the basis of more-flexible interior cabin designs.

The electric motor will also last much longer than its gasoline-powered counterpart because it contains only one moving part. The electric car will be another electrical appliance that runs for years with virtually no maintenance. Just think, when was the last time you needed to have your clothes dryer taken in for an oil change or new spark plugs? They both have similar electric motors. A gasoline car needs something done to it starting around the first three months and then every 3,000 miles—from oil changes to timing-belt replacements, ad nauseam. That in itself is part of the problem in breaking the auto industry away from the gas-engine cars: The industry's business model is based as much on service and parts as it is on sales. Look how much more space at the dealership is devoted to the service and parts department compared to the sales showroom. Clearly, the auto industry will need a better business model than the planned obsolescence that got it so much mileage in the 1950s, '60s, and '70s.

Being so reliable, the electric car may spawn some other novel approaches that would change the way we look at cars. For example, as styling fads change over a few years, instead of buying whole new cars, vehicle owners might just have the recyclable, outer body panels swapped to keep up with the latest trends or just for the sake of change. The auto industry would realize a way to augment money lost on service and parts by marketing newly styled outer panels over the durable electric-drive machinery. GM proposed such a swappable body in its "Skateboard" design, built around a fuel-cell electric vehicle.

Prospects for an "Electric Car Economy"

The electric car economy is one that has eliminated its dependence on oil and transitioned to a vastly more efficient means of powering its cars and trucks. It has removed the addiction to oil that binds consumers to perilous sources of energy. It has removed the issues that distract researchers from developing alternative sources of energy. And it's an economy that provides everyone, businesses and individuals alike, with hundreds of billions of dollars to spend on other things besides the oil they formerly imported to make gasoline. It's an economy that's pumped up by its newly found efficiency. But to create the electric car economy, we first have to make the electric car a real and complete replacement for the gas powered car.

The first thing required to make the electric car a viable replacement for the gasoline-powered car is to create the infrastructure that supports the electric car. This infrastructure will be, by its very far-flung, distributed nature, enormous. According to the U.S. Census Bureau, there are 117,000 gas stations in the United States—or as they prefer to put it, one gas station for every 2,500 people. That's the reason that the gasoline-powered car is so successful—it has a vast gasoline distribution infrastructure.

To be as successful, the electric car needs a comparable infrastructure, but we won't need to start from scratch. Electricity is much simpler than liquid or gaseous fuels, which need to be piped or trucked and then stored in huge tanks at the point of sales. Electricity is available everywhere through power lines. Gas stations already have plenty of electric power to run anywhere from four to 12 big pumps and dozens of high wattage light fixtures. Every gas station will need to conform to a government regulation to have at least one electric car-battery charger to begin with, by a reasonable deadline. Eventually, they'll need more than one charger per station, as people catch on that the electric car can now go further than the city limits. The planned Smart Grid will help accommodate the gradually rising load.

In order for the plan to work, these battery chargers will have to charge a car battery quickly, unlike the home plug-in power sources that take all night. Fortunately, the rapid-charge technology is a reality right now. In fact, one such system, called PosiCharge, was able to charge an electric car battery made by Altairnano in less than 10 minutes.

Standardization is another issue that must be addressed. The batteries and charging-control modules on electric cars have to be standardized so that any vehicle can be recharged anywhere. The plan won't work if you need to go to special recharging stations for a charger that works for your car. At present, different automakers are planning to use different chemistries and internal structures in their batteries. Consequently, not every battery would fit a given service station's charging system. This would put an electric car in the same position a gas-powered car would be in if there was no gas station in the community. How far would a gas-powered car go if there were no gas stations? The government and the auto industry will need to implement standards so that there is a uniform infrastructure of chargers and a uniform code, and that cars everywhere comply with the uniform code. That way, drivers everywhere will be able to quickly charge up their cars without damaging them.

My idea is really quite simple, but it will require some government regulations: Put rapid electric chargers in every gas station, because that's where people already go for gas. Drivers can pull into their local gas station, just as they always had in the past, and quickly charge up their shiny new electrics. Nothing much changes for the driving public except that everyone will be saving that huge amount that was once wasted on gasoline.

The advantages of promoting an all-electric-car economy are manifold, including the enormous savings in money and the substantial reduction in need for foreign oil supplies, which threaten further economic distress. Air quality would improve significantly. The electric-car economy represents a monumental plan that doesn't actually cost that much—an estimated $3.5 billion. With the right organization and determination, a future of clean, efficient, oil-free electric cars is attainable.

Chapter 6

Light-Rail Transit and Economic Development

Tom Brandes *and* Brad Scheib

The concept of transit-oriented development (TOD) began to emerge in earnest in the 1990s, with the planning and development of light-rail transit (LRT) and commuter rail systems connecting the cities of Minneapolis and St. Paul to major growth corridors. Nearly 20 years later, the 12-mile (19.2-km) Hiawatha LRT line, with 17 transit stations, connecting Minneapolis with the Mall of America in Bloomington, has been built. In 2007, the Hiawatha line carried 9.1 million passengers and averaged 27,000 riders per weekday, exceeding preconstruction ridership projections for 2020 by 8 percent.

The 40-mile-long (64-km) Northstar Commuter rail line with six stations is under construction and expected to open in late 2009, while the 11-mile (17.6-km) Central Corridor LRT line connecting the downtowns of Minneapolis and St. Paul is projected to open in 2014.

But even after spending $715 million on construction using federal, state, regional, and county funds, key questions remain. What impacts have investments in transit had on urban development? What has been learned about TOD? Can these lessons be applied elsewhere?

Station area master plans completed along the corridor projected that new development spurred by the Hiawatha Line would generate roughly 7,100 new housing units and 19 million square feet (1.71 million sq. m) of commercial development with up to 68,000 new jobs by 2020. More than 8,000 new housing units have opened or are under construction along the line, with another 6,250 proposed by developers.

Since the Hiawatha line first opened between Minneapolis and Bloomington, a significant amount of new development has occurred within a half mile of station areas. More than 20 new development projects have been completed, four are under construction, and 15 are in the planning/entitlement stages. LRT is credited with being a major factor in stimulating this development.

The Hiawatha LRT line opened in 2004, but LRT was not originally planned for the Highway 55 corridor. Planners first envisioned a freeway connecting Minneapolis/St. Paul International Airport to downtown Minneapolis. In the 1970s, debate began on a dedicated transit way within the corridor, but it was not until the 1990s that this option began to take shape.

Then-Governor Jesse Ventura added political muscle to the debate and made it his goal to ride the train before he left office. Although the line did not open until two years after his term ended, the LRT line was approved and funding secured during his administration.

Using a streamlined design/build contracting approach—one of the first such projects under the supervision of the Minnesota Department of Transportation (MnDOT)—and with help from the federal government, the Hiawatha line was designed and built in less than three and a half years.

Although the TOD concept seemed like a good idea, it was new and untested, and therefore viewed as somewhat risky by local developers. However, Hennepin County, the city of Minneapolis, and various neighborhood groups began to envision TOD projects around each of the stations.

Station area master plans were developed for virtually all of the stations along the Hiawatha Corridor, and significant planning efforts also have been completed for other corridors. Next, developers began to assemble their projects. Each of the Hiawatha line's 17 stations was designed to reflect the unique character of its location.

Bloomington Central Station (BCS), when completed, will comprise 1,063 new residential units (913 for sale and 150 for rent), 300 hotel rooms, 2.55 million square feet (229,500 sq. m) of office development, and 75,000 square feet (6,750 sq. m) of retail development, in a 50-acre (20-ha) site adjacent to an international airport, a national wildlife refuge, and the Mall of America.

The centerpiece of the $1 billion development project is a two-acre (0.8-ha) urban park directly adjacent to the station platform. The first of two 16-story buildings, called "Reflections," opened in 2006 and more than 90 percent of its units have been sold to date—despite today's economic conditions. If not for the LRT station located adjacent to the project, it may not have survived the economic downturn nearly as well as it has.

Households within walking distance to LRT stations are more likely to endure economic downturns than those located farther from convenient access to light-rail systems. This connection appears to be gaining momentum as developers along the Hiawatha corridor continue pursuing aggressive redevelopment projects.

In addition, a large office tower that serves as the corporate headquarters for HealthPartners, a not-for-profit HMO (health maintenance organization), sits directly adjacent to the transit station. According to Mark Fable, project manager for developer McGough Development in St. Paul, Minneapolis, the train has influenced decisions of HealthPartners employees about where to live, with many choosing to live along the corridor. "The train is perhaps the best marketing tool for the project," points out Fable.

TOD is a difficult investment decision to make when a firm commitment from elected leadership at the state level is still lacking. Funding for regional investment faces strong competition from more traditional transportation infrastructure systems, such as roads and bridges.

In theory, TOD projects can demand a price premium, but without the commitment to build the complete system, that premium often goes unrealized. In the Twin Cities, to continue the success of TOD projects near the early light-rail lines—such as the Central, Northstar, or Southwest Corridor—new investment tools and more streamlined land use regulations will be needed to remove barriers to TOD.

A key benefit of being close to transit is that a household may then only need one car; however, until a system—and urban environments—can be designed that allow greater mobility throughout the auto-dominated Twin Cities region, development projects need to continue accommodating off-street parking. There are more than 2,800 free parking spaces near the Hiawatha line.

In the past, American cities were largely designed for cars; however, in the Twin Cities area, this is beginning to change. A number of local governments are including more pedestrian and bike trails in their plans.

Transit systems often are designed to run along preexisting rights-of-way that offer the shortest travel time. A better alternative is to operate transit systems that connect major development nodes, malls, and business campuses. In the case of the Central Corridor, University Avenue was selected over I-94 due to higher ridership projections because moderate high-density development exists close by.

Local residents tend to resist the higher density that TOD relies on because density often results in more traffic, greater demand on services, shadows cast by taller buildings, obstruction of sight lines, and the perception of increased crime. There are areas in the Central Corridor in which the average household size is four people, and 50 to 70 percent of households have one car or no car at all.

Developing a TOD requires time for meaningful dialogue among stakeholders and to find the professional skills to craft necessary mechanisms, including public or private financing, engineering, architecture, entitlements, or planning. Bloomington Central Station, for example, includes a combination of public and private funding initiatives and a creative approach to maintaining common areas.

A major challenge in creating TOD projects often involves a collaboration among many and various stakeholders. The Hiawatha LRT is a prime example. MnDOT was the agency responsible for designing and building the line. The Metropolitan Council is the owner and operating entity. Hennepin County has a stake in the regional transportation system and continues to be an advocate of community planning and development. The cities of Minneapolis and Bloomington played a significant role in local traffic man-

agement, planning infrastructure systems, and neighborhood land use planning and zoning.

Walkability is a key factor in developing a successful TOD. A 2006 study showed that one-third of Hiawatha line riders arrive at stations by walking or biking. Bike racks are available at no additional charge on all Hiawatha line trains, and bike lockers are available at many park-and-ride-lots and LRT stations.

Inside the Bloomington Central Station project is a narrow internal street system that has no speed limit signs. The theory is that people tend to drive the speed limit posted, but with no limit posted, drivers likely will drive a speed appropriate to the place. The environment—street design, landscaping, building patterns, open space patterns—is structured to influence driving behavior positively.

Local governments are gaining a better understanding of the effect transportation improvement projects have on businesses and communities. Business owners along the Hiawatha line, for example, feared the changes that construction and LRT operation would have on their businesses. However, many of these same owners report new opportunities and business growth since the line began operating in 2004.

Business owners along the Central Corridor between downtown Minneapolis and downtown St. Paul also fear the effects LRT will have on their businesses—particularly during construction when parking spaces will be reduced and traffic patterns disrupted.

The Metropolitan Council has established a model for community outreach efforts to help overcome these fears; a diverse team has been charged with ensuring frequent, open communication among business owners; citizens; community leaders and activists; elected and appointed officials; and the project design team (engineers, planners, designers, and architects). The team engages in small group discussions and, in some cases, one-on-one kitchen table discussions that focus on the project's design and progress.

St. Paul's development strategy engages the community in removing barriers to TOD and in improving walkability. Planners along the Central Corridor have identified areas that are potential redevelopment sites, while also emphasizing the need to protect existing stable neighborhoods.

The acceptance of transit and TOD in the Twin Cities area has increased support at the local level, which, in turn, has resulted in a more consistent source of funding for roads, bridges, and transit. For example, a five-cent increase in the state's gas tax—the first increase in 20 years—passed this past year, and a one-quarter-cent sales tax increase for transit projects was adopted by five of seven metropolitan area counties. (For every penny charged, Minnesota's gas tax brings in more than $30 million a year for transportation.)

LRT is no longer the political football it was in the 1970s. Careful planning and collaboration among developers, government agencies, and community groups have helped build trust and increase acceptance of TODs.

Chapter 7

Using Buses for Rapid Transit

Sarah Jo Peterson

Successful transit-oriented developments (TODs) meet demand for compact,
walkable, mixed-use development—the same
markets that are also likely to see an important amenity value in easy access to high-
quality transit service. At the same time, the
more people, jobs, and services that exist
within walking distance of transit service, the
higher the potential transit ridership and fare
generation, and the more cars that can be
pulled off congested roads. TOD is a win-
win for land use and transportation.

TOD would seem to work for both
trains and buses, but rail stations have attracted the most development attention, at
least in the United States, because the infrastructure required for rail service is seen as
both more permanent and more impressive.
The significant investments in rights-of-way,
tracks, and stations, especially when these elements are new, signal the commitment to
make these areas investment priorities. The
flexibility of bus service—in which routes
and service levels can be quickly changed—
works against the bus as an organizing anchor
for TOD.

In addition, rail typically offers higher-
capacity and higher-quality service than do
buses and sometimes even cars. The separate
corridor required for the tracks means that
the train may reach a destination before a car

would, while the bus, trapped on the same
congested roads as cars and stopping frequently, has the reputation of being the slow
horse of the transportation world.

Rail stations also help boost TOD by
contributing to the place making that is a critical component of success. Rail stations not
only function as gateways to a city, neighborhood, or employment center, but they also
are singular in the urban landscape. Mix in
an underground tunnel or an elevated platform, and they become even more interesting.
Recognizing the landmark potential of rail
stations, societies historically have chosen to
invest in high-quality design.

But what if buses provided a high level
of service, traveled through permanent and
impressive infrastructure, and contributed to
place making? Bus rapid transit (BRT) has
the potential to meet all these criteria and, in
the process, turn TOD into BRTOD.

Bus rapid transit is not really just a bus.
It is better described as a movement that is
applying creativity and innovation to bus
service, with a special focus on medium-
length and longer trips. It is in these longer
trips where the *rapid* aspect becomes important—where saving time helps bus service
compete with the automobile. Not all BRT
innovations, however, have the same potential to shape land use. Some innovations im-

Originally published as "Bus Rapid Transit and Land Use," *Urban Land*, Vol. 69, Nos. 7 and 8 (July/August 2010), by the
Urban Land Institute, Washington, D.C. Copyright, Urban Land Institute, all rights reserved. Reprinted with permission.

prove the rider experience, while other innovations begin to make a statement in the landscape—that bus infrastructure no longer means just a sign and maybe a bench by the side of the road.

One way to think of BRT is to imagine a rail line, but with buses instead of trains. In this type of BRT, specially designed and branded buses travel on a bus-only lane or corridor and stop at stations. Stations are typically spaced from a half-mile (0.2 km) to several miles apart. In the full expression of "like-rail" BRT, the corridor is fully grade separated so that the buses only slow to stop at stations. Trips are free from congestion and delays to cross intersections.

The Orange Line in Los Angeles and the EMX Line that travels between Eugene and Springfield, Oregon, are U.S. examples of like-rail BRT.

Bus-only corridors with stations are also a key component of a type of BRT often called busway, or transitway, systems. Busway systems take advantage of the fact that unlike trains, buses can run anywhere there is a road. A bus may start on a neighborhood route, go to the busway to speed downtown, and then circulate on the downtown streets. Busway systems, therefore, can reduce the need for transfers, potentially combining door-to-door service with speed. Busways also can accommodate multiple transit providers: intercity buses, buses from distant suburbs, express buses, local buses, and even private vanpools all could be permitted access to the busways.

Pittsburgh has a busway system dating to the 1970s, and Ottawa, Canada, and Brisbane, Australia, have developed extensive systems of rapid transit on the transitway model. Bus service that uses high-occupancy vehicle (HOV) or high-occupancy toll (HOT) lanes can get a community part of the way toward implementation of a full transitway system.

Bus rapid transit is being unveiled in communities across the United States, following the international trend as BRT spreads from Curitiba, Brazil, to Bogotá, Colombia, to Guangzhou, China, and now to Johannesburg, South Africa. Many of the U.S. BRT projects are much smaller in scale than the leading international examples, but as experience in the suburbs of Minneapolis reveals, thinking anew about land use and buses is still possible.

The Cedar Avenue Transitway is one of two new BRT lines under construction in the Twin Cities metropolitan region. The 16-mile (26-km) route runs from Lakeville through Apple Valley, Eagan, and then on to the Mall of America in Bloomington, where riders can transfer to the area's expanding rail system. The corridor connects these growing suburbs to jobs in downtown Minneapolis and St. Paul and along Interstate 494. The $250 million project is building stations, parking facilities, and bus lanes on the shoulders of the busy, and increasingly congested, Cedar Avenue.

When the first stations on the Cedar Avenue Transitway opened earlier this year, the Minnesota Valley Transit Authority began expanding express service to the region's job centers and linking in local bus routes. Station-to-station service is planned to begin in 2012.

The investment in the Apple Valley Transit Station signals the commitment to high-quality service both to bus riders and to the occupants of the cars that pass under its glass-enclosed pedestrian bridge. Opened in January, its 750-stall parking structure nears capacity on a typical workday; the station also connects to city and county bicycle trails. The $21 million facility shows that bus infrastructure can provide the type of landmark that could boost place making for a neighborhood.

Smaller and supporting less parking than the Apple Valley Transit Station is the Cedar Grove Transit Station, an example of a neighborhood station. The station and its

200 weekday buses are an essential element in Eagan's efforts to promote the redevelopment of an area once occupied by a mall. The transit station is integrated into a plan for a pedestrian-focused, mixed-use neighborhood of residential and commercial uses.

The Cedar Avenue Transitway terminates at the Lakeville Cedar park-and-ride lot. Transit planners thought ahead when selecting the site, currently a surface parking lot in a still-developing area of the suburb. They avoided the prime commercial locations and instead positioned the lot to support shared parking with the commercial development when it eventually reaches the area.

Because BRT technologies are new and evolving and because their use seems to play out differently in every community, it is crucial that transportation and land use decision makers from both the public and private sectors share the specifics about what is being planned and developed. With construction underway on the BRT corridors in the Twin Cities, ULI Minnesota brought together transit providers, local governments, and the private sector for a bus rapid transit forum to learn about the new transit services and share ideas about how to coordinate BRT and land use. Among the issues raised, though not resolved, was whether a development's shuttle bus service would be allowed to use the new transitways and transit stations.

To capitalize on BRT's potential, land use decision makers need to understand what type of BRT is planned. Is it like-rail BRT that will concentrate access at the stations? Or is it a busway system, where land with good vehicle access to the transit corridor may be just as significant as sites within a half-mile walk of the stations? Or does BRT mean better bus service, without much of an impact on infrastructure? Will the BRT line or corridor be "rapid" enough, and—often even more important to transit users—will the buses arrive frequently enough to constitute an amenity to surrounding development?

BRT may open opportunities to coordinate transit service with demand for compact, mixed-use, walkable development in communities that are not large enough to support rail. The same is true for suburban areas not dense enough to support rail. Regardless of the type and service level of BRT, however, the same land use lessons of TOD apply: station area design, attention to security, the placement of parking, and easy and relatively pleasant access into the surrounding neighborhoods or activity centers by foot and bicycle are still the elements of success.

Chapter 8

Building Safe Streets for Citizens

Angie Schmitt

If Ontario Street in Cleveland, Ohio, is any indication, a complete streets policy is no guarantee you'll get a safe place to ride a bike, or even a comfortable place to walk.

Ontario is one of those roads designed to simply funnel traffic to and from a highway—and in fact there's not much to distinguish the street from a highway. It's eight lanes wide and devoid of landscaping, or any obstacles to fast driving, really. The most tragic part is, it's right in front of where the Indians play, Progressive Field, which was sold to taxpayers as a way to enliven the city.

This road just came up for resurfacing, and with the city's complete streets policy, now two years old, it seemed like an ideal time to correct this mistake. Instead, Cleveland's traffic engineering department punted, leaving the road basically as is but adding shared lane bike stencils, or sharrows. (Actual bike lanes would compromise the street's ability to accommodate cars during rush hour, you see.)

And there you have it. A complete streets policy should be a fabulous thing that elevates safety, the economy, and social equity in cities, but it can also amount to nothing more than a few new rules that are easily ducked if officials don't want to follow the spirit of the law.

Some 500 communities and states across the United States now have complete streets policies, so the good work of enacting these laws is well underway. Implementation is the next frontier.

And it's not easy, especially in communities like Cleveland where these ideas still feel new. But some cities are doing a better job than others, says Stefanie Seskin at the National Complete Streets Coalition. Charlotte, for example, developed six key steps to the project development process. Seattle passed a special tax levy to help support safe streets improvements for active transportation. San Francisco, in its "Better Streets" guide, prioritizes pedestrian concerns.

"The cities that I listed are leaders because they've changed a lot in their decision-making process," says Seskin. "It's not like sexy and you don't have pretty pictures, but when you set a goal for an agency and you realign practices to achieve that goal, I think that makes a big difference."

Cleveland, meanwhile, has a complete streets task force, but in practice the decisions still lie with the Department of Traffic Engineering—the same folks who designed an at-grade highway for the front of the city's baseball stadium.

Having good city staff—people who are committed to seeing complete streets implemented and understand why it's important—is crucial. Or, like Charlotte, you can develop

Originally published as "Passing a Law Is the Easy Part: The Challenge of Building Complete Streets," *Streetblog Capitol Hill* (July 11, 2013), by OpenPlans, Washington, D.C. Reprinted with permission of the publisher.

and train a working group or committee to oversee the process.

"You have a lot of people that have been around for years that are used to doing things the way they have been doing them," Seskin said. "You have to change the problem and make them understand they're solving for a new problem."

Another key element is performance measures. What does success look like? Boulder, Colorado, set a goal in the 1990s to reduce traffic. Since then, the city has invested heavily in transit and reduced the percentage of trips taken by car, said Seskin. Indianapolis incorporated a lot of easily "countable" performance measures into its complete streets plan, including the percentage of children walking or biking to school and the number of transit stops that are accessible with sidewalks and curb ramps.

If decision makers in your city are still under the impression that moving cars is the most important factor in street performance, your streets probably won't get a whole lot safer. But some progress is possible even if cities still try to accommodate "peak hour" traffic. Charlotte, for instance, decided to define "peak hour" as the full two hours around rush hour, not the most congested 15 minutes during that

period. As a result, they didn't consider it so imperative for streets to be dangerously wide.

Cities should also be sure to update their design guides. Many communities, after passing complete streets ordinances, develop design manuals that serve as a rough guide for the physical geometry of streets across the city. That way, safety improvements can be applied according to a consistent set of principles whenever streets are repaved, instead of starting from scratch with every street.

"Then, every time a project comes up, it's not a question of whether this is going to be a complete street or not," said Seskin. "It's, 'How can we accommodate all these users.'"

EDITORS' NOTE

The OpenPlans website (http://openplans.org/) lists their organization's goals as working with cities where communities are partners in shaping their neighborhoods, where transportation systems are designed in collaboration with everyone who rides them, and where planners and other professionals are engaging the public in ongoing, productive conversations about positive changes in the future.

The author noted to the editors that cities in the Netherlands and Denmark area are inspirations in their efforts to manage cars, that New York City is a leader in the U.S., and that the City of Vancouver is an example in its efforts to manage vehicular congestion in Canada.

Chapter 9

Technology and Automobiles

Tanya Snyder

As we try to understand why young people are so much less jazzed about driving than previous generations, one possible explanation always comes up: Kids today just love their smart phones.

That is part of it. But the full picture is far more nuanced.

The internet, and the ability to carry it wherever you go, has changed society in so many profound ways it's no surprise that transportation is among them. A new study by U.S. PIRG and the Frontier Group, "A New Direction," illustrates the myriad ways mobile technology has transformed young people's relationship with transportation.

Yesterday, we covered the report's critique of government travel forecasting and its analysis of why young people's driving rates will probably remain lower than those of previous generations. Technology is one of the biggest reasons. Here's why:

Constant connectivity. As you've undoubtedly noticed at the dinner table or on city sidewalks, people have trouble putting down their phones. It's not just compulsive Facebook status checking that keeps people glued to their devices. People perform an increasingly broad assortment of tasks on phones: make travel reservations, go through work email, catch up on the news, diagnose children's ailments—the list is nearly infinite.

While car companies are trying heartily to incorporate digital connectivity and social media into their cars, they still need to battle the fact that such technology is dangerously distracting for drivers. Given the option, many young people would rather take transit, where they can use their phones harmlessly, making far better use of their commuting time.

Alternative social spaces. Older adults may think it's weird when teens would rather text each other than see each other, but hey, the world is a weird place. "A survey by computer networking equipment maker Cisco in 2012 found that two-thirds of college students and young professionals spend at least as much time with friends online as they do in person," write report authors Phineas Baxandall and Tony Dutzik.

Online shopping. More and more people are making purchases online rather than in stores. Young people are leading the way on that, too. And it can be greener than going to the store yourself.

More consumer-friendly transit. Beyond the social sphere, technology is sidelining car travel by making other modes more attractive. Young people are less inclined to view transit as dirty and smelly and only for poor people, partly because the experience of riding transit is improving. Real-time track-

Originally published as "Seven Ways Technology Is Rendering the Automobile Obsolete," *Streetblog Capitol Hill* (May 15, 2013), by OpenPlans, Washington, D.C. Reprinted with permission of the publisher.

ing information, delivered instantly via cell phone, erases the need to wait outside in the elements for a delayed bus. Trip planner apps help riders figure out the best route without having to memorize maps and schedules. Modern transit fare cards make the boarding process quicker and easier, and can be replenished online.

Bike-share. The widespread use of smartphones has enabled whole new transportation options. Imagine a bike-share system that didn't include real-time digital maps telling you where to find available bikes or docks. Or, peeling away another layer of technology, imagine one that didn't have GPS locator capability or electronic payment and security systems. It would be like the free yellow bikes that were sprinkled around the Twin Cities in the mid–90s, then fizzled out a few years later as the bikes were lost to theft or vandalism.

Sharing of all kinds. Car-sharing services like Zipcar could not have thrived with 20th century technology. Every step of the way—from finding an available car online to opening the doors with your magnetic keycard—depends on modern tech. Peer-to-peer car-sharing can use lower-tech cars but still relies on the internet to connect drivers with car-owners. Internet connectivity also enables passengers to match up with drivers offering a ride-share. Plus, countless apps will help you hail a cab or even a limo from the comfort of your barstool.

Telework. Telework saves employers money on office space, and it saves employees valuable commute time. The added flexibility of telework can be especially important to people with families and other responsibilities. It also frees people to live wherever they want—a friend of mine moved to Denver because she loves the mountains but kept her

DC policy-wonk job. Teleconferencing makes it possible for people to scatter around the globe and still have face-to-face meetings when they need to. Online education similarly gives students alternatives to traveling to campus.

In all of these ways, recent technological advances have made it easier and more desirable for people to cut down on driving. They're not reducing their mileage out of a sense of civic duty or environmental commitment; they're driving less because there are simply better ways to do the things they want and need to do. And, as Baxandall and Dutzik write, it's the young people—the millennial generation—that has most readily embraced all the ways technology can save them time and money. According to a recent Zipcar survey they cite, "25 percent of those aged 18 to 34 reported that mobile transportation apps (such as taxi apps, real-time transit information and car sharing) had reduced their driving frequency, compared with only 9 percent of those 55 years of age and older."

It can be tempting to look at these new technologies as the realm of the young, but those young people will continue to demand more and more sophisticated technological solutions as they get older.

EDITORS' NOTE

The OpenPlans website (http://openplans.org/) lists their organization's goals as working with cities where communities are partners in shaping their neighborhoods, where transportation systems are designed in collaboration with everyone who rides them, and where planners and other professionals are engaging the public in ongoing, productive conversations about positive changes in the future.

The publisher noted that the author became *Streetblog Capitol Hill*'s in September 2010 after covering Congress for Pacifica and public radio, and that she lives car-free in a transit-oriented and bike-friendly neighborhood in Washington, D.C.

Chapter 10

The Removal of Roadways

Jeffrey Spivak

Starting a half century ago, highways in North America were built to loop around and slice through downtowns. Today, momentum is building in a growing number of cities to tear down portions of these downtown freeways and replace them with aesthetically pleasing boulevards or parks.

Cities such as Milwaukee, San Francisco, and Portland, Oregon, have already completed freeway removal projects, with notable redevelopment results. Because of these successes, cities such as Seattle, Cleveland, and Oklahoma City are currently moving ahead with their own removal projects, and another dozen North American cities are contemplating or studying similar plans.

Though freeway removals take years to plan and fund, interest in them is growing for a couple of reasons. Highways built 40 or 50 years ago are now crumbling and reaching obsolescence, and governments cannot afford to rebuild them all. In addition, downtowns have been experiencing a residential renaissance, which is making walkable connections and urban aesthetics more important.

Many of the highway removal initiatives share downtown-oriented goals—to open up redevelopment opportunities and reconnect the downtown to the waterfront. "If you were starting from scratch, you'd never build a highway between a downtown and a waterfront," maintains John Norquist, former mayor of Milwaukee and now president of the Congress for the New Urbanism. "Today, there's a new appreciation for urban life and the urban fabric, and the land use impacts you get from a highway aren't so appealing anymore."

In Oklahoma City, construction has begun to relocate Interstate 40 on the southern edge of downtown, with the old stretch eventually becoming a boulevard serving as a new gateway to downtown. Interstate 40's Crosstown Expressway has served as an elevated barrier between downtown and the Oklahoma River, ten blocks to the south. As the state's busiest highway, the expressway carries 120,000 vehicles a day, 67 percent more than its intended capacity. With the roadway in need of massive repairs, the city and state collaborated on a decision to move it instead.

A new ten-lane freeway trench will be built through a warehouse district closer to the river. Meanwhile, the old expressway section will be converted into a tree-lined boulevard by 2014. All told, it is an opportunity to redevelop some 80-city blocks. Among the ideas emerging for the area are a new city park, a new convention center, and new housing.

In Cleveland, the state has committed

to converting three miles (4.8 km) of the West Shoreway highway into a boulevard to improve access to the city's lakefront; the project is in the running for federal money from the economic stimulus package. In Seattle, the state earlier this year approved $2.4 billion in funding for a $4.3 billion plan to replace the one mile- (1.6-km-) long Alaskan Way Viaduct with a tunnel under the Elliott Bay waterfront.

While these projects have government and downtown civic backing, freeway removal plans typically come under fire for their potential to worsen traffic congestion because a highway can handle more vehicles per hour than a surface arterial with traffic signals. One critic, Peter Samuel, editor of the transportation Web site TollroadsNews.com, believes a ten-lane boulevard would be needed to replace a four-lane expressway. "These proposals come mainly from urban planners and designers who seem to have almost zero concern about increasing delays, worsening travel times, and compounding congestion," he says.

But the experiences of a few cities have shown that fears of worsening congestion are not always borne out and that the benefits of removing even short freeway spurs can far outweigh the drawbacks. San Francisco has had the most experience with freeway removals, demolishing two roadways. In the Loma Prieta earthquake in 1989, a double-decked portion of the Central Freeway collapsed, and freeways across the metropolitan area were damaged, including the Embarcadero Freeway, a one-mile (1.6-km) spur at the base of Market Street.

The city had already tried to tear down the 70-foot- (21-m-) high, double-decked Embarcadero Freeway because it hugged San Francisco Bay. But with opponents predicting that removal of the roadway carrying 60,000 vehicles a day would cause gridlock, voters had rejected the plan. After the earthquake, the freeway was closed and drivers found alternative routes. It was finally demolished in 1991, and a six-lane, palm-lined roadway took its place, allowing construction of new neighborhoods oriented to the waterfront.

One portion of the Central Freeway, which ran for two miles (3.2 km) through the center of San Francisco, never reopened after the earthquake, prompting a debate about the fate of the rest of the roadway. California's transportation department decided the freeway was worth saving and developed a plan to demolish the upper deck while expanding the lower deck. When the upper deck was closed, the gridlock anticipated by transportation planners and local politicians did not occur, leading to neighborhood-led petitions to remove the entire freeway and replace it with a boulevard. Voters agreed with the freeway opponents and the replacement road, Octavia Boulevard, opened in 2005. Two years later, San Francisco's department of parking and traffic found that the Central Freeway's flow of 93,100 vehicles had fallen by more than 50 percent to 44,900 on the boulevard. In addition, none of the alternative routes analyzed had experienced more than a 10 percent increase in traffic.

The same was the case in Portland and Milwaukee—the first and the latest cities, respectively, to demolish freeways. Portland's Harbor Drive was a three-mile (4.8-km), ground level freeway that ran along the Willamette River, cutting off pedestrian access from downtown to the river. In the late 1960s, Portland was increasingly interested in developing its riverfront, and Oregon's governor at the time, Tom McCall, wanted to replace the drive with a park. By the early 1970s, additional highway alternatives made Harbor Drive superfluous. The drive was closed in 1974, and the park—later named Tom McCall Waterfront Park—opened in 1978. An urban renewal district was established, high-rise housing was developed, and two decades later, property values in the area had more than tripled.

Milwaukee's Park East was a one-mile (1.6-km) elevated freeway spur left over from more ambitious plans to develop freeways through and around downtown. The roadway divided the northern part of downtown from the rest of the central business district, creating both visual and physical barriers; the adjoining land was used mostly for parking lots. Removing the spur to stimulate downtown redevelopment became a crusade for Norquist. During his last term, in 2002 to 2003, the spur was torn down to be replaced by six-lane McKinley Avenue. Since then, the freed-up land has attracted a company headquarters, as well as development proposals for condominiums and apartment buildings along the Milwaukee River, according to the city development department.

Other cities evaluating what to do with various downtown freeway sections include the following:

• **Baltimore.** The elevated Jones Falls Expressway has long divided downtown from the Johns Hopkins medical campus. The city this spring hired an engineering team to study demolishing a mile-long stretch and replacing it with a landscaped boulevard to "connect the two sides," in the words of Mayor Sheila Dixon.

• **Toronto.** The city last year began an environmental assessment of removing one mile (1.6 km) of the Frederick G. Gardiner Expressway and building an eight-lane boulevard in its place as a way of opening the city to its lakefront. A series of public presentations of the idea continued this spring.

• **Syracuse, New York.** The Onondaga Citizens League civic group has recommended eventually replacing an elevated stretch of Interstate 81 through downtown, and the state is now studying the feasibility of doing that.

These projects—and others like them in Trenton, New Jersey; New Haven, Connecticut; and elsewhere—all share the common goal of creating more pedestrian connections and development opportunities in downtowns.

The interest in freeway removal is ironic. A half-century ago, cities and transportation planners thought highways would keep downtowns alive by paving the way for suburban commuters to get in and out. Today, some of those same highways are viewed as plagues that divide downtowns, wreck adjoining neighborhoods, and block waterfronts.

PART II. THE BEST PRACTICES

Chapter 11

Abu Dhabi, Emirates, Develops New Islands with Light Rail Transit Options

Yasser Elsheshtawy

"The English have a great hunger for desolate places. I fear they hunger for Arabia.... You must be another of those 'desert-loving Englishmen.' ... No Arab loves the desert. We love water and green trees.... There is nothing in the desert.... But you know, in the Arab city of Cordova were two miles of public lighting in the streets—when London was a village! ... I long for the vanished gardens of Cordova."—Sheikh Faisal speaking to Lawrence in the film *Lawrence of Arabia*.

For many observers, urban developments in the Persian Gulf region are synonymous with island reclamation, which is not surprising given the commanding presence of Dubai's Palm Islands in the media. These islands are part of a much larger real estate boom in the region. Two major factors drive these developments: the desire to counteract the cliché of the Arabian desert, and the need to invest capital in preparation for a post-oil economy.

The public's perception of the Arabian Peninsula is dominated by images of the desert—camels majestically roaming its endless horizons and oases miraculously appearing within desolate landscapes. Inhabitants of this region are acutely aware of this perception and in their drive to attract tourists

have embarked on island developments as a way to provide an alternative picture of the area. The dryness and heat of the desert are only one part of the picture. There are also rich waterfronts, lush gardens, and luxurious beaches. These attributes are showcased in new coastal developments and resorts. In addition, the region is expending a great deal of effort and expense to turn the desert green by planting trees and maintaining gardens in metropolitan areas. These efforts, as well as construction on or near water, cater not only to tourists, but also to local residents who desire a respite from the desert.

After 9/11 in the United States, there was a repatriation of Arab capital, which, in addition to an increase in oil prices, led to an oversupply of liquid capital. These monies were being invested in massive real estate and infrastructure projects whose overall value to the Gulf Cooperative Council (GCC) region—made up of Kuwait, Bahrain, Saudi Arabia, Qatar, U.A.E., and Oman—is estimated at $143 billion.

Closely linked to this is the knowledge that oil resources will eventually dry up, so to prepare for a post-oil era, the region needs to diversify its economy. The reclamation and development of islands represent one particularly visible aspect of this effort. The recent global financial crisis, however, has shown the pitfalls of relying on real estate. According to a February 5 listing on gulfnews.com research house Proleads recently reported that about $582 billion of civil construction projects in the U.A.E.—52.8 percent of the country's total civil construction portfolio—are now on hold. The extent and duration of this slowdown remain to be seen, though the region overall, with its high cash reserves, is not expected to suffer as severely as other parts of the world, and significant amount of construction activity continues.

Dubai has been at the forefront of island developments and, over the past two years, its neighbor Abu Dhabi has embarked on a similar path. However, the efforts in these two emirates, particularly in their respective capitals Dubai and Abu Dhabi, are quite different both in type and in a general approach to design. The city of Dubai for the most part is relying on a spectacular mode of development, whereas the capital Abu Dhabi is taking a more measured and cautious approach. Political, geographic, and economic factors have played major roles in these divergent directions.

Brand Dubai

Dubai is no stranger to reclamation and expansion of its coastline. In the 1960s, it embarked on two major projects that transformed the city from what was essentially a small fishing village into a major metropolis.

First, the creek that divides the city into two parts was dredged, enabling boats and *dhows* (traditional wooden boats) to enter the waterway unimpeded. In the process, significant amounts of land were added to the central area of the creek—thus expanding the creek waterfront on which office and government buildings were developed. Second, the Jebel Ali Port was built near the city's border with Abu Dhabi, establishing Dubai as a major center for trade and commerce.

These actions were precursors to the major coastal development projects that began in earnest in the late 1990s with two projects—the Burj Al Arab hotel, built on an artificial island and owned by the Jumeirah Group, and the Palm Jumeirah Island, the first in a series of large-scale reclaimed islands. Both projects are located in the neighborhood of Um Suqeim, considered an integral part of New Dubai and close to Jebel Ali, but distant from the city's central area. These projects helped diversify the economy by focusing both on real estate and on tourism. The urgency and speed with which the two projects were developed resulted from the limited availability of oil in this emirate. According to 2007 estimates, the oil sector's contribution to Dubai's gross domestic product (GDP) is 5.1 percent, compared with 60 percent to Abu Dhabi's GDP.

Nakheel, a fully government-owned developer, is responsible for most of these reclaimed islands, which are known as "Dubai's coastline enhancement projects." After Nakheel began building Palm Jumeirah in 2001, it went on to develop the larger Palm Jebel Ali in 2002, and the Palm Deira in 2004, which is 7.5 times the size of Palm Jumeirah and five times larger than Palm Jebel Ali, with an estimated surface area of 495 million square feet (46 million sq. m). In addition to this "Palm trilogy," all three of which are in the shape of palm trees, Nakheel introduced in 2003 the World, a set of islands whose overall layout resembles a global map, which was followed by the Waterfront, claimed by Nakheel to be one of the biggest offshore projects ever attempted and the largest urban development project in the world. The development was expected to be completed by 2015, but the recent financial downturn cased Nakheel to halt dredging operations on the Palm Deira as well as the Waterfront project.

Nakheel in January 2008 announced another project, the Universe, which will be shaped to resemble the planetary system and be located between the World and the Dubai coastline. Although still at a conceptual stage, the Universe appeared in a recently released master plan for Dubai. While the project is currently on hold due to the financial crisis, it has not been officially canceled.

Nakheel has been criticized by biologists such as Peter Linley and environmental monitoring groups such as mongabay.com for the environmental impact these projects will have on the region. One concern, for example, is how marine life will be affected by changing the coastline and the ocean floor. In response, Shaun Lenehan, Nakheel's environmental manager, said that after 55 separate environmental studies, it was concluded that little coral and few fish exist in the Persian Gulf in the first place, according to a *TimeOut Dubai* magazine article from 2007. In response to a 2005 article on mongabay.com, some environmental scientists at Nakheel have also argued that marine life has flourished due to the construction of these islands.

Another concern pertains to water circulation between elongated earthen shapes on which the island residences are located, which from the air resemble palm fronds. The management of waste, such as garbage, may cause excessive pollution among the fronds. To deal with these problems, the developer has created mechanical systems using pipes to channel seawater and ensure a steady, continuous flow that prevents the water from stagnating.

Nevertheless, as marine biologist Linley pointed out, the real problem starts when thousands of people move in and their waste is not managed effectively. Some criticism has also been leveled at the high density of the houses being built on the frond-shaped areas of the island. Specifically, critics such as Catherine Moyer, writing in the *Daily Tele-graph* in August 2005, say the space between residential units is too small—only 13 to 16 feet (4 to 5 m). According to Nakheel, however, this distance is standard for beachfront development because the main focus is the water.

Also, the location of the newer islands can block views from the older ones. For example, buyers of Palm Jebel Ali, who initially thought they had an unimpeded view of the gulf, have voiced concern that they now face the massive Waterfront development. In short, there is the danger of saturation, which could bring down the iconic status of some of the islands.

Another area of concern is the degree to which these projects are integrated with the city of Dubai. Nakheel officials note that agreements have been signed with the Road and Transportation Authority and the Dubai Electricity and Water Authority to facilitate extension of infrastructure to these islands. Yet, these are exclusive developments—in essence, gated communities that are not accessible to a large majority of Dubai residents. A planned monorail, which will extend along the "trunk" of the Jumeirah island, will allow access to the various destinations within the development, such as shopping areas and hotels. Because it will be linked to the Dubai Metro (see "Dubai Metro")—a light-rail system under construction and expected to cover the entire urban area of Dubai—the monorail should help in overcoming the island's aura of exclusivity by facilitating access to regular visitors, although such access will be restricted to retail and recreational destinations.

New York Times architecture critic Nicholas Ouroussoff, among others, has said the architecture on the islands should be inspiring. Thus, the recent commission of Dutch superstar architect Rem Koolhaas should improve their aesthetic character. Koolhaas developed a master plan for Waterfront City, in the massive Waterfront development, that will "locate a slice of Manhattan in Arabia," according to Ouroussoff.

Others have questioned the unusual shape of the islands. Though unlike those of natural islands, these perimeters succeed in providing an instantly recognizable symbol for Dubai. In effect, these islands function as the company logo, or brand—a well-known marketing device applied in this case to real estate. By directing attention to the various projects being carried out, they help to increase sales. This represents a different approach than that taken by Dubai's neighbor, Abu Dhabi.

Abu Dhabi's Approach

Abu Dhabi's unique geography sets it apart from Dubai. Originally an island in the Persian Gulf that served as a temporary settlement for Bedouins, Abu Dhabi began urban development in the late 1960s when the government started reclaiming land and raising the island's ground level to facilitate construction of roads and buildings. However, the city did not realize the full development potential of the island, which continued to remain in the shadow of its neighbor Dubai.

A transfer of leadership in 2004 led to a number of changes significantly affecting the city's growth and urban form. Chief among these was a change in the property ownership law, which allowed the sale of government-granted land among local citizens and opened up a form of limited ownership to foreigners. Such efforts provided a way to promote growth of the real estate industry, although at a rather limited scale compared with the growth in Dubai. While foreigners are allowed to own property in Abu Dhabi for a period of 99 years, Dubai allows freehold ownership.

(The latter is based on a change in Dubai's property law in 2006 allowing foreigners to receive deeds to their land and register ownership with the Dubai Lands and Properties Department. They are also able to transfer property ownership directly without having to go through the developer. This can only take place within certain designated zones within the city classified as free zones, such as the Palm Islands.)

Real estate accounts for about one-third of the $150 billion that Abu Dhabi expects to spend domestically in the next five years. Projects range from entire new residential and tourist complexes to vast malls and town-sized commercial and industrial developments—as well as development of the vast number of existing islands surrounding the city. One exception is Lulu Island, an artificial island whose reclamation work was completed in 1992. It is the most visible of these islands, lying 2,000 feet (600 m) off the city's Corniche Road. With a total area of 1,050 acres (425 ha), Lulu Island is being developed as a tourist destination by the General Corporation for Development and Investment of Lulu Island. The remaining islands around Abu Dhabi—about 200—are natural and, for the most part, uninhabited, consisting of large stretches of sand, although in some instances, they contain mangroves and have a delicate ecosystem.

Of a similarly monumental scale is Saadiyat Island which is being developed by Tourism Development & Investment Company (TDIC) at an estimated cost of $15 billion. It occupies about 291 million square feet (27 million sq. m). Among its major attractions is a cultural district that will house five major museum and performance centers designed by some of the world's foremost architects: a Frank Gehry Guggenheim museum, the largest in the franchise; a Jean Nouvel–designed Louvre museum; a performance by Zaha Hadid; a maritime museum by Tadao Ando; and the Sheikh Zayed national museum designed by Foster & Partners. The proximity of these buildings presents some unique architectural and urban challenges related to compatibility, coherence, and ultimately their meaning within the larger context of the city. Yet, undoubtedly the presence of these high-profile buildings will be a significant factor in Abu Dhabi's drive to become a major tourist destination.

Other islands being developed include Al Reem and Yas islands. Al Reem Island is being developed by Sorouh Real Estate PJSC and contain a new city called SHAMS Abu Dhabi. More than 100 skyscrapers are planned for a residential population of 53,000 at an estimated cost of $6.81 billion. Yas Island, being developed by Al Dar, will include a special Formula 1 racetrack and Ferrari theme park. Here, it seems, the spectacular as strategy is adapted from Dubai.

These developments are taking place within the framework of the Abu Dhabi Urban Plan 2030 introduced in 2007. Representing a major shift from the initial master plan, the new framework focuses on creating a world-class capital city, with the islands playing a major role in that objective. Abu Dhabi is constructing numerous bridges linking these islands to the mainland. Furthermore, great emphasis is placed on sustainability issues; according to the plan, natural resources such as mangroves and other natural habitats are being preserved. The plan specifically notes that the city should be shaped by its natural environment and be sensitive to coastal and desert ecologies.

Despite the global financial crisis, there have been no announcements in Abu Dhabi of plans to slow down or cancel any ongoing projects; the crisis has not affected Abu Dhabi to the same degree as it has Dubai.

Some of the environmental concerns identified in Dubai—such as waste management, coastline modifications, and change in marine habitat—are sparked primarily by the introduction of artificial islands. In contrast, all islands in Abu Dhabi, with the exception of Lulu Island, are natural. However, concerns still arise because the islands will be inhabited by a large number of people who must receive various services. The environmental impact of such developments still needs to be assessed.

Exporting the Island Model

Both Dubai and Abu Dhabi are breaking new ground in island and coastal development. Dubai particularly is being emulated throughout the region. Similar developments are taking place in Kuwait's City of Silk, Doha's Pearl Island in Qatar, and Oman's the Wave, although these are at a much smaller scale and, in contrast to Dubai, do not represent the typical development in these countries.

The Dubai model also is emerging in distant lands: an Abu Dhabi–based investor, for instance, is developing an island in Russia that will feature a shape based on the map of the Russian Federation. To combat overcrowding in the Netherlands, some thought was given to building an island in the North Sea that would have been shaped like a tulip, although the idea was abandoned due to the high tidal waves and cost.

While such shaped islands can be spectacular, they raise environmental and social concerns. Developments in Abu Dhabi, while also relying on the spectacular, are taking place within a carefully developed master plan that addresses environmental as well as social concerns, and thus may offer a more useful model for urban development.

EDITORS' NOTE

The following information is provided about this best practice case study to facilitate future research.

Name: City of Abu Dhabi
Population: 921,000 (2013)
Region: Central Western Coast
Province/State: Capital Region
Country: Emirates
Official Name: United Arab Emirates
City Website: http://www.abudhabi.ae/

Chapter 12

Addis Ababa, Ethiopia, Explores the Use of Sustainable Transportation Options

Joan Clos

Background: Contemporary Global Challenges of Urban Mobility

Effective transportation networks are fundamental to the functioning of cities and towns across the globe and a precondition for economic prosperity and the well being of their residents. At the same time, the economic and social benefits of mobility are frequently accompanied by negative side effects such as congestion, social exclusion, accidents, air pollution and energy consumption.

Since the mid–20th century, the negative side effects of urban transportation have particularly become apparent in the metropolitan areas of developed countries. Rising car traffic volumes and congestion are increasingly causing lost economic productivity, environmental degradation and affect overall quality of life in cities. With the documented contribution of the urban transport sector to global greenhouse gas emissions, there is a heightened level of urgency to apply new approaches and technologies for mobility in urban areas of developed countries.

Developing countries are increasingly facing similar challenges due to rapid urban-ization and motorization in recent decades, in combination with insufficient investment in transport infrastructure, often accompanied by urban poverty and social exclusion. While vehicle ownership rates in most developing nations are still low in comparison to developed countries, motorization is rising rapidly and is creating major challenges in the expanding "megacities" of the South. Although only 10 to 20 percent of urban residents own a private automobile, cities in developing countries are already facing stifling traffic congestion and worsening air pollution. The annual increase in the motorization rate of many developing countries has approached 10 percent, which is substantially higher than ever experienced in industrialized countries. As a result, energy use by the transportation sector in developing countries has been increasing at over four percent annually in the past 20 years, far exceeding the global 2.7 percent rate of increase.

Consequently, a major challenge for cities all over the world in the 21st century is to meet the mobility needs of their residents in a socially inclusive, economically efficient and environmentally sustainable manner. The provision of adequate, efficient and safe transport infrastructure and services in urban

Originally published as "Bridging the Urban Transport Divide," *Summary Report of the Urban Researchers Roundtable*, World Urban Forum (March 2010), by the Urban Transport Section and Policy Analysis Branch, UN-Habitat, Nairobi, Kenya.

areas is frequently constrained by a complex set of financial, institutional, environmental and political factors. The barriers are not only financial or technical in nature, but arise from political, social and institutional factors preventing progress towards sustainability in the urban transport field.

As a result, severe disadvantages can be observed in terms of the accessibility and affordability of transport infrastructure and services for different societal groups and ultimately in terms of urban mobility. Unequal access to mobility opportunities and therefore employment opportunities, housing and basic services represents "the urban transport divide."

The urban transport divide is conceptualized in terms of the following three pillars of sustainability:

• The social divide: the unequal access to mobility for different groups and locations in urban areas;
• The environmental divide: the uneven distribution of the environmental and health impacts of urban transport within the context of cities;
• The economic divide: the uneven spatial and social distribution of the benefits of efficient transportation systems for employment opportunities and poverty reduction.

The urban transport divide in the world's cities was the focus of the Urban Researchers Roundtable, held in the context of the Fifth Session of the World Urban Forum, which had *The Right to the City: Bridging the Urban Divide* as its overall theme.

The following partners collaborated in organizing the Roundtable:

• Associação Nacional dos Transportes Públicos/National Association of Public Transportation—Brazil (ANTP);
• The International Association of Public Transport (UITP);
• Associação Nacional de Pós-graduação e Pesquisa em Planejamento Urbano e Re-

gional/Brazilian Association of Postgraduate Programmes and Research in Urban and Regional Planning (ANPUR)
• United Nations Human Settlements Programme (UN-HABITAT)

The intention of the Roundtable was to explore and discuss models and approaches that have successfully overcome the urban transport divide and that can be transferred and applied widely. Another purpose of the Roundtable was to inform UN-HABITAT's ongoing work in urban transport and the preparation of the 2013 Global Report on Human Settlements, which will focus on "*Sustainable Urban Transport*" (www.unhabitat. org/grhs). The discussion and outcomes of the Roundtable are highlighted in this summary report.

Case Study Presentations

Corresponding to the overall theme of the Forum—"*bridging the urban divide*"—the Urban Researchers Roundtable centered on a discussion of strategies to bridge the urban transport divide. The event was preceded by an electronic dialogue among prospective participants in late 2009 with several contributors highlighting the importance of bridging the "urban transport divide" in the world's cities.

The Roundtable was facilitated by Mr. Jerome Pourbaix of the International Association of Public Transport (UITP). Following a brief opening movie that outlined the key issues, Prof. Oyebanji Oyeyinka of UN-HABITAT outlined the overall setting of the session within the dialogues of the Forum and stressed its importance for preparing UN-HABITAT's 2013 Global Report on Human Settlements, which will focus on the subject of sustainable urban transport.

To set the stage for the Roundtable discussion, five leading researchers from different regions presented case studies on the urban transport divide and related policy responses.

In her opening remarks, Ms. Leila Christina Dias outlined the work of her organization, the Brazilian Association of Postgraduate Programmes and Research in Urban and Regional Planning. She pointed to the transport challenges in mega-cities such as São Paolo, Brazil and cited the application of restrictive travel demand measures in European cities as a potentially replicable policy response.

In the first case study presentation, Mr. Eduardo Vasconcellos focused on integrated transport systems and his understanding of the "mobility divide." He placed particular emphasis on the inequalities in consumption patterns and access to mobility between low-income residents and higher income groups in Brazil, as well as potential alleviating policy measures.

Mr. Michael Replogle presented the challenges of sustainable urban transport in North America and Europe. Taking the Atlanta metropolitan area as a case study, he explained the multiple disparities and disadvantages faced by low-income households that are unable to afford a car in the United States.

Mr. Peter Wilkinson gave a presentation on informal public transport operations in Cape Town, South Africa. He stressed the need for detailed analysis and caution when designing alternative transport policy solutions, particularly in terms of affordability and political feasibility.

In her presentation on non-motorized transport operations in Jakarta, Indonesia, Ms. Maria Renny Herdanti cited the example of restrictive policies towards tricycle rickshaws (becak) to emphasize the need for transport solutions that take the specific needs of low-income communities into account.

Mr. Xavier Godard's presentation focused on the lessons and experiences of urban mobility and poverty in West Africa. He elaborated on the high share of transport costs for low-income households and examined the potential of non-motorized and public transport to respond to this challenge.

The presentations were followed by a discussion of the key challenges, innovative practices and policies to move towards sustainable urban transport and mobility. In particular, it was stressed that urban mobility is about moving people, not vehicles. This statement, although apparently so obvious, but frequently forgotten, formed the basis of discussions during the Roundtable. Highlights of this discourse will be outlined in the next chapter.

In his closing comments, Mr. Raphael Bostic emphasized that the economic, social and environmental divide should be considered in tandem rather than separately. He further stressed the importance of urban planning for solving transport problems.

Summarizing the event, Mr. Naison Mutizwa-Mangiza of UN-HABITAT emphasized that the Roundtable's outcomes will inform UN-HABITAT's ongoing urban transport work and the 2013 Global Report on Human Settlements.

Highlights of the Discussion and Emerging Issues

The Roundtable discussion focused on the current state of the urban transport divide in both developing and developed countries and effective practices and policies to bridge this gap.

Overall, it was felt that the event provided an important opportunity for urban researchers to share experiences and innovative solutions for addressing the policy challenges related to bridging the urban transport divide in the world's cities. The roundtable was highly successful in communicating a wide range of perspectives for enabling practitioners and policy makers to learn about how to implement sustainable urban transport policies and practices.

Participants focused on the following key issues in terms of implementing solutions for pro-poor urban mobility:

- participants underscored the need to introduce new concepts and transformative practices in urban transport policy;
- participants called for the consideration of the needs of the poor and women in transport policy embodied by the shift in emphasis from "transport" to "mobility";
- participants stressed the need for integrated and interdisciplinary approaches that involve a wide range of institutions which deal with urban mobility;
- participants raised their concern about equity in public transport and the need to address underlying governance challenges.

For the debate on the socio-economic divide, particularly the inputs by Eduardo Vasconcellos, Michael Replogle and Xavier Godard proved to be important catalysts. The presentations showed for contexts as different as Brazil, Western Africa and the United States how poverty is intrinsically related to the lack of affordable transportation. Several speakers stressed that it is important not to take an effect as a cause: transport is not a primary cause of the socio-economic divide, but its inefficiency, poor quality and complete inexistence in some contexts, are mostly the consequences of car-oriented urban plans.

Despite this conceptual conundrum, there is no doubt that the lack of safe and affordable transport options forbids many urban residents to access facilities and basic services such as education, public health, and jobs. Furthermore, without access to urban mobility services, social and economic networks on which particularly the urban poor people depend are impaired.

Poor urban planning was identified as a key factor underlying the current crisis of urban transport. Participants of the Roundtable pointed out that mobility challenges are best addressed within the context of inclusive land policies, participatory processes, supportive political framework and legal basis to enforce change.

Participants also noted the importance of a context specific approach to implementing mobility solutions. For instance, Peter Wilkinson highlighted how the BRT "model" of Bogotá, in Colombia, a world class project, initially failed in Cape Town due to resistance by existing operators. In addition, Maria Herdanti showed how the *becak,* a popular tricycle facing government restrictions, served as a vital form of transport that could be integrated into formal transportation systems.

Finally, despite the huge socio-economic divide related to (the lack of) urban transport, it was emphasized that there are several other "divides" in the urban sphere that must be taken into account: the adults vs. children/elderly divide, the able vs. disabled people, and other social divides. Therefore, it was concluded that it is impossible to think of an inclusive urban agenda without thinking of inclusive urban mobility.

EMERGING ISSUES

The following emerging issues for discussion and action were identified by the Roundtable:

- transport is regarded as an important dimension of the urban divide that affects access to housing, jobs, and urban services;
- there is a need for inclusive urban transport policies that address the needs of the poor and disadvantaged groups, including women;
- bridging the urban transport divide requires reduction of personal automobile use and greater provision of public transport and non-motorized transport;
- in addressing the urban transport divide, emphasis should be placed on mobility of

people rather than on transport modes, and on linking transport planning with other dimensions of urban planning.

Benefits for UN-HABITAT's Ongoing Work

Beyond the fruitful discussions among participants, the Researchers Roundtable on the Urban Transport Divide also provided useful inputs for UN-HABITAT's ongoing work towards promoting sustainable urban mobility worldwide. Outcomes of the discussion and new partnerships established will benefit both normative and operational engagements in this field.

First, the Roundtable resulted in deeper insights into the specific social dimensions of urban mobility and the relationship to urban development as a whole. This knowledge is particularly relevant for promoting inclusive urban transport policies that address the needs of the poor and disadvantaged groups, including women and children. Identified as an emerging issue in the context of the Roundtable, there was consensus that planning for sustainable mobility has to include the needs of marginalized groups in the planning process, particularly by linking lower income residential areas with work places and other urban services.

In this respect, the Roundtable discussion will be highly beneficial for implementing UN-HABITAT's new initiative "Promoting Sustainable Transport Solutions for East African Cities." Launched by UN-HABITAT's Urban Transport Section through support by the Global Environment Facility (GEF), the project will support government agencies in Ethiopia, Kenya and Uganda in the process of introducing improved public transport services and infrastructure for pedestrians and cyclists in the three capitals Addis Ababa, Kampala and Nairobi.

Roundtable presentations and discussions on strengthening non-motorized modes of transport proved to be highly complementary to UN-HABITAT's work in this area, especially in terms of the contribution to the Velo-city conference series, which is a premier international event for exchanging experiences for planning and policies for improved infrastructure for bicyclists.

As emphasized during the event, a main function of the Researchers Roundtable has also been to gather substantive inputs to the preparation of UN-HABITAT's 2013 Global Report on Human Settlements, which will focus on "Sustainable Urban Transport." The report will review key trends, practices and policies on sustainable urban mobility and transportation patterns from cities around the world. Further, the report will assemble models on how to cater for the mobility needs of urban populations in an economically, environmentally and socially sustainable manner. Experiences, innovations and ways to address policy challenges in regard to bridging the urban transport divide that were shared during the Researchers Roundtable will enrich the contents of the upcoming Global Report.

Overall, the Roundtable also presented a rare occasion to link perspectives from developed and developing countries on urban mobility. These unified views on urban transport across the globe have been particularly relevant for UN-HABITAT's participation at the 18th session of the United Nations Commission on Sustainable Development (CSD) in 2010 and the upcoming 19th session in 2011.

Finally, the discussion will also inform urban transport-related deliberations at UN-HABITAT's 23rd Governing Council in April 2011 and the dialogue between governments and Habitat Agenda partners. The aspects identified as emerging issues will particularly be relevant for discussing past resolutions on improved access to basic infrastructure and services and for advocating models to promote livable cities world wide. Overall, the well-attended event provided a significant opportunity for UN-HABITAT to reach out to new audiences and establish new partnerships, which can be particularly useful for expanding the agency's Global Network on Energy in Urban Settlements (GENUS).

EDITORS' NOTE

The following information is provided about this best practice case study to facilitate future research.

Name: City of Addis Ababa
Population: 3,384,569 (2008)
Region: Capital Region/East Africa
Province/State: Addis Ababa
Country: Ethiopia
Official Name: Federal Democratic Republic of Ethiopia
City Website: http://www.addisababacity.gov.et/

The UN-Habitat's website (http://www.unhabitat. org/) has additional information concerning the best practices for sustainable transportation options being used in cities located in countries throughout the world.

Their website also lists an overview of the speakers and panelists that participated in the program titled "Bridging the Urban Transport Divide," the fifth session of the World Urban Forum, which was held in Rio de Janeiro, Brazil. This forum was sponsored by the Urban Transport Section and Policy Analysis Branch of the UN-Habitat, which is located in Nairobi, Kenya.

Chapter 13

Amsterdam, Netherlands, Encourages the Use of Bicycles for Health Reasons

Kenneth W. Harris

I bicycled a lot from about ages 9 to 15. Though I biked little after I got my driver's license at age 16, I took up biking again in my 30s and continued into my 60s. I am going to tell you about 10 trends that are supporting increased bicycling now and will probably continue to do so, as well as five potential obstacles to increased bicycling.

1. More rider-friendly bicycles. Aided by the continuing revolutions in information and materials technology, manufacturers are offering a wide range of bicycles designed to overcome problems many riders have with conventional bicycles designed for the serious competitive or fitness cyclist.

Bicycles with electric motors increase the length of trips for which the bicycle is a feasible transport mode. Riders have their choice of pedal or electric power. For example, the Sanyo Eneloop looks and operates like a standard bicycle until you press a button on the left handlebar that activates a 250-watt motor powered by a lithium-ion battery.

Folding bicycles reduce problems in transporting and storing bicycles. There are now several models, such as the Xootr Swift, which are standard-size bikes but can be folded up and packed into suitcases.

Some bicycles, like the Trek Lime and other folding and electric-assist models, are intended purely for local transportation or for adult riders taking up cycling for the first time since childhood. The three-geared Lime does the gear shifting for you with an automatic shifting system called "coasting." You stop it with the coaster brakes many of us knew as children. It also has a full chain guard to keep grease from the chain off your clothes or bare legs. Now, companies like Denver's Gates Corporation are offering even more elegant solutions to the problem of grease stains on riders' clothes—polyethylene belt-drive systems that substitute for chains and require no lubrication.

If you simply can't stand not to be connected while you ride, you can now buy a weatherproof handlebar mount for your iPhone. Recumbent bicycles have become increasingly popular, mainly because riders don't experience the same chronic back and neck pain as they do when they ride upright bicycles. There are even hand-powered recumbent bicycles for riders who have lost use of their legs.

2. New bicycle infrastructure. The infrastructure development necessary to support a major modal shift toward bicycle and walking transportation is taking place, as envi-

Originally published as "Bike to the Future," *The Futurist*, Vol. 45, No. 2 (March–April 2011), by the World Future Society, Bethesda, Maryland. Reprinted with permission of the publisher.

sioned in a Rails-to-Trails Conservancy study titled *Active Transportation for America,* partly with public support and partly as a result of market forces. The change is taking place relatively quickly in Europe and gradually in the United States.

Dedicated bicycle traffic lanes are a key element of bicycling infrastructure. When I was in Amsterdam in 2009, I was impressed by the extensive network of bike lanes in that city and by the large number of cyclists using the lanes. The system even included special traffic lights for bikers. I learned to watch for both bicycles and cars when I crossed the street, and I found that bicyclists there were no more forgiving of pedestrians than car drivers are in the United States.

Cities and towns throughout the United States are creating designated bike lanes on streets and highways. Downtown Washington, D.C., now has 50 miles of designated bike lanes, including lengths of Pennsylvania Avenue, and the city plans to expand the network to 80 miles. Chicago and Portland, Oregon, also have extensive networks of bicycle lanes and plan major expansions.

Secure parking facilities are just as necessary for bicycles as for cars. During my visit to Amsterdam, I was impressed by the huge bike parking area near the main railway station. I don't believe there is any bike parking facility of that magnitude yet in the United States, but there are plenty of small-scale facilities, such as the bike racks and lockers at Washington's Metro stations.

Of course, if we are to make ourselves dependent on bike transport, we need convenient places to rent bicycles, just as we can easily rent cars at airports and hotels. Such bike rental programs are coming into existence. The best-known one is Paris's Velib, which makes 15,000 bicycles available for rent at 1,000 stations. In the United States, there are bike rental programs in Washington, D.C., and Irvine, California. There are slight variations in operation, but you rent the bicycles by paying an annual subscription fee or with a credit card for a short period of time, much as you would rent a car from Zipcar.

Some hotels now offer bike rentals to their guests. Some employers are also providing needed bicycling infrastructure, such as showers, changing facilities, and wellness programs that offer financial incentives for weight loss.

3. Medical community advice to exercise. As we have heard for many years, medical authorities are urging everyone to exercise more. They cite a growing body of scientific evidence that regular exercise prevents or mitigates a wide variety of health disorders, especially obesity, cardiovascular disease, diabetes, substance abuse, and mild emotional and psychological disorders.

Bicycling is a particularly good way to exercise because you can use your bike for transport or purely recreational purposes. Furthermore, many people will not get enough exercise for good health unless they bike to work or to and from errands, or otherwise set aside some of their leisure time for biking or another form of exercise.

The medical advice for people to exercise more has promoted cycling among what used to be considered the geriatric set. National Sporting Goods Association (NSGA) data show that the percentage of Americans aged 45–65 participating in cycling has grown steadily from 11.4 percent in 1993 to 20.2 percent in 2009, while participation by Americans 65 and older increased from 4.4 percent to 5.0 percent.

4. Believe it or not, people have more leisure time. A study by the National Bureau of Economic Research concluded that Americans of working age had an average of more than 35 hours per week of leisure in 2003 (compared with 31 hours in 1965), even excluding time spent in necessary personal care, sleeping, and paid employment. The Bureau of Labor Statistics Time Use Survey shows that Americans over age 15 spent 5.25 hours daily on purely leisure activities in 2009—including 2.82 hours watching TV—but only about 20 minutes a day on sports and exercise.

The Time Use Survey also shows that leisure time is becoming more and more fragmented, and while people do have more leisure time than they think they do, they aren't getting out much more. Now, watching television and bicycling are no longer mutually exclusive activities. In January 2010, Nintendo released an exercise bike called the Cyberbike to go with its Wii video game system. The game features 18 levels and allows people to compete with friends and other bike riders around the world remotely. Because it is a home bike, it offers an extra level of convenience for people who feel time-stressed (even though they actually do have the time to exercise).

5. Changing laws, regulations, and social attitudes. Participation in sports and exercise used to be considered an activity only for young males, especially upper-class males. No more! Thanks to changing laws, regulations, and social attitudes, women's and girls' participation has dramatically increased.

In the United States, the biggest factor contributing to more women exercising has been the passage and enforcement of Title IX of the Education Amendments of 1972. This required schools and colleges to offer equal access to sports participation for females. School and college sports participation by women and girls subsequently increased from 300,000 when the law was passed to more than 3 million today.

I believe the increase in female participation in school and college sports for more than a generation has helped create an attitude that adult women should participate more in sports and fitness activities, including biking, after high school or college. NSGA data show that cycling is still male dominated, but a significant minority of women participate. Since 1993, more than 50 percent of men and 40 percent of women have participated in cycling annually.

6. Charities and others organize bike rides. Participating to finish endurance athletic events rather than competing to win has become a new ethic, and charities are taking advantage. They organize many athletic events, including bike rides to raise money, and thousands participate. Prominent health foundations, such as the American Lung Association, the Arthritis Foundation, and the National Multiple Sclerosis Society, sponsor a lot of rides.

The National Multiple Sclerosis Society chapters sponsor about 100 bike rides annually throughout the United States. I learned about the MS rides when my daughter became special-events coordinator for the Washington chapter of the MS Society. I participated in several of their rides. One memory I will always have was one year at the start there was a young man crippled with MS sitting on a chair. Beneath him was a sign, "Your legs help mine!" That's effective marketing! I bet it brought a lot of people back the next year.

There are many other rides organized to promote the areas where they take place. A great example is the annual Seagull Century that takes place each fall on Maryland's Eastern Shore. The 100-kilometer (62 miles) ride starts and ends at Salisbury State University in Salisbury. I have participated several times and have been continually amazed by the extent of participation. In 2009, 8,300 riders from 39 states and Canada participated.

7. Popularity of exercise vacations, especially bike touring. Exercise vacations have become popular, and one of the most attractive options is bicycle touring. Many companies offer guided bicycle tours. Typically, the tour companies lay out the routes, rent the bicycles if participants don't bring their own, provide mechanical support, carry the riders' luggage in support vehicles, and arrange the riders' meals and lodging, which range from rustic to luxurious.

I have been on several that involve biking from country inn to country inn. The tours cover a wide range of distances. Some circle around small parts of a state, like the Vermont Bicycle Touring's Champlain Valley and Islands Tour in Vermont. Others tour across the entire United States, like the Adventure Cycling Association's Southern Tier tour from San Diego, California, to St. Augustine, Florida.

8. Creation of rail trails. A significant development for biking and other forms of exercise in the United States has been the creation of rail trails. Today, there are more than 1,600 rail trails extending 19,000 miles, with another 9,000 miles planned, compared with only 200 in 1986. Much of the rail trail mileage is in urban areas, where most Americans live. These trails are on abandoned railroad rights-of-way or on rights-of-way shared with intra-city freight rail or intra-urban light-rail transport.

The climate for creation of these trails has been highly favorable. The U.S. railroad network shrank from its peak size of 270,000 miles in 1916 to about 140,000 miles currently as a result of substitution of trucks for rail freight transportation, as well as railway consolidations and mergers. These industry shifts left thousands of miles of railroad rights-of-way unused.

Because the parcels of land included in these rights-of-way would be difficult to reassemble if they ever were needed for rail transport again, Congress passed the Rails-to-Trails Act in 1983, which gave the federal government authority to regulate disposition of these rights-of-way and save them for trail use by "railbanking" them. Railroads have been willing to turn over the rights-of-way for trail use because they are relieved of the associated property taxes and maintenance costs, and because they could still reclaim the rights-of-way for transport later, if necessary.

9. Environmentally friendly local transport. Substituting walking and nonmotorized or electric motor-assisted cycling for automobile use can provide substantial pollution reductions. The *Active Transportation for America* study concluded that short trips of three miles or less make up half of all trips taken in the United States; shifting these short trips to biking and walking could reduce CO_2 emissions by at least 12 million and up to 91 million tons a year.

That study also pointed out two important secondary environmental benefits of active transportation. First, people will use fuel-efficient public transportation more and drive less if they are able to walk or bike to the train station or bus stop. Second, the more that active transportation substitutes for motorized transportation, the less congestion there will be on the highways. Fuel savings and emission reductions will follow.

10. Government support. Governments are giving a lot of support to bicycling both for transport and health. The U.S. government authorized $370 million to support bicycling during fiscal years 2004–2009 and enacted numerous laws and regulations favorable to the creation of trails.

In Europe, Norway set a goal of having bicycle travel constitute 8 percent of all travel by 2015, compared with 4 percent in 2007. Sweden hopes to have bicycle travel constitute 15 percent of all travel. And the European Union adopted a goal of eliminating 6 percent of all emissions from cars by means of bicycle trips.

Five Factors Inhibiting a Biking Future

I believe that these 10 trends favoring more bicycling will continue, but change will come slowly. Here are five reasons why:

1. People are slow to adopt healthy lifestyles. Look no further for evidence than the quarter of the U.S. population who still smoke more than 40 years after the first Surgeon General's report on smoking and health. People who are not exercising enough now will likely be harder to persuade than those who are already active.

2. Alternative approaches to fitness are being promoted. The medical community's current advice that you can get the exercise you need in episodes of as little as 10 minutes may make people more favorably inclined to forms of exercise other than bicycling, especially if they are currently inactive.

3. Bikes on the budgetary chopping block. Many governments are likely to cut their budgets sharply in the next few years to pay for the massive debts they incurred during the economic downturn, and bicycling support programs will be tempting targets. There will be major political "tugs of war" between motorized transport lobbies and bike advocacy organizations, such as the Rails-to-Trails Conservancy and League of American Bicyclists.

4. Conflicting infrastructure priorities. The U.S. population is expected to grow by another 100 million people by mid-century. If there is prolonged fiscal austerity, growth in bicycle infrastructure might not keep up with demand. The automobile will remain the primary transport mode. Demands for more auto infrastructure will have priority. This will also be the case in other countries with growing populations, such as India and China.

5. Conflicting leisure time priorities. Many people may have less leisure time in the future than they do now. Harder economic times may force some adults to work multiple jobs, for instance. Retired adults may be preoccupied with taking care of frail or sick friends and relatives, or becoming "parents" again for their grandchildren. Children and adolescents may continue to have their leisure time organized for them by their parents and schools, with less time left over for individual exercise.

Biking for a Healthier Future

Continued world population growth will likely be accompanied by growing amounts of resource consumption and, hence, pollution. Advances in communications technology may also make unhealthy sedentary lifestyles less avoidable. These two threats to human health alone suggest that the world community must invest in local transportation solutions that are less polluting and that promote sufficient physical activity for the sake of everyone's good health in the future.

The trends described above indicate that the bicycle could be a part of the answer to these significant challenges. Transportation and health authorities and segments of the general public already embrace this partial answer; imaginative and continual public education, as in antismoking campaigns, is necessary to achieve total public acceptance.

EDITORS' NOTE

The following information is provided about this best practice case study to facilitate future research.

Name: City of Amsterdam
Population: 810,084 (2013)
Region: Capital Region
Province/State: North Holland
Country: Netherlands
Official Name: Kingdom of the Netherlands
City Website: http://www.amsterdam.nl/

Chapter 14

Barcelona, Spain, Facilitates the Redesigning of Cars for Inner-City Use

Ryan Chin

How can you design a city by designing a car? Today's automobiles are driven by an increasing number of users who live in cities. The United Nations reported in 2007 that migration patterns and population growth have created an equal split between inhabitants of cities and rural areas for the first time in human history. This general trend will continue for the next several decades and will produce a very urbanized world.

In 1950, New York City was the only megacity on the planet, with 10 million occupants. Today, there are 25 megacities that are mostly in developing countries. To verify this trend, we need only to look at the rapid urbanization in China to see the mass migration of the rural poor to urban areas for economic opportunity. Population experts project that most of the urban growth will occur in Asia and Africa for the next several decades. Simultaneously, humanity's thirst for personal mobility will continue to grow. History shows that, as countries develop economically, so does their use of four-wheeled motorized transportation.

The world's automobile fleet is currently estimated at 800 million cars that serve the 7.8 billion people living on Planet Earth. In the developed world, roughly seven out of 10

people own a car, whereas in the developing world, it's two out of 10. The continued economic development of Brazil, Russia, India, and China will fuel the growth of this fleet to more than 1 billion cars by 2020. The continued use of this personal transportation model is simply unsustainable given the combination of energy inefficiency, environmental consequences of fossil-fuel usage, potential disruptions to fuel supplies, urban sprawl created by automobile reliance, and congestion caused by inadequate alternative modes of transport. What we need is to radically rethink the problem by examining not only the automobile itself, but also how it is used in cities (where most of us are currently living).

Size and Weight

2010: Today's automobiles weigh an average of nearly 4,000 lbs., approximately 20 times the weight of the driver. Today's automobiles also have a footprint of approximately 100 square feet, which is nearly 15 times the amount of space required for a comfortable office chair. But the size requirements don't stop at the footprint of the vehicle, if we consider the space that cars oc-

Originally published as "Sustainable Urban Mobility in 2020," *The Futurist*, Vol. 44, No. 4 (July–August 2010), by the World Future Society, Bethesda, Maryland. Reprinted with permission of the publisher.

cupy on the road, in parking at home, work, and other destinations; add to that the space for maintenance and repair and it quickly grows to approximately 1,200 sq. ft. per vehicle. In midtown Manhattan, a 1,200 sq. ft. condominium would cost you upwards of $2 million to own.

2020: Tomorrow's automobiles will be more lightweight and smaller. Size, weight, and energy efficiency are three factors that intimately interconnect in the design and engineering of automobiles. The lighter the vehicle, the more energy efficient it will be to move the mass of the car. The smaller the vehicle, the less mass you have. This set of relations forms a set of positive and negative feedback loops that ultimately affect the design of the vehicle. It will be imperative to incorporate technological improvements in lightweight materials, and composites will certainly help to make vehicles leaner, but this is not enough. Vehicles must also become more compact. These changes will not only improve energy efficiency, but also the vehicles' overall footprint.

Range and Speed

2010: Today's automobiles have a fuel range of about 300 miles (meaning they can travel 300 miles or so on one tank), can go from 0 to 60 mph in less than 10 seconds, and top out at more than 110 mph. This is great for intercity travel, but most Americans don't travel that far. More than 80 percent of daily commutes in America are less than 40 miles (round trip). With more than 81 percent of Americans living in metropolitan areas, you simply don't need to go 100 miles an hour down a city street. If you travel to Shanghai today, the average speed in the city is 9 mph. Bangalore, India, has achieved 24-hour congestion. Today's vehicle is simply over-engineered for most practical purposes in cities.

2020: Tomorrow's automobiles will not need that much refueling autonomy. BMW recently finished a series of user experiments to examine "range anxiety"—the fear of running out of electricity in electric cars—and discovered that their new electric mini (with 100 miles of range) has two to three times the range required for practically all trips. Users don't need to have five to six times the range, and they quickly learned to adapt to the constraints (and benefits) of this new vehicle type. The introduction of electric charging infrastructure in the upcoming decade will virtually eliminate range issues in urban areas. Cities like San Francisco, Portland, Paris, Madrid, and Barcelona all have initiatives to bring a network of charging stations in their respective metropolitan areas. Car makers are introducing plug-in options for many models that enable the electrical charging from a common 110V household outlet.

Gasoline Versus Electric

2010: Today's vehicles are predominantly powered by petroleum-based fuels. An internal combustion engine is terribly inefficient (approximately 15 percent) in converting chemical energy into mechanical work to drive the wheels of your car. Hybrid vehicles are better at conserving energy at the cost of a more complex power train, but projections for the next five years call for less than 12 percent of the total new car market. The remaining alternative fuels, like compressed natural gas, hydrogen, compressed air, and biofuels, have varying levels of efficiency, but are utilized in even fewer numbers than hybrids. Battery electric vehicles utilize electric motors that are more than 90 percent energy efficient, but these have not taken over mainstream markets because of limitations of battery technology.

2020: Tomorrow's automobiles will be

increasingly electrified. The emergence of new battery chemistries such as lithium ion nanophosphate have allowed battery manufacturers to produce cells that have higher energy density and lower internal resistance, thus allowing rapid charging in less than 30 minutes. In fact, my colleagues at the MIT Electric Vehicle Team have been able to rapid-charge these new cells in less than 7 minutes with just a 10 percent degradation in capacity after 1,500 cycles. For comparison, lithium ion cells in your laptop today have roughly 1,000 cycles of usable life. The ability to rapid-charge will enable users to top-off their batteries in about the time it will take to order and drink an expresso, thus opening up new opportunities to create an ubiquitous charging network distributed throughout cities. No longer do we need to charge only at home or the workplace where our cars sit waiting for six to 10 hours.

Driver-Controlled Versus Autonomous Driving

2010: Today's cars are driven by human operations. Drivers have a number of telematics devices that aid in driving, such as antilock brakes for safe stopping, adaptive cruise control for the highway, parking sensors to help avoid scratches to the bumpers, and GPS for navigating unfamiliar places. However, we still have more than 50,000 deaths a year in the United States under the current driving paradigm. Today's drivers sit in traffic for more than 50 hours a year and endure the stop-and-go driving experience.

2020: Tomorrow's cars will be increasingly autonomous. The annual DARPA Urban Challenge has consistently proven to be a tremendously useful catalyst for innovations in autonomous driving. The most recent challenge shows that autonomously driven vehicles can navigate in busy city streets without incident. The potential of autonomous vehicles to self-drive and coordinate with other autonomous vehicles is to smooth traffic flows. In urban environments, top speed is not necessary; it is the orchestrated movement of vehicles within a speed regime that will improve congestion. The introduction of semi-autonomous systems such as self-parking and automated highway systems has provided useful lessons in the benefits and challenges of autonomous driving. Continued federally funded research in this area, combined with improvements in computational power, will enable the miniaturization of autonomous technologies, thus making autonomous driving commercially viable for mass markets in the coming decade.

Private Versus Shared Ownership

2010: Today's automobiles are designed for private ownership. The burden of ownership includes the cost of the vehicle, depreciation, tires, licensure, taxes, registration, insurance, maintenance, fuel, and parking. These individual direct costs are compounded by what economists call "negative externalities," which include congestion and pollution leading to global warming—that is, costs to society not immediately felt by the individual user. Privately owned commuter vehicles that may drive two hours a day (round trip) will sit doing nothing useful for 92 percent of the day. During this state, the car takes up valuable real estate and doesn't move people around. Single passenger occupancy also doesn't help in this situation; if I stand on Memorial Drive in Cambridge, Massachusetts, I could wait up to 20 minutes before seeing a vehicle with two occupants. In that same city, approximately one-third of the land area is devoted to the servicing of automobiles (this includes roads and parking for cars) that are principally used by private individuals. This is not an atypical land-use percentage devoted to the automobile throughout the United States.

2020: Tomorrow's automobiles will increasingly utilized in cooperative or shared-use models. The emergence of car-sharing and bike-sharing schemes in urban areas in both the United States and Europe have established alternative models and markets for fractional or on-demand mobility. Zipcar, the world's largest car-share program, has grown from just a handful of cars to a fleet of 6,000 cars and 275,000 drivers in 49 cities in just under 10 years. It's very difficult to own one-quarter or one-tenth of a car with traditional ownership, and let's not even talk about fractional insurance. Shared ownership provides users fractional ownership that allows them access to any vehicle in the fleet whenever they please and for as long as they need, just like video on demand or print on demand.

Radical Rethinking Required

Since 2003, the Smart Cities group at the MIT Media Lab has developed solutions to directly tackle these problems. We have designed an electric two-passenger vehicle called the CityCar, which utilizes in-wheel electric motors called Wheel Robots that have incorporated drive, suspension, and braking directly inside the wheel. Each wheel is independently controlled with by-wire controls (no mechanical linkages) and is capable of 120 degrees of steering, which provides very high maneuverability. The CityCar can turn on its own axis (zero turn radius) and can make sideways turns by turning the wheels perpendicular to the primary driving axis.

The Wheel Robots eliminate the need for traditional components like drivelines, transmissions, and gearboxes. We have taken advantage of this freedom by rethinking the architecture of the vehicle. Since there is no driveline, we can make the vehicle very compact by folding the chassis. The CityCar can fold up to half its length to just under the width of a traditional parking space. The CityCar, when folded, is less than 60 inches in length and 100 inches when unfolded (comparable to the Smart Car). Three City-Cars when parked can fit into one traditional parking space. It weighs just 1,000 lbs., thus making it very lightweight and energy efficient, and the new architecture allows us to rethink entry and exit. We have designed a front ingress solution that easily allows the driver and passenger to safely exit the vehicle onto the curb rather than the street. The folding mechanism complements this feature by articulating the seats so that the user can eronomically and elegantly exit at an elevated position. CityCars are designed to park nose-in to the curb, which allows the user to use the sidewalk rather than the street. Finally, the in-wheel motors will provide plenty of low-end torque, thus making the CityCar fun to drive in urban areas.

Simply redesigning the vehicle is only one part of the solution. We have also created a new use model, called "Mobility on Demand" (MoD), which utilizes a fleet of lightweight electric vehicles (LEVs) that are distributed at electric charging stations throughout a metropolitan area. The LEVs are designed for shared use, which enable high utilization rates for the vehicles and the parking spaces they occupy. The use model mimics the bike sharing systems made popular in Europe, whereby users simply walk up to the closest charging station, swipe a credit card, pick up a vehicle, drive to the station closest to their destination, and drop off the vehicle.

Our group has designed our CityCar to fit into these MoD systems, thus creating a complementary network that can solve what transportation planners call the "First Mile Last Mile" problem of public transit—that is, how to bridge the distance between your real origin (i.e., your home) to the transit station and from the transit station to your real final destination (i.e., your work-place). Often these distances are too long to walk, thus encouraging private automobile use.

The expansion of MoD into a sustainable urban eco-system can be achieved by introducing additional shared-use vehicle types like electric bicycles and scooters. (Smart Cities has also designed an electric folding scooter called the "RoboScooter" and an electric bike called the "GreenWheel.") This will offer flexibility and convenience while allowing for asymmetric trips. For example, a user can drive a GreenWheel to the supermarket, then go home with a CityCar that can carry groceries.

We believe that MoD systems will work better than private automobiles in cities because you never have to worry about storing the vehicle. In many cases, a MoD charging station will be closer to your final destination than if you had to park in a private lot. A typical urban trip is short, however; much of the time spent is not actually driving, but rather walking to the vehicle and finding parking once you get there. A recent study by the Imperial College in London showed that, during congested hours, more than 40 percent of total gasoline use is by cars looking for a parking space!

In 2020, I expect the shift from private gasoline powered use to shared electric vehicles will be on its way. There are three primary factors that will accelerate this trend:

1. Economic and environmental pressure to transition away from petroleum fuels.
2. Technological innovations.
3. Political leadership to promote new regulations and policies for this type of innovation.

In 2010, China has become the world's number-one automobile market, surpassing the United States, in the total number of cars purchased. The increased consumption of fossil fuels and the emissions of CO_2 will be part and parcel of this economic development. This will all but guarantee increased demand for petroleum and set the stage for political responsiveness.

Luckily, most of the technologies required to make the CityCar real already exist today, such as highly efficient electric motors, computational horsepower, new battery technologies, wireless network communications, lightweight composite materials, advanced sensing, and GPS. The only thing that limits us is the inherent difficulty of breaking away from our preconceived notions and embracing this radical rethinking.

NOTE

Vehicle-to-Grid Energy

Industrial research has been conducted in the last decade on the benefits of Vehicle-to-Grid (V2G) charging. This enables cars to charge from renewable power sources and also feed power back into the grid, which can be sold at a premium back to the utility. Utilities will be able to load level the electric grid by "peak shaving" during the hottest days when everyone has the air conditioning running.

EDITORS' NOTE

The following information is provided about this best practice case study to facilitate future research.

Name: City of Barcelona
Population: 1,620,943 (2009)
Region: Capital Region
Province/State: Catalonia
Country: Spain
Official Name: Kingdom of Spain
City Website: http://www.barcelona.cat/

Chapter 15

Beijing, China, Is Working on a High Speed Rail System That Is a World Model

Center for Design Excellence

It's time for a New Deal for America—building the 21st century green economy to solve our problems and set us up for a prosperous, sustainable future

We need to embark on a major government project to fix America like President Roosevelt initiated in 1933 and 1935. We need another New Deal that will create millions of jobs and stimulate our economy. But that's not enough. We also need to solve our oil dependence by reducing our car dependence, and we have to address global warming in a big way too. To accomplish all this, we need a new direction—we need all hands on deck! Can we do it? **"Yes we can!"**

Investing in New Roads IS NOT the Solution

More roads increase our oil and car dependence. Roads are the problem. We need a complete change of direction in spending on transportation. We have limited time, money, and resources, so we need to get this right by addressing all our problems together with the most comprehensive solutions—*as quickly as possible*. If we don't enact real, long-term sustainable solutions, we will end up back in this same situation a year or two from now when

oil prices skyrocket again. We are running out of time and options to permanently solve our problems.

Investing in New Trains IS the Solution

Train system construction has all the benefits of road construction in creating jobs, but train construction puts into place the solution to all the other problems at the same time. Trains take us away from our oil and car addiction, and move us towards a truly sustainable, green economy and country.

China is Building a Massive National Rail System, *Quickly*

China is well on its way converting their entire country to sustainable, green transportation. Abandoning their plan to create a car culture rivaling America, China quickly switched to building an extensive train system nationwide. They realized the era of cheap easy oil was over just as they had arrived to the party. China is currently building 5,000 miles of brand new high-speed rail comparable to the French TGV (200+ mph), plus 36 brand new, full size metro systems—each to cover an entire city. The new Shanghai metro system will be the largest in the world when complete. This will all be open for business in

Originally published as "New Deal National Rail Plan," *State of the Art Sustainable Transportation* (2009), by the Center for Design Excellence, Alexandria, Virginia. Reprinted with permission of the publisher.

just a few short years! China's massive, fast track green transportation construction project is unprecedented in the history of the world, and will completely transform China towards sustainability by drastically reducing their need for cars and oil. They have also begun large scale manufacturing of wind turbines to power the trains and green their nation's energy. If China can accomplish all this in such a short time, we can too... *Yes we can!*

5 Serious Problems We Must Solve Quickly

1. Failing economy and rising job losses. Our economy is crumbling right before our eyes. Major corporations are going bankrupt or disappearing one after the other. Job losses are rising every day, and are predicted to get far worse. At the root of our economic problems is the cost of our oil addiction—$700 billion each year for the purchase of oil. This is unsustainable, and is expected to rise dramatically over the next couple of years. The big problem is that our entire economy—especially our transportation system—is built upon cheap and plentiful oil—which is now gone forever. *"Business as usual"* is no longer possible. We need a new business for America.

2. Global warming and climate change. The planet is in peril, and little has been done in America to deal with this crisis. In fact, there have been considerable efforts to delay any real action. Millions of lives are at stake, our cities, our prosperity, and our entire food supply is vulnerable to irreversible damage if we don't act quickly. We face a planetary emergency and we need to act as we would in any emergency with fast action and solutions as big as the problem. Building more roads adds to the problem.

3. Peak oil and energy security. According to leading experts, world oil supplies have peaked resulting in less oil available for our consumption each year from now on. We need fast action to drastically reduce our oil and car dependence. Many experts say peak oil is more serious than global warming. Our entire economy is dependent on oil, along with 98 percent of our transportation and 99 percent of our food supply. Our nation is dangerously vulnerable to the volatile global oil situation, which will only get worse as we move deeper into the era of world peak oil. We need to transition our society away from oil and cars—*quickly.* We are currently at war trying to secure the last remaining oil reserves, but this war has destroyed our economy and put us deep into debt. We can no longer afford the huge costs of war, both financially and in human lives and suffering. And we certainly can't afford to burn up massive amounts of the remaining scarce oil fighting wars for oil.

4. Crumbling infrastructure. We have neglected the repair and maintenance of our transportation infrastructure nationwide to the point where bridges are collapsing, roads are falling apart, and our rail systems are unable to function at a reasonable level of service, or meet the rapidly rising demand. The collapsing systems are due to age, poor maintenance, and being overloaded. The collapsed bridge was never designed to carry the loads it was carrying, and thousands more bridges are in the same condition. In 2005, the American Society of Civil Engineers gave the nation's infrastructure a "D" rating, just above complete failure, and estimated the cost to repair it to a safe level at $1.6 trillion! This doesn't even include expanding the systems to meet the projected growth in demand. It will be far cheaper to build a new national rail system!

5. Mobility crisis nationwide. Our entire national transportation system is in disrepair and overloaded to a point near paralysis. It's a time-consuming nightmare to get anywhere in America. We waste countless hours of our time and billions of gallons of precious fuel sitting stuck in traffic on our roads and runways. We are spending more money on waste than it would cost to build a new national high-speed rail system. We are paying hundreds of billions of dollars for an outdated transportation system that fails to provide reasonable, efficient mobility. Building more roads simply grows the problem, and has proven over and over to create more traffic, and digs us deeper into our oil and car addiction. We clearly need a new direction in transportation policy and funding.

One Solution For 5 Problems

New Deal National Rail Plan 2009

A new direction! One project can solve all our problems together. Building a new world-class rail system across America will address all 5 problems simultaneously, and put us on a course to sustainability and prosperity. This is the fastest, most efficient way to deal with all these huge problems together. Solving 5 big problems with one solution is smart, efficient, and a real bargain compared to what it would cost in time and money trying to solve them individually.

A Safe, Affordable, Green Transportation System

This is not New in America—We Already had an Extensive Rail System
In 1922, America had more than 44,800 miles of green, electric streetcar rail systems in 80 cities, plus thousands of miles of regional and national rail systems. More than 90 percent of Americans lived in walkable cities with great train service right outside the door, transporting them everywhere.

A New National Rail System Solves Many Problems:

• Creates millions of green jobs nationwide building the new rail infrastructure and manufacturing the rail cars
• Pays for itself by significantly reducing our $700 billion a year oil purchase trade deficit
• A major step toward solving global warming by reducing our oil consumption and emissions
• Drastically reduces our oil addiction and lowers our risk from the coming peak oil crisis
• Lowers our dependence on costly military operations securing oil flow around the world
• Lowers our national security risk, and ends wars for oil
• *Freedom from oil*—Powered by clean electricity from renewable energy sources: wind, solar, geothermal, ocean/tidal
• Safe, affordable, green transportation for everyone
• Saves lives (43,000 Americans die each year in car accidents)
• Provides efficient mobility that moves people and goods without delay and waste
• Puts in place a high quality infrastructure setting us up for prosperity, mobility, efficiency, and a sustainable future
• It lays the foundation for building walkable, affordable green communities surrounding the train stations
• Makes cities more livable, safe, healthy, and beautiful by removing cars, traffic, noise, pollution, and parking lots

The New Rail Plan

A New Safe, Affordable, Green Transportation System for All Americans
Build a new world-class national rail system made up of an extensive network of connecting train lines in a 3-tiered, seamless system. The trains would run on clean electricity powered by a combination of wind, solar, geothermal, and ocean/tidal renewable green energy.

A. National High-speed Rail System

This top level train would serve as the national fast system now covered by airplanes and distance car travel. It would consist of all high-speed train lines connecting central cities together in a web of train lines across the nation. The trains operating at this level would be state-of-the-art TGV/Eurostar type trains that travel at 200–220 mph. This high-speed rail system is a high quality, high capacity system transporting more passengers than highways and airlines put together—using a fraction of the energy, for less than a quarter of the cost.

The 800-mile California High Speed Rail project—just voted in by the people—is the first piece of this national system. Propelling California into the 21st century, the new train will link all major cities from Sacramento to San Diego with 220 mph trains.

B. Regional rail systems

This level of trains would serve as the medium-speed regional system linking the many regional destinations together and to the high-speed train station. These regional trains would connect to all the smaller cities, towns, and significant destinations within each region.

This includes metro systems as well as commuter and regional trains. These new trains would serve as the backbone of a new regional planning effort to convert low density suburban development into a series of walkable, transit oriented developments along the new train lines.

C. Local light rail, streetcar, trolley & tram systems

This level of trains would serve as the local collector system connecting to the regional trains. It would have stops in all parts of cities, neighborhoods and central gathering places, as well as employment centers, retail locations, and sports and recreation facilities within each community.

Ideally, these trains would never be more than a few blocks walk from all loca-tions within cities and towns. Much like the original 44,800 mile streetcar system in America, this new system would enable a large percentage of Americans once again to live in walkable cities without the need for a car.

PARTNERSHIPS

A green retooling of the U.S. transportation industry is needed. Our transportation systems were built around cheap oil—which is now gone for good. No amount of biofuels, used french-fry oil, hydrogen fuel cells, and hybrid cars are going to be able to move 300 million Americans into the future. We need a new 21st century transportation system for a new age! *"We need all hands on deck!"*

All the companies now in transportation need to retool and be included in this new plan. This would save as many jobs as possible, and minimize competition and resistance to the new systems. The retooling would include train system design, manufacturing, operations, and maintenance, and could take place as follows:

Companies now known as airlines, rather than limited to managing air travel, would become "transportation providers" and invited to operate train company franchises. Airplane and auto manufacturers could start building trains, track, and parts. Airport operators could become train station operators. The FAA could change into the agency that oversees the entire operation. The Department of Transportation could plan the train network, instead of planning roads. Road builders can become train infrastructure builders.

There are also a number of other American companies outside the transportation industry that would benefit greatly by getting involved in a new train system. Real estate developers would build walkable urbanism surrounding the train stations. Resort, hotel, theme park operators, and travel companies would all see increased business. Shipping and delivery companies would all save money. Defense contractors could get involved building the energy, signaling, and control systems. In addition, there are many train operators and manufacturers in Europe and Japan that would be more than willing to participate in building and operating a high-speed train network in America.

RETOOL AMERICAN

Retooling industry is essential for fixing America. We are in the midst of a sea change in our society that requires us to fundamentally change our transportation and many of our industries to build the new green economy. This is the new business of America! Continuing "business as usual" is no longer possible.

1. Retool Car Manufacturers. All three American car manufacturers are on the edge of bankruptcy and are pleading for a massive bailout from the government to the tune of tens of billions of dollars—far more then their total net worth. Even with the bailout, these companies are no longer viable entities, since continued car manufacturing makes little sense in light of peak oil and climate change. There is an enormous need for large scale manufacturing of trains in America. Retooling the car factories can be done quickly to build trains while saving millions of jobs. A complete retooling of the car factories was accomplished in a matter of months back in the 1940s to meet the wartime need for tanks and airplanes. We can do the same thing now just as quickly. *Yes we can!*

2. Retool Car Parts Suppliers. In addition to trains, millions of bicycles will be needed in America as we transition away from cars. Rather than import them from China, we should manufacture them here in America and create millions of green jobs. Car parts suppliers can retool into making bi-cycles since there will be a big reduction in the need for car parts.

3. Retool Airplane Manufacturers. There will be a great reduction in the need for airplanes as we enter the peak oil era. Since most trips will take place in trains, the majority of airplane manufacturing will become obsolete. Currently, there is a huge demand for wind turbines, and manufacturing is unable to keep up with this demand. Airplane manufacturing plants are ideal for retooling into producing wind turbines.

4. Retool Road Builders. As we transition away from cars, it makes no sense to spend any more money building roads that have no future. Roads and cars for the masses only made sense when there was plenty of cheap oil, but it's now gone forever. Currently, the huge need is for new train systems all across the nation. We need many thousands of miles of train infrastructure built as quickly as possible.

We need train tracks, train bridges and tunnels, and many new train stations built. This will be one of the nation's largest construction projects ever. Road builders are the ideal group to retool and lead the way building the nation's new green transportation system.

5. Retool Real Estate Developers. Since the era of cheap oil is over, our drive-in utopia will no longer be possible. Future development needs to be compact walkable urbanism surrounding train stations. This designs away the need for cars and oil. Walkable urbanism and trains are the future, and the building blocks for a sustainable society—creating livable, affordable, healthy, and enjoyable communities for all.

6. Retool Defense Contractors. We need to rethink our national defense strategy since everything is changing as we enter the era of peak oil. We need to focus more of our efforts on reducing our dependence on oil. This needs to become a central mission of our national security. We need to redirect a portion of our huge defense budget (currently half our entire nation's annual budget) towards changing our transportation to reduce our need for oil.

Peak oil and global warming represent a far greater national security threat than terrorism or any potential enemy. Defense contractors are ideal companies to manufacture products such as solar panels, wind turbine parts, and train computer control systems.

EDITORS' NOTE

The following information is provided about this best practice case study to facilitate future research.

Name: Beijing Municipality
Population: 20,693,000 (2012)
Region: Capital Region
Province/State: Hebei
Country: China
Official Name: People's Republic of China
City Website: http://www.ebeijing.gov.cn/

The Center for Design Excellence's website (http://www.urbandesign.org/) has additional information concerning the best practices for state-of-the-art rail transportation systems that are being implemented in cities in various nations throughout the world.

Chapter 16

Berlin, Germany, Builds Regional Transit Station to Promote Economic Development

Brian Baker

When the 1990s building boom in Berlin slowed at the end of the decade, several tracts of land across the center of the previously divided city remained underused or derelict. The Berlin Wall and its environs had taken a significant amount of land out of use, and for 30 years two distinct cities existed in Berlin, both physically and politically.

Notable redevelopment projects were completed during the boom period, including the large-scale mixed-use Potsdamer Platz development and the new government quarter adjacent to the reconstituted Reichstag, but the German economic downturn and the financial difficulties of Berlin have left much still to be accomplished.

One vital public sector project was realized during the early years of this decade. Beginning in 1994, the German government, Berlin, and the national rail company Deutsche Bahn worked on the design and construction of the largest railway station in Europe—the Berlin Hauptbahnhof—and in May 2006, it was officially opened by German Chancellor Angela Merkel.

Designed by Hamburg-based von Gerkan, Marg, and Partners, the five-story, glass-and-steel structure has three levels of re-

tail space, two levels of railway—one 33 feet (10 m) above street level—and two 151-foot-(46-m-) high office towers. The station building measures 525 by 130 feet (160 by 40 m) with 753,000 square feet (70,000 sq. m) of floor space. The project, which includes 161,000 square feet (15,000 sq. m) of retail space and 538,000 square feet (50,000 sq. m) of office space, is set to become the catalyst for development of 732,000 square feet (68,000 sq. m) of surrounding land. Fortunately for its prospects for success, this iconic structure, which evokes the large 19th-century cathedral-like rail stations across Europe but in a modern composition, was completed as the German economy improved.

"Berlin was unique and significant in the turbulent history of Europe in the 20th century. We believe it can be an important international city in the 21st," says Berlin deputy mayor Ingeborg Junge-Rever. "By creating a national and European transport hub in the center of the city, we have made it accessible for people across the former west-east divide. The approach we have taken to developing the sites around the new *hauptbahnhof* [main station] reflects the crucial role these developments will have in knitting back to-

Originally published as "Berlin's Hauptbahnhof Spurs Development," *Urban Land*, Vol. 66, No. 7 (July 2007), by the Urban Land Institute, Washington, D.C. Copyright, the Urban Land Institute, all rights reserved. Reprinted with permission.

gether the two parts of our formerly divided city." The city is investing heavily in the public realm on all sides of the station and in the adjacent area leading to the new government quarter, she adds.

Berlin is seeking to create a diverse, unique urban place using the opportunity for waterfront development in its proposal for the adjacent mixed-use Humboldthafen property to the east of the station, she says. Also planned is a "cube" building that will form one side of the perimeter of the new Washington Platz looking over the Spree River. To the north, across Invalidstrasse, the east-west road that runs along the northern perimeter of the station property, more development opportunities exist, especially close to the Museum of Contemporary Art, says Junge-Rever.

"The areas around the Hauptbahnhof form a unique location that we think can attract investors from around the world to develop buildings of distinction offering office, hotel, residential, and retail uses," she continues.

The original proposals for the land immediately around the rail station were the subject of a 1994 master plan by now retired German architecture legend Oswald Unger.

"The main issue in 1994 was that we wanted to create a defined urban area around the station," explains Karl-Heinz Winkens, now of Winkens Architekten and formerly with Ungers, who worked on the plan. "The challenge was how to achieve a typology around such a sculptured building. We found the solution by using the block form, which typifies the surrounding areas of the Mitte district to the east and west, and the more dramatic buildings close to the station entrances on the south and north elevations."

Proposals for areas east of the station around the original city harbor and the Berlin Spandau Canal were launched as the Humboldthafen project at the 2007 MIPIM exhibition in Cannes, France, in March.

In 2005, the Senate asked Winkens to revise the master plan because it was not attracting investors, says Hilmar von Lojewski, head of Berlin city center planning; more density and mixed uses were needed, he says. The new proposal calls for 1.2 million square feet (110,000 sq.-m) of gross floor area on a 377,000-square-foot (35,000-sq-m) site, which can be developed in flexible parcel sizes; some can be aggregated. Envisioned are nine building plots with development potential of 43,000 to 248,000 square feet (4,000 to 23,000 sq. m).

The Senate has invested $399,000 (€300,000) to prepare the harbor area for sale and development, though more than that was spent by Deutsche Bahn and the federal government to decontaminate the site and divert the Spree River as part of the railway station project, notes von Lojewski. Proposals call for a series of seven-story buildings that will be linked and augmented by smaller arcaded structures. All will front the water, where marinas and restaurants are planned. Uses will include residential space, offices, and hotels.

While land to the east of the station is currently owned by the city-state of Berlin, property on most of the other three perimeters is held by Deutsche Bahn or Vivico, a federal government entity that specializes in urban infill developments. Vivico has secured preliminary zoning and development approval for seven buildings totaling 1.6 million square feet (144,900 sq. m). It is not clear yet if Deutsche Bahn will develop its land in the northwest perimeter or sell it.

To the southwest of the railway station, detailed plans are being finalized this summer for the Lehrter Stadtquartier development, five seven-story buildings that will include apartments, offices, retail space, and hotels. Some properties will look over the Spree River with views of buildings in the government quarter 1,000 feet (300 m) away.

"At present, we are completing the zoning and deciding on the best concept; we will be marketing to investors later this year," says Michael Burrack, head of Vivico's Berlin office. "We do not intend to build speculatively for this development." The project will respond to market preferences for uses, with one of the main goals being creation of a lively place, he says. If Vivico decides not to develop residential space at the site, it will develop hotels with retail space and restaurants on the ground floors, Burrack said.

Vivico may well need to be flexible if it is to make early progress because doubts exist about market demand. At both Lehrter Stadtquartier and Humboldthafen, the heights and density are determined, but there is flexibility with design and materials.

Berlin currently has about 19 million square feet (1.75 million sq. m) of vacant office space. "Berlin never gained the importance we thought it would in the commercial sector," says Inga Schwarz, principal researcher at Cushman Wakefield in Frankfurt. "Its office market is heavily dependent on the public sector."

However, there is strong interest in Berlin among foreign investors, Schwarz reports, and she suggests they may find the unique character of the station area attractive. "It is clearly likely to be a good long-term investment, but I think the proposed uses will be significant in determining early development. With its waterside attraction and the proposals for some residential use, the area to the east of the station may well go forward more quickly than the Vivico estate," says Schwarz. "Waterside living is not as mature a market in Germany as elsewhere, but apartments in current [waterfront] schemes in Frankfurt and Hamburg have sold for very high prices recently," reflecting pent-up demand.

With 1,100 international, national, regional, and local trains arriving daily, the station generates a large amount of traffic. Its signature roof, the most striking architectural

feature of the area, has led to controversy and litigation. Project architect Markus von Gerkan originally specified a span of 1,053 feet (321 m), which would have extended the roof well beyond the core building in both directions, but in 2002, construction was curtailed by Deutsche Bahn in order to meet the deadline for reopening the railway. In its completed form, the span is 692 feet (211 m). Litigation over the late imposed changes to the roof structure is now settled, but a lasting consequence of the change is that the noise levels at some locations in the surrounding properties are higher than would have been the case originally.

Vivico also has tentative approval for construction of the cube and tower buildings. The tower is to be north of the station, but likely will be constructed only once a major tenant has signed on. The current approval is for a height of slightly less than 328 feet (100 m), but, Burrack says, "I'm convinced we could get approval to go a little higher if it would attract a major company headquarters to the city."

The cube will be built for a company that wants to show off its business, he says. "Its main use will be offices, but this may be combined with a use motivated by its special location," he adds. Some areas allowing public access are also likely to be included in the project, he says.

"We found the Albert Dock area in Liverpool in the U.K. an especially appropriate inspiration for the harbor area—especially the idea of the high density of buildings there," says Winkens. "Also, the buildings open to connect to the surrounding neighborhood and to views of the rest of the city."

To the northeast of the waterfront, where the harbor becomes the narrower Spandau Canal, the land parcels will probably be developed as two predominantly residential blocks. "Of the Humboldthafen plots, those in the northeast area are likely to be the second ones to be marketed," notes von Lojewski. "Marketing began with the southeast plots in May because they are in a prominent location closest to the government quarter, and because the ground there is not affected by ongoing underground railway construction."

According to von Lojewski, *baugruppen*, or private builder/owner groups, have expressed interest in developing the northeast plots for cohousing. However, all plots will be sold to the highest bidder with a conforming proposal.

Beyond Invalidstrasse, there is more developable land around older buildings associated with the former Berlin Hamburger station, now the Museum of Contemporary Art. Vivico owns adjacent buildings and intends to launch an art campus proposal there this year, which will involve converting the smaller buildings, currently in industrial use, to galleries.

Von Lojewski says he thinks it will take longer to build out the vacant land parcels that surround the museum and other older buildings than the parcels on the perimeter of the station site. "It will take time to build the idea of the area north of Invalidstrasse as a residential address," he says. "I think the developments around the station will be medium term, and those near the contemporary art museum may take longer, perhaps ten years or more."

While industry professionals are unwilling to speculate on the prices the land parcels will reach at public auction or on the likely value of the developments that will emerge, no city in Europe other than Berlin has such large, centrally located sites available on the market. For long-term international investors in particular, the sites—and subsequently the buildings—closest to the transport interchange and the government quarter are likely to prove the most attractive.

EDITORS' NOTE

The following information is provided about this best practice case study to facilitate future research.

Name: City of Berlin
Population: 3,397,469 (2013)
Region: Capital Region
Province/State: Berlin
Country: Germany
Official Name: Federal Republic of Germany
City Website: http://www.berlin.de/

Chapter 17

Bogotá, Colombia, Promotes Non-Motorized Transportation for Its Citizens

Felipe Morales *and* Carlos Felipe Pardo

The transformation of Bogotá's urban transport has had various components, one of which is the implementation of bicycle-related infrastructure, policies and promotion strategies. The key issues for Bogotá have been integrating these policies into a wider sustainable urban transport context, adapting existing regulations and policies to a NMT-promoting agenda, and overcoming political barriers in order for projects and policies to have continuity between each political term of office. Various stakeholders have been involved in this process; and their participation has in fact been strengthened throughout the past decade.

The model used for work done in terms of urban planning in Bogotá, such as the Bike Path Master Plan can be replicated in cities with similar socio-economic characteristics: it can be realized with low budgets especially when compared with other heavy infrastructure projects.

Importance of the Issue

The theme of non-motorized transport (NMT) policy is important in Bogotá because it provides a historical background to all the changes in transport policies and projects in the city. It is also very relevant globally as Bogotá provides an example to other cities interested in implementing similar policies. Bicycle-related developments in the city (e.g. the establishment of 350+ km of bike paths) have increased citizens' access to goods and services, reduced their travel times and improved their perception of their travel mode (bicycle use has increased from 0.5 percent in 1998 to circa 5 percent in 2010).

In essence, bicycling is a transport mode that has the following advantages: it is environmentally friendly, cheap, efficient, fun and versatile. Although its use is recommended for short trips (about 4.5 km on average) it can be combined with other modes of transport for longer trips providing an excellent alternative to the private car. Furthermore, the physical exercise provided by using the bicycle enables a healthy lifestyle, by reducing heart disease etc. Bicycles consume much less public space than most other vehicles, and by virtue of the low purchase and maintenance costs, it is also a mode of transport that is more accessible to vulnerable groups (elderly and children) or the poor strata of the population.

Originally published as "Building a Plan to Transform Non-Motorized Transport in Bogotá, Colombia," *ICLEI Case Studies*, No. 165 (August 2013), by ICLEI–Local Governments for Sustainability, Bogotá, Colombia. Reprinted with permission of the publisher.

The City Context

Bogotá is the capital and largest city of Colombia. Motorization in the city, as in the rest of the country, has reached record levels since 2006 (every year a new local record is broken in terms of car sales). The Urban Development Institute (IDU) and the Secretary of Mobility (SDM) are in charge of all mobility projects (IDU in charge of infrastructure development, SDM in charge of regulation and traffic), and in recent years the city has had various transport projects which have been mostly directed towards increasing public transport. The TransMilenio bus rapid transit (BRT) system is one example, in addition to increased efforts to develop non-motorized transport.

During the period reviewed here, from 1998–2011, the city has had 4 different mayors (Enrique Peñalosa 1998–2000, Antanas Mockus 2001–2003, Luis Garzón 2004–2007 and Samuel Moreno 2008–2011). Since 1998, the city has undergone a complete transformation of its public space (i.e. destroyed or inexistent sidewalks were redeveloped, parks were built, dusty areas were transformed into dynamic public spaces).

Urban Planning Instruments

In the late 1990's new city regulations came into force in Bogotá and resulted in the development and provision of bicycle paths. The intention of these "acts" was to highlight the most relevant aspects of bike path management contained in the following policy instruments:

- The Land Use Plan
- The Mobility Master Plan
- The Public Space Master Plan

Additionally, in 1998 the Urban Development Institute realized the need to formulate a Bike Path Master Plan. Even though this plan did not become part of the city reg-

ulations, it served as a technical foundation for building the bicycle paths project. The Bike Path Master Plan is divided in three parts: Diagnosis, Evaluation and Plan formulation.

In the diagnosis phase, planners identified the potential and ease associated with bicycle use as an alternative means of transportation and as a complement to existing public transport nodes. A network of bike roads was identified and integrated into the transport plans of Bogotá. During the evaluation, the feasibility study of the project was conducted, and the optimal network was defined among several alternative options. This was done according to criteria and indicators obtained from the diagnosis.

The formulation of the plan incorporated various components, such as the preparation of policies, a description of the system to the definition of the stages of implementation, the administrative/financial requirements and the indicators to measure the performance of the plan and the measures to operate it.

The network was designed in a grid with total coverage of the city, consisting in a main network, secondary and complementary routes.

Inter-institutional Coordination

The implementation of the Bike Paths Master Plan was only possible thanks to the joint efforts of various law enforcement district entities (planning and mobility sectors) and utilities, along with strong corporate management.

Construction and Maintenance of Public Works

Having decided on the implementation of the Bike Path Master Plan, a complex process of feasibility, design and construction of public infrastructure began, which allowed for the transformation of the urban space.

The formulation of the Bike Path Master Plan included the development of a bike path design manual. This included looking to build high-quality urban designs that offered complementary services such as parking for bicycles, street furniture and landscaping, to contribute to the environmental quality of the city. The IDU in charge of executing the public works acquired expertise in the design process and construction (including land management, environmental, social, network utilities, and other technical aspects).

To ensure the smooth operation of the network, investment of public funds was also necessary for the upkeep of the network. This was realized through a community service scheme of social work, where vulnerable sectors of the community can get involved and appointed to maintain the upkeep of this system.

Results

There was an increase of bicycle use (daily trips and reported travel mode) from 0.58 percent in 1996 to 4–5 percent in 2006—(results obtained from Origin-Destination surveys and phone surveys). In a city where cycling was previously not an option people considered this a noteworthy achievement.

There have been significant improvements of infrastructure conditions for bicycle users (i.e. building 357 km of bikeways from 1998). As seen below, in the 1990s and (to a lesser degree) in the early 2000s the emphasis was on creating new cycle-paths, and from 2006 more effort was put in to maintain existing paths through the community service scheme.

Bicycle policies in Bogotá, as other

transport policies, have had a strong political influence. Mayors have been very proactive in promoting bicycle use and ensuring the construction of the necessary infrastructure.

There is now clearly a greater possibility for citizens to take the bicycle as a main mode of transport, for different uses.

There is also a growing citizen awareness and involvement in urban transport policy, something which was not previously evident before this decade.

There is now clearly a greater possibility for citizens to take the bicycle as a main mode of transport, for different uses according to the following figures:

There is also a growing citizen awareness and involvement in urban transport policy, something which was not previously evident before this decade.

Lessons Learned

• Political will and commitment is fundamental to promote non-motorized transport.

• Bicycle-related Institutions must be established to support the efforts being developed to promote non-motorized transport policies.

• Infrastructure is a crucial component in order to provide a basis for increased bicycle use for all user groups (including children and women).

• Regulations and policies related to bicycle use must be addressed to enhance the potential of infrastructure for bicycles.

• Citizens must be included in the development of bicycle use-related policies.

• Advocacy efforts are a very useful complement to infrastructure and policies that promote bicycle use in a city.

• Maintenance of infrastructure is often undervalued in infrastructure development but is fundamental to include into NMT policies.

Replication

Bogotá, capital of a developing country has encouraged its public investment generating infrastructure for sustainable mobility through urban renewal that has occurred with the construction of TransMilenio and the bike paths, amongst others green economy initiatives.

These projects have generated citizens' confidence in public entities. Today Bogotá is known for having a notable transport system covering the transport needs of the vast majority of citizens, however it still needs improvements. In a world crowded by the use of individual motorized transport, the implementation of mass transit and non-motorized systems is essential in order to develop sustainably.

To achieve this, one of the most important factors to encourage the use of bicycles as a daily mode of transport has been the implementation of a promotional plan, comparable to a marketing plan of any commercial product. Ambitious advertising campaigns, accompanied by an institutional presence have led to greater use of bike paths in Bogotá. The promotional campaign has also generated benefits such as time and money savings, increased civil involvement and cooperation as well as an establishing an overall improvement in Bogotá's transport infrastructure. Finally, the campaign has created awareness of health and environmental issues.

Budget and Finances

The average cost of a kilometer of a cycle-path built in Bogotá is US$ 600,000 while the cost of a kilometer of a 30 meters wide road (including public utility networks) is about US$ 6,500,000.

The construction of cycle paths resulted in spending over US$ 200 million. In terms of maintenance; the city has spent approximately US$560,000 since 1998 to 2008.

However, in most cases it is difficult to know precisely the investment since the construction of bicycle paths also includes other interventions such as renewal of networks for public utilities, construction of sidewalks, etc.

Investment has been done exclusively with public resources from the municipality of the city where the main sources of income are fuel (gasoline) surcharges and others such as the income from traffic tickets and land value tax. The contribution from value tax is an actual duty from land properties, subject to a registration earmarked towards construction works, plans or a group of construction works of public interest. The duty is imposed on owners of those properties that benefited with the development of those works.

EDITORS' NOTE

The following information is provided about this best practice case study to facilitate future research.

Name: City of Bogotá
Population: 7,674,366 (2013)
Region: Capital District
Province/State: None
Country: Colombia
Official Name: Republic of Colombia
City Website: http://www.bogota.gov.co/

The "Acknowledgements" section of the Case Study listed Santosh Kodukula, Global Coordinator for EcoMobility, ICLEI-Local Governments for Sustainability, world headquarters, Bonn, Germany, as a contributor to this case study.

Chapter 18

Bologna, Italy, Prohibits Vehicles but Promotes Walking and Bicycling Downtown

Cleto Carlini

Inhabitants of Bologna are proud of the city's historical nature. Bologna residents and the local government have worked together to protect the heritage. A law disallowing pollution-emitting cars from the city center and infrastructure for bikers and pedestrians allow residents a safe and efficient way to travel the city and avoid damaging the city's culture.

A Car-free City Center

In the last decade, there was a significant increase in the number of cars entering the city center on a daily basis. This increase caused traffic chaos because more cars were entering the city than the roads allowed. Eighty percent of the city center has been converted to a pollution-limiting area and car traffic is strictly controlled. Only residents of this zone, public transport vehicles and drivers of electric cars may receive a permanent permit to drive in the restricted zone. Private cars can buy day tickets for 5€ or a four-day ticket for 12€. There is a limit of three one-day tickets or one four-day ticket per vehicle per month to limit the over-all number of trips in the city. Suppliers wishing to enter the city center may purchase a one-year permit at a cost of 25€ to 100€ depending on the level of pollution their vehicle emits. With these restrictions, the yearly number of vehicles entering the city center has decreased more than 25 percent.

Commuter Statistics

Of the one million residents of the metropolitan area of Bologna, 650,000 of them live in what is referred to as the "commuter belt." With a per capita vehicle ownership rate of 522 cars per 1,000 residents (compared to the 601 cars per 1,000 residents in Italy, second rate in the World), the city must have sufficient infrastructure to allow the residents without cars to get to their destinations and to reduce the number of residents with cars driving to their destination. The city of Bologna has a transportation modal share of 28 percent car drivers, 7 percent car passengers, 26 percent public transit users, 21 percent pedestrians, 11 percent motorcycle drivers, and 7 percent bicyclists.

Originally published as "Reducing Car Traffic to Protect City Heritage in Bologna, Italy," *ICLEI Case Studies—EcoMobility* (October 2011), by ICLEI–Local Governments for Sustainability, Bonn, Germany. Reprinted with permission of the publisher.

An Overview of the Bus System

Bologna has a limited public transportation system, if compared to the best European cities but one that is widely used. The bus network contains routes from the metropolitan area through the city center. This simplifies the system for customers by reducing the number of changes customers need to make. The system also contains two circular lines to transport customers within the city. Most buses run once every five minutes. Almost the whole bus fleet is monitored by means of Automatic Vehicles Monitoring system and the schedule of buses and real-time tracking information are communicated to riders at many bus stops.

A City Fit for Pedestrians and Bicyclists

Pedestrians in Bologna may take advantage of 45 km of covered streets. These create a pleasant environment for commuters wishing to avoid the sun and the rain. To further increase the share of pedestrians, Bologna plans to extend the pedestrian area towards the university neighborhood. This link would create a walking environment throughout most of the city. The city also promotes bicycles as an alternative to cars. In the last four years, the city has created 128 km of safe, well-recognized bike paths along 14 different routes. The city strives to significantly increase the share of cyclists. To boost it, a new bike-sharing system, based on magnetic card technology, will soon be implemented in the city to make available more than 1,000 bicycles to all citizens. Such a new system will run beside the already existing one based on mechanical technology and specifically targeted to commuters. The city hopes these measures will increase the appeal of cycling as a viable alternative to traveling by more motorized and pollutant vehicles.

The City of Bologna is the seventh largest city in Italy and the capital of the region of Emilia-Romagna in Northern Italy.

The metropolitan area has a population of approximately one million people. The city has a density of 2,700 people per km². It is known for its historic center and university. The economy of Bologna is industrial and is based on footwear, textiles, and engineering. Bologna has been an ICLEI member since December 1992.

A Major Participant of European Mobility Week

The city of Bologna is a strong participant in European mobility week, which aims to make citizens more sensitive to the effects of a rise in urban traffic, such as increasing pollution. The program stresses ways to reduce this traffic (and subsequently the emissions) in order to improve the quality of life in the city. Another goal of this week is to make the public more aware of public transit and infrastructure available to pedestrians and bicyclists and to discuss investment in new infrastructure. The program requests that local authorities prioritize alternative transport modes by following certain guidelines. Examples include planning the city so residents do not have to travel as often or as far as they currently do, to make safe routes through the city for pedestrians and bikers, and to work with local schools and businesses to establish better travel plans. The edition of 2010 saw the active and enthusiastic participation of more than 3,000 citizens.

EDITORS' NOTE

The following information is provided about this best practice case study to facilitate future research.

Name: City of Bologna
Population: 384,038 (2012)
Region: Emilia–Romagna Region
Province/State: Bologna
Country: Italy
Official Name: Italian Republic
City Website: http://www.comune.bologna.it/

Chapter 19

Bremen, Germany, Uses Intermodal Transportation System to Promote EcoMobility

Michael Glotz-Richter

Bremen is a leading Eco-Mobile city, with only 40 percent of commuters using cars or motorcycles. This can be attributed to Bremen's intermodal transportation developments. Bremen has a large car sharing system, improved biking infrastructure, and a public transportation system with a new S-bahn system as of 2010.

Bremen Sets Goals High, on Track to Exceed

In Bremen, 60 percent of trips are already made by sustainable means. In 2008, this 60 percent comprise 14 percent trips by public transportation, 20 percent walking, and 25 percent biking. An increase in this percentage is promising through expansion of existing public transportation and creation of new systems. The 2020 target strives to increase the biking percentage to 30 percent since a bike is ultimately the most plausible sustainable form of transportation. Focusing on intermodal passenger transportation systems sets a goal to reduce the dependence on the automobile as the main mode of transportation and increase use of public trans-

port in order to decrease greenhouse gas emissions and fossil fuel consumption.

Restructuring Busy Roads

In the past few years, Bremen has improved conditions for walking and biking by restructuring wide roads that were formerly dominated by car traffic to have a wider sidewalk and a smaller road. With wider sidewalks, there is more room for walkers and safe, clearly-marked bike paths that do not interfere with pedestrian or automobile traffic. The housing areas have speed limits of 30 km/h and almost all one-way streets here are opened for cyclists in contraflow direction.

A Growing Car Sharing System

A car sharing system, where people can rent cars for short or longer periods of time, allows customers to access cars without having to own one. These rentals are often by the hour and are attractive to customers occasionally needing a vehicle or those who need a different

Originally published as "Bremen, Germany: Rapidly Growing Intermodal Transportation," *ICLEI Case Studies—EcoMobility* (October 2011), by ICLEI–Local Governments for Sustainability, Bonn, Germany. Reprinted with permission of the publisher.

type of vehicle than the one they own. Thirty-three new vehicles were added amongst nine new cars sharing locations in the past year, making a total of 43 car sharing locations with 160 vehicles. As a result, the number of clients increased by 39 percent. As of 2010, of the 547,000 inhabitants of Bremen, 5,700 were car-sharing customers. But Bremen is ambitious and intends to reach 20,000 customers by 2020. Car sharing has shown many positive impacts. People now can use the appropriate size cars for each trip, which has led to a down-sizing of owned cars. In addition, customers are now able to use cars with higher emissions standards as they become available instead of keeping the same lower emission standards car for the life of the car. Another achieved benefit was that 1,500 fewer parking spaces were needed throughout the city, causing savings of €20–40 million for parking infrastructure.

Expansion and Growth of Public Transportation

In 2010, a new regional S-bahn system began operation. Four lines were created with a total of 35 stations. Trams are the backbone of public transport on the local level and contribute significantly to the annual ridership of more 100 million passengers (2010) in the city of Bremen. The tram network is under extension—also into neighboring communities and also using freight train tracks in mixed use. Public Transport uses low-floor-level and low-emission vehicles. Clean vehicles such as taxis, trucks, and buses have also been introduced. In January 2011, there were approximately 350 CNG (compressed natural gas) vehicles in Bremen that resulted in a 60 percent decrease in NOx emissions. There is a lower car mileage (around 500,000 km avoided per year) travelled due to higher use of public transportation and bikes. This decrease in car mileage has resulted in a reduction of 85,000 kg of CO_2 emissions.

Knowledge—The Crucial Element

Although travel behavior in Bremen is highly EcoMobile, the percentage of car commutes is considered too high. In 1995, there was an average of 176 public transport trips per capita. This increased to 187 trips in 2010. Every year, Bremen invests in providing better access to information about schedules, routes, and fares in order to further increase the number of public transport users. Improved intermodal information systems are available on pre-travel (esp. Internet-based information for Public Transport, for cycling but also for taxi use etc.) and on-travel (Real-Time Passenger Information at stops and information in the PT vehicles). The website of BSAG is visited more than 500,000 times per month. Also, a prepaid "BOB" card was introduced to attract non-frequent travellers—whereas the season tickets have anyway their frequent users. The BOB-Card is a post-payment system that keeps track of a passenger's destination and stores this information in a database that automatically charges the customer's bank account upon zero balance. Up to now, the number of BOB Card users increased to more than 65,000 citizens.

The City of Bremen is a commercial port and trade city on the Weser River in northern Germany. Bremen is the tenth largest city in Germany. The city has a population of 547,000 and an area of 400 km². The economy of Bremen has been dominated by trade and shipping. The city is also strong industrially with its shipbuilding and automobile industries.

EDITORS' NOTE

The following information is provided about this best practice case study to facilitate future research.

Name: Municipality of Breman
Population: 547,976 (2012)
Region: Bremen/Oldenburg Metropolitan Region

Province/State: Bremen
Country: Germany
Official Name: Federal Republic of Germany
City Website: http://www.bremen.de/

A note at the end of this case study mentioned that the Municipality of Bremen has been an ICLEI member since 1992, that Bremen has been a pioneer city in the field of EcoMobility for many years, and that they were responsibility for the development of the concept of car-free neighborhoods.

Chapter 20

Changwon, South Korea, Develops a Public Bicycle System to Benefit Its Citizens

Seong Jae Park

Changwon's aim was to introduce a user-friendly bicycle system that would become part of the city's urban landscape. The city has managed to create a bicycle system matching its own particular needs by researching other cities' bicycle programs, analyzing Changwon's physical conditions and by applying advanced technologies. The new system, NUBIJA, has lead to improvements in citizens' health, job creation and has also laid the foundation for a low-carbon transportation culture. The extensive use of information technology and implementation of a cyclist's insurance system are among NUBIJA's unique characteristics.

The Importance of Bicycles

The bicycle has enjoyed popularity since it was introduced in the early nineteenth century. Even though it lost some of its popularity with the advent of the automobile, many still use a bicycle as a means of transportation in their daily lives. The bicycle has the potential to contribute even more to urban sustainability and curbing greenhouse

gas emissions. This is why cities must enable their citizens to use bicycles by adapting infrastructure or by building public transportation that accommodates bicycles. This is already happening in many cities throughout the world.

In many Asian cities, cycling retains a high modal share and plays a large role in the transportation of people and goods. In China, particularly in some smaller cities such as Tianjin and Shi-Jia-Zhuang, more than half the population commutes by bicycle. Even in Shanghai 3.5 million bicycles are in circulation, accounting for 31 percent of all commuting trips. Some good examples are also found in South America; cycling in Bogotá, Colombia, for example, has been slowly increasing.

Bicycles are also a big player in European transportation: Bicycle share in all journeys in Netherlands was 26 percent in 2009 and was the highest share in Europe. In some cities in the Netherlands, the mode share of bicycles exceeded 30 percent, for example, Groningen 38 percent, Zwolle 37 percent, Leiden 33 percent, Ede 32 percent and Veenendaal 32 percent.

Originally published as "Changwon, Republic of Korea: The Nearby Useful Bike, Interesting Joyful Attraction (NUBIJA) Project," *ICLEI Case Studies*, No. 119 (October 2010), by ICLEI–Local Governments for Sustainability, Bonn, Germany. Reprinted with permission of the publisher.

The City Context

Changwon, located at the center of the Republic of Korea's southern Kyeongnam province, is the engine of regional industry alongside neighboring cities Masan and Busan. While it experiences four distinct seasons, Changwon's weather is often mild and warm. The city's well-developed roads have prompted the rapid acquisition of cars; there was an average of 7.6 percent growth in car ownership between 2002 and 2007. Bicycle ownership was at 3.2 percent in 2006.

Changwon identifies climate change as the most important problem facing the planet and views adaptation and mitigation as top priorities—for the welfare of its population and for the survival of its local industries and economy. With these issues in mind, Changwon is also set to host the First International EcoMobility Exchange Congress in October 2011, convened by ICLEI and the Global Alliance for EcoMobility.

Changwon: Pedaling Toward a Sustainable Future

Changwon instituted the NUBIJA program out of the desire to be a leading model of urban sustainability. Prior to NUBIJA, Changwon citizens perceived biking as a leisure activity only and bicycles were seen as private property rather than as a means of public transportation. The goal of NUBIJA is to make the bicycle a common means of urban transportation for Changwon's citizens.

Changewon applied state-of-the-art technologies to develop NUBIJA including a bicycle developed specifically for the program, called the NUBIJA Bicycle. The NUBIJA bicycle is equipped with:

- a special handle,
- a self-lock supplementary device,
- program signs and logos, which ensure

safety and security while also establishing the visual presence of NUBIJA in the city

Bicycle storage points were installed where cyclists can lock and unlock the Radio Frequency Identification (RFID) device used on every NUBIJA bicycle. Kiosks were set up to manage integrated loaning and returning information, to search the locations of other NUBIJA terminals and to provide security at terminals. A central control center was also established to operate and survey the NUBIJA program.

In addition to technological investment, the city held events such as public workshops, bicycle promotion campaigns, bicycle riding lessons and bicycle safety training to increase public awareness and encourage riding. Changwon took the step of introducing citizen bicycle insurance—a first for the Republic of Korea—which compensates Changwon citizens involved in a bicycle-related accident.

Results and Impacts of the Project in the Community

Changwon applied innovative ideas and cutting-edge technology toward the development of NUBIJA and has set the foundation for a low energy consumption transportation culture in the city. Cycling was not a traditional means of late-night transportation prior to NUBIJA, now commuters use bicycles for short distances during the night—even after midnight. The program has:

- Improved cyclists' physical and mental health, according to popular opinion;
- Reduced the transportation-related burden on household budgets; bicycles, when used as a primary mode of transportation, can save about 80 percent of a person's total transportation expenses if he/she previously depended on a car;
- Created jobs from an expansion of

bicycle-related industries—approximately 3,600 new positions each year. NUBIJA has also stimulated more activity in the advanced technology bicycle industry;

• Raised the transportation mode share of bicycles from 3.2 percent in 2006 to 7 percent at the end of 2008. Changwon targets it up to 20 percent in 2020;

• NUBIJA had 36,820 members as of September 2009. The program offers weekly, monthly and yearly memberships; 51.5 percent of NUBIJA users have a yearly membership;

• Helped raise Changwon's climate change protection profile because of its environmental, economic and social achievements;

• Saved 1,061 million KRW ($915,000 USD) through reduced oil consumption and lowered the city's CO_2 emissions by 1,486 tons per year.

Lessons Learned

The idea of a public bicycle system posed logistical challenges in Changwon. For example, how would the city handle loaning and returning bicycles and how many bicycle loaning stations would suffice? Many obstacles were addressed prior to the implementation of the project by researching bicycle programs in other urban centers. Overarching challenges were addressed in the following ways:

Infrastructure: Improvements to Changwon's infrastructure is a key factor in the success of the NUBIJA program. As part of its effort to create a bicycle-friendly environment, the city repaired bicycle paths, bicycle-pedestrian paths, crossroads at intersections, created new paths and improved security along cycling areas. The city has also lowered the speed limit for cars and narrowed vehicle lanes to create more room for bicycles—a process called "road diet."

Public incentive: In addition, Chang-

won created the Republic of Korea's first-ever bicycle insurance program as an incentive for prospective cyclists. The NUBIJA program showcases the importance of integrating technological innovation into a municipal bicycle program, particularly with regard to creating a bicycle loaning system. For example, the NUBIJA developers introduced a Global Positioning System (GPS) to track bicycles and prevent theft. GPS is a satellite-based navigation system, which tracks location and time information.

Background research: The NUBIJA project developers thoroughly researched bicycle programs in other cities and carefully assessed Changwon's physical compatibility with bicycles as well as how the city's infrastructure would accommodate an influx of bicycles.

Political leadership: Consistent support from Changwon's local leaders has played a significant role in the success of the NUBIJA program. When challenges arose, policymakers made a decision in an efficient manner to ensure NUBIJA's successful launch.

Stakeholder involvement: Efficient and fast responses to public complaints and suggestions has proved invaluable to securing strong connections with NUBIJA consumers. Even before NUBIJA's launch, the city held several open committee meetings designed to collect citizens' feedback.

Replication

Changwon is open to sharing NUBIJA's development process with other municipalities and would also explore partnerships to replicate the program. Promotion and expansion of the NUBIJA program will be especially valuable in conjunction with the 1st International Ecomobility Exchange Congress to be held in Changwon in October 2011.

The NUBIJA model has strong potential for replication in cities where local leaders are politically committed to tackling climate change and where reforming urban transport is a key priority.

Cities should consider their strong and weak points before undertaking an urban bicycle plan. This should include: an analysis of bicycle accessibility issues and a city's level of ease—among its leaders and citizenry—with information technologies such as GPS systems.

It is not easy to introduce a sustainable transportation system to a city, such as Changwon, whose planning and organization caters to automotive transportation. Changwon has managed to conquer this obstacle, and several others, by frequently communicating with its citizens about the program, soliciting public opinion, using technology in an effective way and benefiting from consistent support from local policy-makers.

The NUBIJA program is funded through public resources and does not benefit from private sector assistance. In cities where public resources are limited, city-to-city partnership funding, or international climate funding could be considered.

Budget and Finances

The NUBIJA program was launched in March 2008 and will be completed by 2012. The total cost of the program, which is funded by Changwon's municipal budget and a federal subsidy, is 15,000 million KRW ($12.5 million USD). Changwon plans to invest these funds over a total of five years from 2008 to 2012:

• 1,600 million KRW (1.3 million USD) comes from federal government sources.
• Up to the end of 2009, 7,500 million KRW ($6.3 million USD) was invested in

city infrastructure, NUBIJA bicycles, and the monitoring system's development.

• Due to limited human resources, most work on the NUBIJA project (until August 2010) was completed by one individual, Ha Seoug-Woo, with some assistance from colleagues.

What's in Store for the NUBIJA Project:

• Introducing a Korea-manufactured NUBIJA bicycle for better quality and management;
• Introducing a transit discount system to facilitate transfer between NUBIJA bicycles and city buses;
• Offering NUBIJA data via cell phone;
• Installing of a bicycle terminal canopy which uses solar energy;
• Building a global alliance among major cities which have public bicycle loaning programs: The "Global Alliance for Public Bike Cities."

EDITORS' NOTE

The following information is provided about this best practice case study to facilitate future research.

Name: City of Changwon
Population: 1,089,406 (2013)
Region: Yeongnam Region
Province/State: Gyeonggi
Country: South Korea
Official Name: Republic of Korea
City Website: http://www.eng.changwon.go.kr/

The "Acknowledgements" section of the case study listed Emma Wadland as the editor; thanked the City of Changwon for their collaboration and cooperation; and also thanked Nuno Quental, EcoMobility Officer, Global Alliance for EcoMobility, ICLEI.

Chapter 21

Copenhagen, Denmark, Evolves into a Pedestrian Friendly City

Center for New Urbanism

Designing great places for the comfort and enjoyment of the pedestrian is one of the most important aspects of New Urbanism. Taken to the highest level of urbanism, the finest places in the world are cities with entire networks of car-free streets, known as pedestrian cities.

Pedestrian cities are growing in popularity in many top regions around the world. The incredible beauty, enjoyment, and convenience a network of connected pedestrian streets and squares provides to the residents on a daily basis are unsurpassed. Being able to walk to a mix of shops, restaurants, newsstands, coffeehouses and open-air markets within car-free neighborhoods and work centers delivers the highest quality of life, and adds great variety and vitality to an area. Jane Jacobs calls this "an intricate and close-grained diversity of uses that give each other constant mutual support, both economically and socially." There is a growing demand for entire city districts to be made pedestrian, and directly connected to a train line.

Venice, Italy is considered the greatest pedestrian city in the world because it contains the largest pedestrian street network completely free of cars. The entire city has no cars operating on its streets. The city is quite dense, yet the most relaxing and pleasant city in the world.

Copenhagen is another of the world's great pedestrian cities. A recent issue of "Metropolis" magazine talks about Copenhagen and its growing pedestrian street network. Although it's blessed with certain inherited characteristics—such as a narrow medieval street grid—the city has worked steadily to improve the quality of its street life. In the 40 years since Copenhagen's main street was turned into a pedestrian thoroughfare, city planners have taken numerous small steps to transform the city from a car-oriented place to a people-friendly one. "In Copenhagen, we have pioneered a method of systematically studying and recording people in the city," says Jan Gehl, a Danish architect and co-author of "Public Spaces-Public Life," a study on what makes the city's urban spaces work. "After twenty years of research, we've been able to prove that these steps have created four times more public life." Here is Copenhagen's program for a more pedestrian-friendly city:

Copenhagen's 10-Step Program

1. Convert streets into pedestrian thoroughfares. The city turned its traditional

Originally published as "Copenhagen, Denmark: Copenhagen's 10 Step Program," *Pedestrian Cities/Quality of Life Case Studies* (July 2013), by the Center for New Urbanism, Alexandria, Virginia. Reprinted with permission of the publisher.

main street, Stroget, into a pedestrian thoroughfare in 1962. In succeeding decades they gradually added more pedestrian-only streets, linking them to pedestrian-priority streets, where walkers and cyclists have right-of-way but cars are allowed at low speeds.

2. Reduce traffic and parking gradually. To keep traffic volume stable, the city reduced the number of cars in the city center by eliminating parking spaces at a rate of 2–3 percent per year. Between 1986 and 1996 the city eliminated about 600 spaces.

3. Turn parking lots into public squares. The act of creating pedestrian streets freed up parking lots, enabling the city to transform them into public squares.

4. Keep scale dense and low. Low-rise, densely spaced buildings allow breezes to pass over them, making the city center milder and less windy than the rest of Copenhagen.

5. Honor the human scale. The city's modest scale and street grid make walking a pleasant experience; its historic buildings, with their stoops, awnings, and doorways, provide people with impromptu places to stand and sit.

6. Populate the core. More than 6,800 residents now live in the city center. They've eliminated their dependence on cars, and at night their lighted windows give visiting pedestrians a feeling of safety.

7. Encourage student living. Students who commute to school on bicycles don't add to traffic congestion; on the contrary, their active presence, day and night, animates the city.

8. Adapt the cityscape to changing seasons. Outdoor cafes, public squares, and street performers attract thousands in the summer; skating rinks, heated benches, and gas lit heaters on street corners make winters in the city center enjoyable.

9. Promote cycling as a major mode of transportation. The city established new bike lanes and extended existing ones. They placed bike crossings—using space freed up by the elimination of parking—near intersections. Currently 34 percent of Copenhageners who work in the city bicycle to their jobs.

10. Make bicycles available. The city introduced the City Bike system in 1995, which allows anyone to borrow a bike from stands around the city for a small coin deposit. When finished, they simply leave them at any one of the 110 bike stands located around the city center and their money is refunded.

Quality of Life

New Urbanism is creating and restoring walkable, diverse, compact towns and cities that enable a higher quality of life by offering new choices for living.

Pedestrian Friendly Urban Places

This is the highest quality environment possible for living. It includes a full range of services within a 5–10 minute walk of every residence. At minimum, this would include grocery stores, deli's, bakeries, newsstands, coffeehouses, vegetable stands, open-air markets, personal services, parks, and green spaces. A full range of entertainment and cultural activities are also desirable, all in an attractive, friendly atmosphere.

European cities are some of the finest examples of pedestrian friendly living forms. Venice is the best example of this because cars were never allowed to enter the city—the entire city is composed of all pedestrian streets. Venice also has the most complete, most varied and beautiful continuous urban fabric. Each neighborhood has its own central square or campo that acts as its heart and soul. These are within walking distance of all the residents, and offer a full range of services as well as social interactions.

Cities and Towns as Works of Art

The combination of beautiful architecture with great urbanism creates the most beautiful places to live, places that express a life of richness and tradition, and act as a comfortable stage for the drama of life.

Places Free From Danger and Toxins

An environment offering a high quality of life is a place free from noise, pollution, toxins, radiation, and danger. This includes safe streets everyone can walk along, clean air to breathe, clean and healthy water and food.

A Safe, Comfortable, and Efficient Transportation System

An integral part of a high quality environment is a quality transportation system that everyone can use to easily get around locally and regionally.

EDITORS' NOTE

The following information is provided about this best practice case study to facilitate future research.

Name: City of Copenhagen
Population: 562,379 (2013)
Region: Capital Region
Province/State: None
Country: Denmark
Official Name: Kingdom of Denmark
City Website: http://www.kk.dk/

The Center for New Urbanism's website (http://newurbanism.org/) has additional information on international transportation initiatives being undertaken in cities throughout the world.

Chapter 22

Dar-es-Salaam, Tanzania, Promotes Cleaner Fuels to Achieve Sustainable Urban Mobility

Thomas Melin

The United Nations Advisory Committee of Local Authorities (UNACLA) was established by UN-HABITAT in 2002. The Committee is comprised of mayors representing the broad range of local authorities from all global regions. The purpose of UNACLA is to advise the UN-HABITAT Executive Director on important issues concerning the implementation of the Habitat Agenda.[1] The UN-HABITAT Executive Director, in turn, reports on a regular basis to the UN Secretary General on the work and recommendations of UNACLA.

Each year, the Committee focuses on a specific thematic issue that is of importance to cities and towns worldwide. At the last regular Committee meeting held in Nairobi on 10 April 2011, the following themes were defined and agreed on for the next few years:

2011/2012: Sustainable urban mobility
2012/2013: Job creation and local productivity
2013/2014: Flood protection and environmental resilience
2014/2015: Municipal fiscal systems and finances

Addressing Sustainable Urban Mobility in 2011/2012

Functioning transportation networks are a key element for cities and towns across the globe and a precondition for economic activity and access to basic services. However, urban travel is often accompanied by congestion, social exclusion, accidents, air pollution and energy consumption.

Against the background of the related challenges worldwide, the thematic emphasis of the UNACLA meeting in April was placed on urban mobility and an exchange of experiences for establishing effective public transport systems as a key element for sustainable urban development in general. In the context of this meeting, it was agreed that activities during the course of the year 2011/2012 should focus on the following components important for sustainable urban mobility:

Linking Transportation to Urban Planning to Reduce the Need for Motorized Travel
Encourage coordination of land-use and transport planning, especially spatial settle-

Originally published as "Dar-es-Salaam, Tanzania: Work Program on Sustainable Urban Mobility," *UN Advisory Committee of Local Authorities Report–2011/2012* (April 2011), by the United Nations Human Settlements Program, UN-Habitat, Nairobi, Kenya. Reprinted with permission of the publisher.

ment patterns that facilitate access to such basic necessities as workplaces, schools, health care, places of worship, goods and services, and leisure, thereby reducing the need to travel.

Example: Eco-Cell in Tianjin Eco-City, China[2]

The basic building block of the Eco-city Master Plan is a single cell, or "Eco-Cell", that serves to integrate the different land uses within a modular 400m by 400m grid. Educational institutions, commercial areas, workplaces and recreational areas are distributed within these Eco-Cells and located close to the residential areas to minimize commuting. Together, these Eco-Cells add up to form neighborhoods, districts, and eventually the urban centers.

Establishing Effective Public Transport Systems

Expand or create more effective, affordable, physically-accessible and environmentally-sound public transport and communications systems, giving priority to collective means of transport with adequate carrying capacity and frequency that support basic needs and the main traffic flows.

Example: Jakarta, Indonesia[3]

TransJakarta was designed to provide Jakarta citizens with a fast public transportation system, which helps to reduce rush hour traffic and thus green house gas emissions. The buses run in special lanes with elevated platforms for rapid boarding and alighting. TransJarkata serves approximately 250,000 people every day.

Expanding Non-motorized Transport Infrastructure

Expand or establish comprehensive and safe infrastructure and services for pedestrians and cyclists in cities since cycling and walking are the fastest, most sustainable and easiest in low-cost means of transportation.

Example: Mexico City, Mexico[4]

The world famous Plaseo de la Reforma in the heart of Mexico City has recently been redeveloped with designated bicycle lanes and improved signage for pedestrians. Along with the initiative, the avenue is closed for cars every Sunday turning it into one big public space, including more than 10,000 bicyclists.

Mobility Management for Integrated Service Solutions

Mobility management is a general term for strategies that result in a more efficient use of transportation resources as opposed to increasing transportation supply by expanding roads, parking lots, etc. There are many potential mobility management strategies with a variety of impacts. Some improve transportation diversity (the travel options available to users). Others provide incentives for users to change the frequency, mode, destination, route or timing of their travel. Some reduce the need for physical travel through mobility substitutes or more efficient land use. Some involve policy reforms to correct current distortions in transportation planning practices.

Example: London, United Kingdom[5]

Since February 2003, the city of London has charged a fee for driving private automobiles in its central area during weekdays as a way to reduce traffic congestion and raise revenues to fund transport improvements. This has significantly reduced traffic congestion, improved bus and taxi service, and generates substantial revenues.

Facilitating More Efficient Vehicle and Fuel Technologies

Fuel quality (unleaded and low sulfur fuels) is not only necessary to reduce or eliminate certain pollutants (e.g. lead, particulate matter) directly but is also a precondition for the introduction of many important pollution control technologies. Further, one critical advantage of cleaner fuel has emerged: its rapid impact on both new and existing vehicles. For example, tighter new car standards can take ten or more years to be fully effective whereas eliminating lead in gasoline will reduce lead emissions from all vehicles immediately.

Example: Dar-es-Salaam, Tanzania[6]

Air quality monitoring studies carried out in the city of Dar es Salaam show that vehicles are a major source of pollution. As a result of the findings, the Dar Rapid Transit Agency (DART) in 2009 organized a media campaign to promote cleaner fuels, in particular low sulphur diesel for use in the Dar Rapid Transit System. The campaign resulted in the Government adopting new standard for diesel with sulphur levels at 500 parts per million (ppm) down from 5000ppm from January 2011. The low sulphur diesel is required for use in the cleaner buses (Euro III) that will operate along the BRT. This will significantly reduce the level of particulate matter emission from transport.

Activity Components

Work on the five themes is being undertaken through the following four key activity components:

A. Documentation of case studies and best practice examples on urban mobility interventions

UNACLA is gathering case studies to show how specific cities and towns in different global regions are implementing programs and solutions for sustainable urban mobility. The main product will be an electronic and printed compilation/publication, which can be utilized both at country level as well as for drafting recommendations to the United Nations to influence future strategies, partnerships and programs targeting sustainable urban mobility and collaboration with local authorities in this area.

B. Development of eResources and knowledge exchange platforms

This component centers on developing eResources on mobility and establishing knowledge exchange platforms between UNACLA members on the topic. In this context, it is envisaged to establish a presence on the new UN-Habitat Urban Gateway portal (www.urbangateway.org), undertake an inventory of existing tools, reach agreement with partner on content management to ensure sustainable approaches, and undertake

dissemination and promotion of knowledge compiled in the context of UN-Habitat's overall work.

C. Initiation of Peer Exchange and Twinning Programs

This component draws on the discussion at the regular meeting in Nairobi, where several members with extensive experience in establishing public transport systems and infrastructure provision for pedestrians and cyclists expressed their interest and availability for implementing Peer-Exchange or Twinning programs to support members with a need for capacity building. This activity component will center on identifying areas and effective ways of exchange between interested UNACLA members. For instance, advisory services and exchange of knowledge could cover public transport investment strategies, how to set-up transport institutions, specific advice on transport solutions such as BRT, referral services to suppliers of expertise and financing, etc.

D. Outreach—regional meetings and contribution to major international events

This component envisages the implementation of regional meetings for UNACLA members to review the work and exchange perspectives on the different work elements. In addition, the Secretariat will ensure representation at key international conferences.

FOOTNOTES

1. The Habitat Agenda is the main political document that came out of the Habitat II conference in Istanbul, Turkey on 3–14 June 1996. Adopted by 171 countries at what was called the City Summit, it contains over 100 commitments and 600 recommendations on human settlements issues. http://ww2.unhabitat.org/declarations/habitat_agenda.asp

2. See www.tianjinecocity.gov.sg/masterplan.htm

3. See www.itdp.org/documents/TransJakarta%20Final%20Report%205.pdf

4. See *ITDP (2010): Our cities. Ourselves—10 Principles for Urban Transport in Urban Life.*

5. See www.vtpi.org/london.pdf

6. See www.unep.org/transport/pcfv/PDF/Dart
2_WorkshopProceedings.pdf

EDITORS' NOTE

The following information is provided about this best practice case study to facilitate future research.

Name: City of Dar-es-Salaam
Population: 4,364,541 (2012)
Region: Dar-es-Salaam Region

Province/State: Province of Dar-es-Salaam
Country: Tanzania
Official Name: United Republic of Tanzania
City Website: http://www.vtalia.com/Dar-es-Salaam/

The UN-Habitat's website (http://www.unhabitat.org/) has additional information concerning the best practices for sustainable transportation options being used in cities located in countries throughout the world.

Chapter 23

Dubai, Emirates, Develops Transportation Systems to Sustain Future Growth

Faisal Durrani *and* Daniel Seleanu

Dubai's acute traffic problems is one of the few things that everyone in the booming city-state complains about. After all, being crowned as "the Most Congested City in the Middle East" is hardly something Dubai residents are proud of. To help rectify the situation, ULI Middle East North Africa (MENA) organized a transportation roundtable that was held on May 20, 2008, at the Dubai World Trade Centre Complex in the United Arab Emirates. Regional business and industry leaders came together to discuss the problem and propose solutions. Guests speakers included Abdul Mohsin Al Younes, CEO of strategy and corporate governance at the Dubai Road Transport Authority (RTA), and Robert Dunphy, then senior resident fellow of transportation and infrastructure at the Urban Land Institute.

The Problem

According to Al Younes, "...55 percent of the congestion in Dubai is due to insufficient transportation infrastructure, 11 percent is due to road diversions, and 8 percent is due to poor driving habits." Another key factor is the rate of car ownership in Dubai, which rose by 17 percent last year. At 541 cars per 1,000 people, Dubai ranks well above New York City and London, which have 444 and 345 cars per 1,000 people, respectively. Al Younes estimated that traffic congestion costs Dubai's business community $1.25 billion annually.

Meanwhile, Dubai's explosive growth and development are expected to continue. According to Al Younes, Dubai's population—currently 1.7 million—is expected to surpass 5 million by 2020. He said that to accommodate this phenomenal growth, Dubai's total urban area is likely to expand from 193 square miles (500 sq. km) now to more than 849 square miles (2,200 sq. km) by 2020.

Strategic Plan for 2020

As such, Dubai is racing not only to meet current demand, but also to develop sophisticated transportation solutions capable of sustaining future growth. In 2007, the RTA announced the development of its Strategic Plan for 2020 in order to accomplish these goals. Anticipating a total cost of a staggering $12 billion on this effort, the

RTA is currently enforcing ambitious construction deadlines, employing state-of-the-art technology, and introducing innovative new schemes to reduce the number of cars on the road.

A key aspect of the Strategic Plan for 2020 is the development of an integrated public transportation system that will attract millions of daily users. In 2006, for example, the RTA contracted U.A.E.–based Right Angle Media to build the world's first air-conditioned bus shelters to improve the comfort and convenience of daily commutes. By September 2008, 350 shelters were operational, with more than 650 underway. The RTA recently spent AED 1 billion (U.A.E. dirhams) on 625 new buses, which will bring to 1,200 the total number of buses in service by the end of 2009.

Meanwhile, an international consortium lead by Mitsubishi Heavy Industries is building for Dubai the world's longest 43-mile (70 km), fully automated rail system. Once completed, the Dubai Metro is expected to carry 1.2 million passengers daily and 355 million passengers annually. Its first segment, the Red Line, is ahead of schedule and will begin operating in September 2009 with a total of 29 stations. A second line, the Green Line (with an additional 18 stations) is 60 percent complete and will be operational by March 2010. Four more rail lines are being finalized, with tenders to be issued in the near future. Through these investments, the RTA aims to increase the number of trips made by public transit passengers from 6 percent to 30 percent by 2020.

Parallel to its ambitious mass transit system, the RTA devised the Mobility Management Programme (MMP) to cut vehicle use in Dubai by half. To achieve this, a Mobility Management Unit within the RTA will coordinate efforts with the private sector to provide transport solutions, including carpooling programs, flexible working hours, a network of air-conditioned pedestrian bridges, and company bus services. In particular, the RTA expects that flexible working hours and telecommuting from home will reduce traffic congestion by up to 30 percent. The MMP will also discourage individual car use by increasing the number of toll gates, known as Salik Toll Gates. Salik, which means "clear" in Arabic, was introduced in 2007. Today, there are a total of four Salik Toll Gates in operation throughout Dubai. The toll gates, which are operational 24/7, have been positioned at strategic traffic congestion points in the heart of the city. Two toll gates have been placed on Sheikh Zayed Road, Dubai's main arterial highway. Two other Salik Toll Gates have been placed on two key bridges across Dubai Creek–Al Maktoum Bridge and Al Garhoud Bridge.

The success of these investments hinges on the willingness of Dubai's residents to give up their cars, which the RTA admits will be difficult. Ssays Al Younes, "We will introduce policies to deter car ownership; we will probably have higher [car] registration fees, and [will] increase parking fees after the [Dubai] Metro opens and more Salik tolls are introduced." In addition, the RTA created the Dubai Award for Sustainable Transport to promote a sense of awareness, responsibility, and initiative among everyone in the community, but especially those at the corporate level. The award consists of three categories: Management & Streamlining of Mobility Operations, Transport Safety, and Conservation of Environment. Through this awards program, the RTA hopes to encourage improvements in mobility, safety, and environmental protection while also involving a wide cross-section of government agencies.

Major Components of the Strategic Plan for 2020

• More than 310 miles (500 km) of new roads.

• An increase in the number of lanes crossing Dubai Creek from 47 to 100

• 95 new interchanges added; 25 existing interchanges improved.

• Nine new mini-ring roads to define nine of the city's most prominent central business districts.
  • 70 new pedestrian bridges.
  • 360 (580 km) of bicycle trails.
  • 1,243 miles (2,000 km) of new bus routes.
  • 2,500 new buses.
  • A 43-mile-plus (70 km plus) rail system (the Dubai Metro).

View from the United States

In a stark contrast to Al Younes's description of Dubai's impressive infrastructure program, Robert Dunphy highlighted the inability of the United States to keep up with its changing infrastructural needs. According to the Joint Economic Committee of the U.S. Congress, for example, flight delays alone cost the U.S. economy $41 billion in 2007. Poor organization, infrastructure failure, and extremely limited planned future investment mean that if current problems are not addressed, the United States will face a wide-ranging infrastructure crisis. Meanwhile, emphasized Dunphy, India, China, and the United Arab Emirates have emerged as "high-growth regions," which he defined as places characterized by vigorous infrastructure development and investment.

Toward the close of his presentation, Dunphy drew some interesting similarities between Dubai's current growth and that experienced by the United States in the past. He praised the RTA for tackling Dubai's congestion problems before they got any worse. He did, however, caution the RTA to bear in mind the historical, inverse correlation between employees' distance from work and the likelihood that they will use mass transit. This relationship could pose difficulties for Dubai, given that the majority of Dubai's residential developments are located in its quickly expanding suburbs. Dunphy stated that the RTA "must think about the end user—this is the way forward." He explained that during the planning of megacities, such as Dubai, a user-oriented design was the only way for mass transit systems to be successful.

Wrap-Up

During the extensive Q&A session, Al Younes was asked to comment on the effectiveness of the Salik road toll system. He defended its introduction in 2007 as necessary in the absence of a mass transit system. He asserted that "Salik has reduced congestion in Dubai and Salik is working." He further emphasized that Salik represents a targeted approach meant to deter traffic in Dubai's growth corridor, while avoiding driver penalties in other areas.

When asked to comment on how the RTA plans to attract a large user base for the Dubai Metro, Al Younes explained that bus fares would be lower than those of taxis. In addition, Dubai's transit map will be divided into geographic zones, similar to London's model, and fares would vary for interzone and single-zone travel. He also remarked that traveling in and around Dubai would remain cheaper than in London; the Central London Congestion Charge is £8 (56 dirhams) daily, while Salik's maximum daily charge is 24 dirhams.

In concluding the discussion, Al Younes addressed environmental sustainability and spoke briefly about the RTA's plan to introduce a fleet of low-emission, hybrid taxis and to launch a public awareness campaign to promote the benefits of Dubai's new public transit model.

The key conclusion of the roundtable was that Dubai's ambitious transportation infrastructure development program is pushing the boundaries of technological and political innovation. By promoting sustainable growth, involving the private sector, and providing attractive commuter options, the RTA is on track to relieve Dubai's now-legendary traffic congestion.

EDITORS' NOTE

The following information is provided about this best practice case study to facilitate future research.

Name: Dubai Municipality
Population: 2,106,177 (2013)
Region: Eastern Coast
Province/State: Emirate of Dubai
Country: Emirates
Official Name: United Arab Emirates
City Website: http://www.dm.gov.ae/

Chapter 24

Egedal, Denmark, and Other Cities, Work to Link Bike Lanes to Their Nation's Capital

Lars Wilms *and* Tommy Poulsen

Compared to other countries, Denmark is small in population and size but great in democratic tradition and strong in local political and administrative power. With 5.5 million inhabitants and a size of 43,000 square kilometers, Denmark has a simple two-tier structure with national authorities at one level and regional and local authorities at the other.

A relatively high level of taxation on income, property, companies, and consumption is the financial basis of a public sector second to none. The public sector bridges wealth disparities, stretches out a social safety net for those in need, and directly runs or subsidizes a range of activities from education to employment, from cultural to environmental matters, and from transportation infrastructure to university research and development.

Our welfare system is often referred to as the Scandinavian welfare model, which is based on our specific historical and cultural background in this part of Europe regarding, for instance, a tradition of consensus politics, equal rights to social security, education for all as a key priority, and the fact that Denmark is recognized as a nation with virtually no corruption at all.

This efficient, transparent, and demo-cratic public sector may be one of the reasons for Denmark being cited as one of the best countries to live in by such magazines as *The Economist*.

The expenditure of local governments amounts to almost 50 percent of the total public expenditure in Denmark. That is, half of the total public expenditure is taken care of by local government authorities in 98 municipalities, leaving the other half to five regions and the state. These 98 municipalities employ, all in all, 500,000 employees and cover a broad range of public responsibilities, handled in close contact with the local residents.

A municipality is, at the same time, an authority and a service provider for the residents from the cradle to the grave. As such, the municipalities are the residents' main entry to public service in Denmark.

City management, therefore, is a job category of interest to many people by offering a wide range of services under a unified municipal umbrella, whether individuals want to manage social, health, educational, cultural, environmental, technical, or financial matters. Thus, a career as city manager in local government is something to strive for in Denmark.

Originally published as "Denmark's Local Governments Press On," *Public Management*, Vol. 95, No. 3 (April 2013), by the International City/County Management Association, Washington, D.C. Reprinted with permission of the publisher.

This does not mean that Danes, including Danish city managers, are just happy people riding their bicycles on the many specially constructed bicycle lanes in cities, as an American television program once told the Americans. We do have our share of problems and challenges in our everyday working life.

An average Danish community with 56,000 inhabitants employs 5,100 employees spread out in city hall, kindergartens, schools, nursery homes, utility works, road maintenance departments, senior citizen caregivers, and so forth. And it goes without saying that an organization this size constantly gives managers new challenges, especially when interacting with local, regional, national, and worldwide societies in constant changes.

Managing the Challenges

What, then, are the greatest challenges to managers in executive positions these days?

First of all, we are still following up on the efficiency requirements in the Danish local government reform that came into force in 2007. From a city manager's point of view, taking part in a process of merging two or more local governments into one—and, at the same time, taking over new responsibilities from other parts of the public sector—is a once-in-a-lifetime experience. And successful it was!

The Danish government announced the municipal reform in 2004 as a voluntary process towards larger municipalities providing more tasks close to the residents, and with the aim of creating an even more efficient, transparent, and democratic political and administrative structure in Denmark. The reform focused on (1) the size and structure of municipalities; (2) the distribution of tasks between state, regions, and municipalities; and (3) the financial transfers of the equalization system.

In order to make municipalities able to meet the demands of tomorrow, one of the main arguments from the government was: Size matters if you want to develop economic and professional sustainability in local government. As a result, the previous 271 municipalities were restructured into 98 in 2007, with an average size of 56,000 inhabitants against 20,000 before the reform, and now with only 7 percent of the municipalities with less than 20,000 inhabitants against 76 percent before the reform.

Without going into details about the fascinating local decision-making process in those formative and difficult years before the actual mergers took place, which would take yet another article to describe thoroughly, it is possible to summarize the main result of the municipal reform: an improved municipal sustainability with larger units, more specialization, greater professionalism, and expanded digitalization

The municipal reform, and of course the technological development in itself, has in particular brought along many internal challenges of using new technologies in the digitalization of municipal organizations and in the way we manage our relations with residents. Along with Local Government Denmark (the national association of Danish municipalities), the Danish government has decided on an ambitious digital strategy for public institutions that aims at both optimizing and renewing the entire public sector, including an extensive use of digital self-service solutions aimed at residents.

Thus, executive city managers operate in a complex field in which they have to implement national strategies on digitalization, as well as apply these to the wishes and needs of local administrators, politicians, and residents.

Economic and Environmental Issues

And here we are today in our larger communities but in a totally changed environment affected by the worldwide financial crisis. Like in most other countries, we are trying to survive an economic crisis where the town councils have to cut budgets and make difficult priorities between activities of need-to-have and nice-to-have. As managers, it is our responsibility to prepare and carry out these decisions when our political bodies have made their choice between "worse or worst."

In this atmosphere of change, we are, as well, being faced with external challenges beyond our immediate control; that is, the increasing climate changes.

Climate change has already left visible traces in Denmark. In the summer of 2011, Copenhagen and surrounding areas were hit by a cloudburst of unprecedented precipitation. The enormous amount of water caused extensive damages at an estimated cost of more than $515 million U.S. dollars. Since then, more cloudbursts have occurred in other parts of the country.

Although Denmark has a well-developed sewage system, the dimensioning of the pipes will never be able to solve the problem of disposing extreme quantities of water over a very short period of time, a problem that the local governments have been forced to address. Therefore, we are currently in the process of mapping the possible problem areas.

Once the problem areas are identified, plans for the transport of sudden water flows must be drawn up. This may include new ways of thinking in relation to landscape planning with, for example, the location of parking areas in lower terrains than the surrounding areas to allow flooding, flooding of playing fields, or the utilization of available water for recreational purposes.

Demand for Innovative Thinking

In short, these external challenges force the municipalities—and our private counterparts—to think innovatively and outside the box, avoiding major investments in order to limit the negative effects of climate change.

All in all, the municipal reform, the priorities made in consequences of the economic crisis, and the constant internal and external challenges have been an incentive for city managers in Denmark to work within a framework of "more for less." That is, in spite of less available resources and lower budgets, we—and, for that matter, also the many private and market-based service providers—develop and motivate employees to take part in the creation of more productive and efficient municipal services for the benefit of residents.

This makes it easier for town councils, when reconsidering municipal service levels, to make their decisions according to available funds, according to local political values, and, of course, according to their legitimate wishes of maintaining their position in the eyes of the local electorate.

Commuting by bike generally improves health conditions of the population. Some 22 municipalities are working together to build a vast net of biking lanes that will connect the inner city of Copenhagen with the surrounding suburban municipalities.

Editors' Note

The following information is provided about this best practice case study to facilitate future research.

Name: Egedal Municipality
Population: 41,799 (2012)
Region: Capital District
Province/State: Region Hovedstaden
Country: Denmark
Official Name: Kingdom of Denmark
City Website: http://www.egedalkommune.dk/

Chapter 25

Freiburg, Germany, Uses Public Tram System and Bikes for Transportation

EcoMobility Alliance

Freiburg's long-lasting ambition to encourage sustainable mobility shows successes: Due to the affordable and convenient alternatives to car use, more than one third of Freiburg residents do not own a car. Latest statistics from 1999 indicate that 18 percent of all journeys within the city are done by public transport, 27 percent by bikes, 23 percent by walking and only 32 percent by car.

EcoMobility Since the 1960s— Freiburg's Mobility History

In the 1960s, when traffic congestion in Freiburg was at an all-time high, officials decided to maintain and develop the tram system. This decision was different from many other German cities in which the vision of an automobile city resulted in enlarging the streets and reducing public transport infrastructure. Since these days—much earlier than later sustainability debates—public transport is given priority within city development and trams build the backbone of the system.

In Freiburg, it is mainstream to use public transportation and bikes. Investments are done in all systems constantly so they are kept

modern. It is normal to find local leaders, business people, professors and sports idols in trams and on bikes, together with students, elderly people and others. How does it work?

Public Transportation

The tram system is constantly extended, new lines are built and existing lines are prolonged. In each city development public transport must be there first, is it in new housing areas or commercial zones. Trams are fast: they have mainly own tracks independent from car roads and they get automatic priority at traffic lights. 65 percent of Freiburg residents have a tram stop within 500 meters of their home.

It's not only convenient to use public transport, it is also not expensive: As first city in Germany, Freiburg took over a model from Basel, Switzerland in the 1980s: An unpersonalized mobility card which can be used for one month by anybody. In 1991 a regional mobility company was formed and the card transferred into a "Regio card" which since then allows using all local trains, trams and buses in a wider region. During weekends not only one but also two people including their

Originally published as "Freiburg, Germany: Successfully Reducing Automobile Traffic," *ICLEI Case Studies–EcoMobility* (October 2011), by ICLEI–Local Governments for Sustainability, Bonn, Germany. Reprinted with permission of the publisher.

children may use the one card. In 2011, one out of five inhabitants of the region purchases such a card each month and 1,5 Mio monthly passes are sold per year.

The secret of Freiburg's tariff approach is: offer public transport for low prices, increase the services constantly, extend the use and thus become one of the cheapest but highly competitive systems in Germany.

Priority to Pedestrians

Since the 1980s the city center remains open only to pedestrians, cyclists, buses and trams. The local economy has enormously benefited, unfortunately rents for centrally located stores are among the highest in Germany meanwhile. Since most of the city center is a pedestrian area, walking makes up 23 percent of all travels in Freiburg. The city promotes walking by reducing difficulties and delays. For example, the maximum waiting time at pedestrian crossings is sought only 30 seconds. In most parts of the city, the speed limit has been reduced to 30 km/h to make safer travel conditions for those traveling by bike and other means of EcoMobility.

Increasing Bicycle Use

Freiburg became famous through its bikes. Since the 1980s, the use of bicycles has doubled in Freiburg. Currently, bikes account for 27 percent of all journeys. The city has over 400 km of bike paths and new bike fast lines are built to cross the city without stops, this also in expectation of the faster e-bikes. Significant investment has also gone into bicycle parking facilities. The city has 9,000 parking spaces for bikes in the city center and at "Bike & Ride" locations at bus or tram stops. In 2011 the city council decided to set-up a by-law on bicycle parking which, among other requests that new buildings must offer bike parking facilities, an obligation which is well known for cars.

Impacts Are Obvious: Living Without a Car is Easy in Freiburg

Due to the affordable and convenient alternatives to car use, more than one third of Freiburg residents do not own a car. Over the past 10 years, there has been a 100 percent increase in public transportation use. Every day, 200,000 residents make use of the system of four tram lines and 26 bus lines. Freiburg has the lowest automobile density of any city in Germany with 423 cars per 1,000 people. The increase of car trips in Freiburg over the last 15 years was only 1.3 percent while the total trips increased 30 percent. Public transport passengers have increased 53 percent and bicycle trips have risen by 96 percent since 1976.

The City of Freiburg is located in southwestern Germany near the Black Forest with a population of 220,000 in the city and 615,000 in the region. The city is known for its university and for its advanced environmental practices. The main economies of Freiburg are public administration, university, electrical and medical engineering. Freiburg has been an ICLEI member since January 1990 and is the seat of the ICLEI European Secretariat.

EDITORS' NOTE

The following information is provided about this best practice case study to facilitate future research.

Name: City of Freiburg
Population: 218,043 (2012)
Region: Southeastern
Province/State: State of Baden-Wurttemberg
Country: Germany
Official Name: Federal Republic of Germany
City Website: http://www.freiburg.de/

Chapter 26

Groningen, Netherlands, Is Known as the World's Cycling City

Gary Toth

Would you use a rototiller to get rid of weeds in a flowerbed? Of course not. You might solve your immediate goal of uprooting the weeds—but oh, my, the collateral damage that you would do.

Yet when we try to eliminate congestion from our urban areas by using decades-old traffic engineering measures and models, we are essentially using a rototiller in a flowerbed. And it's time to acknowledge that the collateral damage has been too great.

First, an explanation of what I call the "deadly duo": travel projection models and Levels of Service (LOS) performance metrics. Travel projection models are computer programs that use assumptions about future growth in population, employment, and recreation to estimate how many new cars will be on roads 20 or 30 years into the future.

Models range from quite simplistic to incredibly complex and expensive. Simple models deal primarily with coarse movements of vehicles between cities, while complex models deal with the intricacies of what happens on the fine grid of urban areas. To be truly accurate, growth projection modeling can be expensive. Therefore, absent compelling reason to do otherwise, most growth projections tend to be done using less expensive techniques, which usually lead to overestimates.

Levels of Service (LOS) is a performance metric which flourished during the interstate- and freeway-building era that went from the 1950s to the 1990s. Using a scale of A to F, LOS attempts to create an objective formula to answer a subjective question: How much congestion are we willing to tolerate? As in grade school, "F" is a failing grade and "A" is perfect.

Engineers decided that LOS "C" was a good balance between overinvestment in perfection and underinvestment leading to congestion. In urban areas, a concession was made to accept LOS D, representing slightly more restricted but still free-flowing traffic. LOS is commonly (actually, almost always) calculated using travel projections for 20 to 30 years into the future.

Using basic traffic models and LOS C/D to plan and design the interstate system was a no-brainer in the 1950s, '60s and '70s. When deciding how many lanes to build on a freeway connecting major cities, a sensitivity of plus or minus 10,000 trips a day could be tolerated, and the incremental difference in cost to plow through undeveloped land was relatively insignificant.

Originally published as "Levels of Service and Travel Projections: The Wrong Tools for Planning Our Streets," *Cycling and Trails, Public Transportation and Parking, Resources* (August 2012), by the Project for Public Spaces, New York, New York. Reprinted with permission of the publisher.

Good Approach, Wrong Setting

I'm not going to look back and quibble with the general philosophy of how the interstates and the associated high-speed freeways were planned and designed. On many levels, the approach made sense.

But it became increasingly less persuasive when applied to the rest of our road network. Unlike interstates and freeways, most roads exist not just to move traffic through the area, but also to serve the homes, businesses, and people along them. Yet in search of high LOS rankings, transportation professionals have widened streets, added lanes, removed on-street parking, limited crosswalks, and deployed other inappropriate strategies. In ridding our communities of the weeds of congestion, we have also pulled out the very plants that made our "gardens" worthwhile in the first place.

It's worth remembering, too, that not all congestion is bad. John Norquist, former Mayor of Milwaukee and current CEO and President of the Congress for New Urbanism, suggests that congestion is like cholesterol: there is a good kind and a bad kind.

What makes the prevailing situation even more troubling is that there are no comprehensive requirements dictating the use of either LOS or travel modeling in transportation planning and project design. The "Green Book" from the Association of American State Highway and Transportation Officials (AASHTO) (more formally known as "A Policy on Geometric Design of Highways and Streets") clearly states that these are guidelines to be applied with judgment—not mandates. So does the Federal Highway Administration's "Highway Capacity Manual."

The idea that we must rid our roads of any and all traffic congestion is, in fact, a self-imposed requirement. As Eric Jaffe wrote in an article for Atlantic Cities in December, 2011:

Although cities aren't required to abide LOS measures by law, over the years the measure hardened into convention. By the time cities recognized the need for balanced transportation systems, LOS was entrenched in the street engineering canon.

Worse yet, many designers size a road or intersection to be free flowing for the worst hour of the day. Sized to accommodate cars during the highest peak hour, such streets will be "overdesigned" for the other 23 hours of the day and will always function poorly for the surrounding community.

If that isn't troubling enough, LOS is often calculated using traffic predicted 20 years into the future, even in urban settings. Until the forecasted growth materializes, the roadway will be overdesigned, even during the peak hour. Overdesigned roadways encourage motorists to drive at higher speeds, making them difficult to cross and unpleasant to walk along. This degrades public spaces between the edges of the road and the adjacent buildings, encourages people to drive short distances, and generally unravels a community's social fabric.

Let me repeat: Contrary to what you may hear, there is no national requirement or mandate to apply LOS standards and targets 20 years into the future for urban streets. This thinking is a remnant from 1960s era policy for the interstate system, and has erroneously been passed down from generation to generation.

So What Are the Right Approaches?

Asking the simple question, "Do you want congestion reduced at a particular location?" is a question out of context. It's like asking you whether you want to never be stung by a bee again. Of course, the answer will be yes. But what if I told you that to in order to never suffer a sting again, every plant within a several mile radius would have to be destroyed—and that you could never leave the area of destruction?

You would have a completely different answer, I'm sure.

The question that needs to be asked in urban settings is not whether you ever want to sit in congestion again. Who does? The question is whether you want to eliminate congestion on your Main Street 24 hours a day, 7 days a week, 365 days a year—knowing that the consequence would be a community with decimated economic and social value, increased reliance on car use, increased crashes, and, ultimately, more congestion.

Recognizing the need for balance, a number of entities are beginning to promote approaches sensitive to the context.

I was the New Jersey Department of Transportation's project manager for the "Smart Transportation Guide" (STG), adopted jointly by the state DOTs in Pennsylvania and New Jersey. The STG directs DOT designers to consider the tradeoffs between vehicular LOS and "local service." It goes on to say that if the street in question is not critical to regional movement, that LOS E or F could be acceptable—and that designers may actually need to design to *slow down cars*.

The Institute of Transportation Engineers, an "international association of transportation professionals responsible for meeting mobility and safety needs" also promoted this concept in its landmark "Context Sensitive Solutions Guidelines for Urban Thoroughfares." Florida DOT has adopted multimodal LOS standards, and cities like Charlotte, N.C., have elevated pedestrian and bicycle LOS to the level of that for automobiles. We have a long way to go, but the door is opening.

Creating balanced standards for roadway design will benefit transportation as well. In the Netherlands, the "Livable Streets" policy led to a remarkable improvement in safety on their roadways. They started in the 1970s with a crash rate 15 percent higher than in

the U.S., and now have a crash rate 60 percent lower.

Design with the Community in Mind

It's time for communities and transportation professionals alike to accept that we have been using the wrong tools for the wrong job. LOS and travel modeling may be effective when sizing and locating high-speed freeways, but are totally inappropriate in every other setting. If travel modeling with high rates of growth is used to make street decisions, your community may be doomed to a series of roadway widenings or intersection expansions. If vehicular LOS C or D performance measures are adopted as nonnegotiable targets, major road construction will be heading your way.

Village, suburban and city streets need to be designed with the community in mind using the PPS principle of Streets as Places to create a vision for a great community and then plan your streets to support that vision.

Let's not be fooled by the appearance of science behind Levels of Service and Traffic Modeling. As I pointed out in an interview with Wayne Senville that was published in the November 2010 "Planning Commissioner's Journal," LOS standards are easy to understand—and that's exactly what makes them so dangerous.

It's no secret that just about anywhere you go in the Netherlands is an incredible place to bicycle. And in Groningen, a northern city with a population of 190,000 and a bike mode share of 50 percent, the cycling is as comfortable as in any city on Earth. The sheer number of people riding at any one time will astound you, as will the absence of automobiles in the city center, where cars seem extinct. It is remarkable just how quiet the city is. People go about their business running errands by bike, going to work by bike, and even holding hands by bike.

The story of how they got there is a mix of great transportation policy, location and chance. You'll learn quite a bit of history in the film, but essentially Groningen decided in the 1970s to enact policies to make it easier to walk and bilk, and discourage the use of cars in the city center. By pedestrianizing some streets, building cycle tracks everywhere, and creating a unique transportation circulation pattern that prohibits vehicles from cutting through the city, Groningen actually made the bicycle—in most cases—the fastest and most preferred choice of transportation.

EDITORS' NOTE

The following information is provided about this best practice case study to facilitate future research.

Name: City of Groningen
Population: 198,355 (2013)
Region: North End
Province/State: Province of Groningen
Country: Netherlands
Official Name: Kingdom of the Netherlands
City Website: http://www.gemeente.groningen.nl/

The Project for Public Spaces' website (http://www.pps.org/) has additional information concerning the best practices for placemaking being used to improve neighborhoods in cities throughout the world.

Chapter 27

Halifax, Canada Is Among the Most Walkable Cities in North America

Dan Burden

This is one of the most important and necessary questions anyone should ask before settling down in a permanent location. Many corporate leaders looking to expand or move locations are now looking for towns offering appropriate start up breaks, but also where they and their middle managers want to live many years, raise a family and retire. Our website has a 12-step program for defining and achieving or strengthening community walkability.

But finding a walkable town is a different task. So, I have built a list of the 12 most important things to rate when searching for a Walkable Community. Note that there are many walkable communities in America that are declining, due to poor politics, staffing or a lost vision. And there are some communities on the cusp of becoming walkable that have strong leadership and direction. Given a choice, I would move to the community that is up and coming.

You can, of course, move into a new Walkable Community, such as Seaside, Celebration, Abacoa, Florida; Kentlands, Maryland, The Crossings, Mountain View, California; Fairview Village, Orenco Station, Oregon; Northwest Landing, Washington; and now hundreds of others. I know these

places well. I return to them often, photographing, walking and measuring their essences. The paint, the grass, everything is fresh and new there. Some of these new urban villages are rather complete, and fit well into the fabric of the greater town or region they share.

But if you don't want to wait for these places to become organic, go for the real towns of America ... they are abundant, old, tried and proven, and they need many defenders of their greatness. This article is mostly on how to find existing Walkable Communities. They are way too numerous to list more than a fraction.

This article is also a little bit on how to protect these delicate real places of the heart. As I write this, I am sitting in East Lansing, one of my favorite Walkable Communities. I am eager to go out for a walk. But I am also 100 miles from Holland, Michigan. I am torn—I'd like to go there, right now, take in the color of the tulips, walk its streets and listen to the outward pride and laughter of its people.

You can either be a passenger on the train to change, or get up in the engine helping stoke the fire, taking in the gusty winds of change feeling the sting and smell of hot

Originally published as "How Can I Find and Help Build a Walkable Community?" *Walkable Communities Resources—Articles* (August 2013), by the Walkable and Livable Communities Institute, Port Townsend, Washington. Reprinted with permission of the publisher.

cinders burning the hair off the nape of your neck. These up and coming communities may be more affordable, and are likely to be fun places to place your energies. But before you move, truly check out the politics of change.

Good towns come in all regions of the country. The best are often small places like Keene, New Hampshire; Winter Park, Florida; Flagstaff, Arizona; Crested Butte, Colorado or Los Gatos, California ... or they include big cities like Seattle, Washington; Chicago, Illinois; Milwaukee, Wisconsin; Minneapolis and St Paul, Minnesota; Portland, Oregon; or San Diego, California that have many small, well designed compact, intact neighborhoods, each with a village center and a character and personality of its own.

In some of these villages, strong enclaves of Hispanic, Jewish, Polish, German, Asian, Afro-American or gay cultures are found, taking pride building or maintaining their communities. Other villages are fully mixed, rich in diversity of people, age, abilities and wealth. You can live in a town that is sprawling itself to death, and still lead a healthy life in several great neighborhoods. Note that top rated towns in this listing either already have or are now developing many villages in their city.

Finding the Great Walkable Community. My wife, Lys, and I left Central Ohio the day after we got married in June, 1970 and moved west in search of a great place to live. We struck gold, almost by accident, in our first search for a town. We settled into and lived in Missoula, Montana without a car for nearly ten years, very happy, healthy, and highly engaged with every level of community life. We knew, felt ownership and took pride in the many good places. We walked and watched over green, canopied streets almost everywhere. We felt the courtesies of drivers who watched out for us. We knew each park, each of the five valley neighborhoods and other places in the pre-sprawl portions of town.

It seems we came to know everyone, and everyone knew us. We had many dozens of friends and hundreds, if not thousands of associates. During our evenings we bicycled into and up the Rattlesnake Creek, Grant Creek, Pattee Canyon, the Hells Gate or, when we had the time, out to French Town or Lolo. Our first child, Jodi, who maintains this web site, was born there. Our small company, Bikecentennial (now Adventure Cycling), was started there 25 years ago, and is still a small but healthy addition to the local economy.

Missoula has a healthy downtown. In the summer a weekly farmers market is held on Saturdays. Many hundreds of people walk or bicycle in to buy their fruit filled pastries, breads, fresh fruits, and organic vegetables. Others come for coffee, listen to music, watch people dance, or just visit. Missoula also has a Friday noon gathering on the rebuilt Clark's Fork River front. People come almost like a weekly pilgrimage for more food, more music and more fun. And just across the street from our little red ginger bread house at 317 Beverly, in Bonner Park, people came on Wednesday nights to hear the small but good community band. Some who bring their cars to these events park them blocks away, some too embarrassed to be seen arriving by car, but not knowing the beauty of walking there.

One immigrant, poor in money, rich in pride of being an American, conceived and built with his own hands, along with the 50–60 volunteers he and former Mayor Daniel Kemmis brought together, the newest and best post World War II carousel in the nation. Missoula also boasts a variety of pricing and sizing of housing stock, great waterfront and trails and a pleasant college campus.

Like many Walkable Communities, today Missoula is also a hearty sprawl place. One only has to look to the down slopes of the mountains to see the ugly brutality of unregulated, un-walkable growth patterns. But

Missoula, like all vision directed towns, has and continues to build upon its walkability, while other parts of the same town and county hold contempt for walkability, watering down, isolating and making more distant healthy lifestyles in order to cash into the hungry car culture, complete with all of its demands and droppings.

Like many good places, Missoula is a town highly conflicted, ever in balance. Goodness is not always understood by all people living in a place. There are many short-term investors milking and robbing from long-term accomplishments. It is all too easy for decision makers to close down good, well located and sized schools, healthy and vital local parks, and well located small churches, grocery stores or other retail in order to build big. It always appears to be cheaper to provide the same function on the bigger and cheaper parcel farther out. These farther out places are locations where cars appear to be happy. These outward parcels are cheaper yes, but as we destroy the essences of a good neighborhood, forcing ourselves into a car to have what we need we whittle away the many reasons we came to invest here in the first place. If you move to a walkable community, you must understand its value then learn the skills of building and defending its goodness.

Places more abandoned of walkability, health and vitality have few conflicts. Their sense of place, pride and community values have been lost, or chased away.

All towns in our nation have some degree of walkability. Some hold less than 5 percent, where microscopes are needed to find the remaining shredded and often buried fragments. Some, such as Littleton, New Hampshire, where they are too poor to afford sprawl, have nearly 98 percent walkable scale and features. When you find a town with good walkable features, such as Keene, New Hampshire, you keep returning to recharge. I know I do. I go back often, settle into a nice center town hotel, hang out at local eateries, listen to the town chatter, walk the main street day and night, over and over 2–4 days at a time.

Walkability Items to be rated are always on a scale. A 1–10 scale can be personalized and applied to each of the below twelve categories. Common sense and powers of observation are used to make these determinations. The categories are in no particular order. Never pick a town that you have not visited. Always ask for second and third opinions.

If I were making a commitment to move to a town I would want the town to have high scores on 6 or more of the following 12 categories:

Walkable Communities Have:

1. Intact town centers. This center includes a quiet, pleasant main street with a hearty, healthy set of stores. These stores are open for business a minimum of 8 hours a day. The stores include things like barbers/beauticians, hardware, druggist, small grocery/deli, sets of good restaurants, clothing, variety store, ice cream shop, stores that attract children, many youth and senior services, places to conduct civic and personal business, library, all within a ¼ mile walk (5 minutes) of the absolute center. If this is a county seat, the county buildings are downtown. If this is an incorporated town the town hall is in the town center. The library is open for business at least 10 hours a day 6–7 days a week. There is still a post office downtown.

2. Residential densities, mixed income, mixed use. Near the town center, and in a large town at appropriate transit locations there will be true neighborhoods. Higher densities are toward the town center and in appropriate concentrations further out. Housing includes mixed income and mixed use. A truly walkable community does not force lots of people to drive to where they work. Aspen, for example, is a great place to shop and play ... but fails to provide housing for anyone who works there. Granny flats, design studios and other affordable housing are part of the mix in even the wealthiest neighborhoods.

3. Public Space. There are many places for people to assemble, play and associate with others within their neighborhood. The best neighborhoods have welcoming public space within ⅛th mile (700 feet) of all homes. These spaces are easily accessed by all people.

4. Universal Design. The community has a healthy respect for people of all abilities, and has appropriate ramps, medians, refuges, crossings of driveways, sidewalks on all streets where needed, benches, shade and other basic amenities to make walking feasible and enjoyable for everyone.

5. Key Streets Are Speed Controlled. Traffic moves on main street and in neighborhoods at safe, pleasant, courteous speeds. Most streets are designed to keep speeds low. Many of these streets are tree lined, have on-street parking and use other methods that are affordable means to keep traffic speeds under control. There is an absence of one-way couplets designed to flush downtown of its traffic in a rush or flight to the suburbs. In most parts of the nation the streets are also green, or have other pleasant landscaping schemes in dry climates.

6. Streets, Trails are Well Linked. The town has good block form, often in a grid or other highly connected pattern. Although hilly terrain calls for slightly different patterns, the linkages are still frequent. Some of the newer neighborhoods that were built to cul-de-sac or other fractured patterns are now being repaired for walking by putting in trail connectors in many places. These links are well designed so that there are many eyes on these places. Code for new streets no longer permits long streets that are disconnected.

7. Design is Properly Scaled to ⅛th, ¼
and ½ mile radius segments. From most homes it is possible to get to most services in ¼ mile (actual walked distance). Neighborhood elementary schools are within a ¼ mile walking radius of most homes, while high schools are accessible to most children (1 mile radius). Most important features (parks) are within ⅛th mile, and a good, well-designed place to wait for a high frequency (10–20 minutes) bus is within ¼ to ½ mile. Note that most of these details can be seen on a good local planning map, and even many can be downloaded from the web.

8. Town is Designed for People. Look for clues that decisions are being made for people first, cars second. Does the town have a lot of open parking lots downtown? Are a lot of streets plagued with multiple commercial driveways, limited on-street parking, fast turning radii on corners. Towns designed for people have many investments being made in plazas, parks, walkways ... rarely are they investing in decongesting intersections on the far reaches of town. Towns designed for people are tearing down old, non-historic dwellings, shopping plazas and such and converting them to compact, mixed use, mixed income properties. Ask to review the past year of building permits by category. Much is told about what percentage of construction that is infill and independent small builder stock versus big builder single price range housing or retail stock.

9. Town is Thinking Small. The most walkable towns are boldly stepping forward requiring maximum parking allowed, versus minimum required. Groceries and other important stores are not permitted to build above a reasonable square footage, must place the footprint of the structure to the street, etc. Palo Alto, for instance, caps their groceries at 20,000 square feet. This assures that groceries, drug stores and other important items are competitive at a size that is neighborhood friendly. Neighborhood schools are community centers. Older buildings are rebuilt in place, or converted to modern needs. Most parking is on-street.

10. In Walkable Communities There Are Many People Walking. This sounds like a silly statement at first ... but think again. Often there are places that look walkable, but no one walks. Why? There is always a reason. Is it crime? Is it that there is no place to walk to, even though the streets and walkways are pleasant? Are the downtown stores not open convenient hours? You should be able to see a great diversity of those walking and bicycling. Some will be very young, some very old. People with disabilities will be common. Another clue, where people walk in great abundance virtually all motorists are courteous to pedestrians. It is true.

11. The Town and Neighborhoods have a Vision. Seattle, Washington, Portland, Oregon and Austin, Texas are just three examples where neighborhood master plans have been developed. Honolulu sets aside about $1M per year of funds to be spent by each neighborhood. Visionary, master plans provide direction, build ownership of citizens, engage diverse people, and create opportunities for implementation, to get past sticky issues, and deal with the most basic, fundamental, necessary decisions and commitment. There are budgets set aside for neighborhoods, for sidewalks, trails, links, parks. The community no longer talks about where they will get the money, but how they will change their priorities.

12. Decision Makers Are Visionary, Communicative, and Forward Thinking. The town has a strong majority of leaders who "get it". Leaders know that they are not to do all the work ... but to listen and respond to the most engaged, involved, broad-minded citizens. They rarely are swayed by the antigroup, they seek the opinions and involvement big brush citizens and retailers. They are purposefully changing and building policies, practices, codes and decisions to make their towns pleasant places for people ... rein-

vesting in the town center, disinfesting in sprawl. These people know the difference between a green field, brown field and grey field. They know what Active Living by Design is all about. The regional government understands and supports the building of a town center, and is not attempting to take funds from the people at the center to induce or support sprawl. Often there is a charismatic leader on the town board, chamber of commerce, planning board, there is an architectural review team, a historic preservation effort, and overall good public process. Check out the web site of the town ... if they focus on their golf courses, tax breaks, great medical services, scenic majestic mountains, or proximity to the sea ... fail to emphasize their neighborhood schools, world class library, lively downtown, focus on citizen participation ... they are lost, bewitched and bewildered in their own lust and lure of Walt Disney's Pleasure Island.

Finding walkable communities is a great quest we should all make together. I have many personal favorites. They come in all sizes. Each must be tested out using the above criteria before investing in these places. All are in various stages of healing or becoming more diseased, often at the same time.

Generally, I like a town to be on the small side, but larger towns are on my list if they have many good neighborhoods and villages. Some highly favored towns (Crested Butte, Colorado) have as few as 1400 people, many, such as Littleton, New Hampshire, pop 7,000) 5–15,000. A good size town that is complete can provide good services when populated by 30–50,000 people. When towns get up to 100,000 or more, many added services, like efficient transit, are a must to remain walkable and fun.

EDITORS' NOTE

The following information is provided about this best practice case study to facilitate future research.

Name: Halifax Regional Municipality

Population: 390,016 (2011)
Region: Eastern
Province/State: Province of Nova Scotia
Country: Canada
Official Name: Canada
City Website: http://www.halifax.ca/

The attachment to this article showed "Walkable Communities by Region" in North America. The most walkable communities in Canada were listed as follows: Halifax, Montreal, Ontario, Quebec City, Toronto, Vancouver, and Victoria

Chapter 28

Hangzhou, China, Has Developed the World's Largest Bike Sharing Program

EcoMobility Alliance

In May 2008, Hangzhou launched China's first bike sharing system to support a more EcoMobile transport system. Meanwhile, it became the world's largest bike share program. Residents and visitors may rent a bicycle and take advantage of the hundreds of kilometers of dedicated bike lanes.

Start-up and Regulation

The bike share system in Hangzhou was designed, built, and funded by the local government in order to cover the last kilometer from the public transportation stop to the customer's destination or vice-versa. Several hundred million Chinese yuan (approximately 30 Million Euro) were invested at the start-up of the system. Strong local government involvement helps to ensure the financial sustainability of the bike share system, prevent vandalism, and improve the service level.

How the Bike Rental Works

This municipally owned and operated the system which uses a card in conjunction with the city's bus system and parking. Over 80 percent of the rental stations in Hangzhou are unmanned service stations. At one of these self-service kiosks, the customer inserts his or her card into the machine unit. Then, a bike is unlocked and the docking station flashes a green light. A deposit of 200 Chinese yuan (22€) is then deducted from the card and the rental period has begun. To return a bike, the customer simply puts the bike in the open slot and places the card in the machine. The deposit is then returned and the rental period is over. The appropriate rental charge is then deducted from the card's balance.

A Growing Bike Sharing Community

In May 2008, Hangzhou had 61 bike sharing stations with 2,800 bicycles. One year later, there were 640 stations with 16,000 bicycles. At the end of 2009, there were 2,000 stations with 50,000 bicycles and the system has since expanded to 2,200 stations with 60,600 bicycles. A station can now be found

Originally published as "Hangzhou, China: The World's Largest Bike Sharing Program," *ICLEI Case Studies–EcoMobility* (October 2011), by ICLEI–Local Governments for Sustainability, Bonn, Germany. Reprinted with permission of the publisher.

every 100 meters—almost 3.6 bike stands per km2. Since its opening, the daily use per bicycle has increased from less than one ride to five rides. There are approximately 240,000 daily usages of the system, with the highest single day usage being 320,000 rides.

Bicycle trips in Hangzhou account for 43 percent of all trips, and the city's bike sharing system is partly to credit for that. Daily bike sharing trips cover about 1,123,200 km. An automobile covering the same distance would produce more than 200,000 kg of CO_2 emissions. Given these figures, and the goal of reaching 175,000 public bikes by 2020, there is potential for further greenhouse gas emission reductions.

Fee Structure and Business Model

Since many people use the system for the first or last kilometer of a trip, 96 percent of trips are under one hour, with an average ride time of 23 minutes. Three percent of trips are between one and two hours, 0.6 percent are between two and three hours, and only 0.4 percent are greater than three hours. Since bikes are free during the first hour of rental and most trips are under one hour, the bike system itself does not generate much revenue. Advertising on the bikes is the main

source of funding. Since advertising revenues are large, bikes are available to customers at a very affordable rate. For a use of one to two hours, the fee is one yuan (0.11€). For two to three hours, it is two yuan (0.22€). After three hours, the fee is three yuan (0.33€) per hour.

The City of Hangzhou is a city in Eastern China, located on the Yangtze River 180 kilometers southwest of Shanghai. It is the capital city of the Zhejiang province. Hangzhou is made up of six central urban districts which make up 683 km² and are populated by over 2.2 million people. Hangzhou's economy is based on light industry, agriculture, textiles, medicine, and information technology.

EDITORS' NOTE

The following information is provided about this best practice case study to facilitate future research.

Name: City of Hangzhou
Population: 6,242,000 (2012)
Region: Eastern China
Province/State: Zhejlang Province
Country: China
Official Name: People's Republic of China
City Website: http://www.hangzhou.gov.ch/

A chart at the end of this municipal case study noted that the City of Hangzhou's Public Bicycle Program had only a few thousand bikes in 2008 (2,000 or 3,000), and now has well over 60,000 bikes (2011), at the time that this case study was researched and written.

Chapter 29

Hilden, Germany, Reduces Vehicular Traffic and Promotes Public Transport and Cycling

Project for Public Spaces

Developed in Europe, traffic calming (a direct translation of the German "vekehrs-beruhigung") is a system of design and management strategies that aim to balance traffic on streets with other uses. It is founded on the idea that streets should help create and preserve a sense of place, that their purpose is for people to walk, stroll, look, gaze, meet, play, shop and even work alongside cars—but not dominated by them. The tools of traffic calming take a different approach from treating the street only as a conduit for vehicles passing through at the greatest possible speed. They include techniques designed to lessen the impact of motor vehicle traffic by slowing it down, or literally "calming" it. This helps build human-scale places and an environment friendly to people on foot.

Besides its power to improve the livability of a place, the beauty of traffic calming is that it can be applied inexpensively and flexibly. The strategies outlined below in The Traffic Calming Toolbox can be employed by painting lines, colors and patterns; using planters, bollards and other removable barriers; eliminating or adding parking; or installing sidewalk extensions or similar structures with temporary materials. All provide an opportunity to test devices, combinations and locations, fine-tuning the approach according to results. Traffic calming, along with other small-scale improvements, can enhance a place immediately, while being tested and refined to meet long-term needs. When funds are available, the right combination of devices can be transformed into permanent improvements and extended over a broader area. Regardless of what traffic-calming action is undertaken, the benefit to a community is greater when the technical improvements are strengthened by visual enhancements like trees, flowers and other amenities.

The Traffic Calming Toolbox

1. Diagonal Parking.

Cars park diagonally, jutting out from the curb, rather than parallel to it. The benefits:

- Simple and inexpensive
- Changes both the perception and the function of a street
- Shortens the "peering distance" for people crossing the street
- Drivers pulling out must be alert to approaching traffic

Originally published as "Traffic Calming 101," *Walkable Communities Resources—Articles* (December 2013), by the Walkable and Livable Communities Institute, Port Townsend, Washington. Reprinted with permission of the publisher.

- Oncoming drivers must be alert to the cars pulling out
- All of this added driver awareness creates more awareness of pedestrians
- Can add up to 40 percent more parking space than parallel parking

2. Changing One-Way Streets to Two-Way.

Single or double traffic lanes, either face-to-face or with a median, sometimes flanked by parking. The benefits:

- Less driving, less confusion, and better traffic access
- Eliminates the need to drive blocks and blocks out of the way
- No need to make extra turns to get to nearby destinations
- Drivers can get directly to their destination
- Increases commercial traffic and business
- Decreases the speed of traffic

3. Widening Sidewalks/Narrowing Streets and Traffic Lanes.

These techniques provide a flexible way to take back space from the street for non-motor-vehicle uses. Traditional traffic engineering calls for 12- to 13-foot lanes, citing "traffic safety" standards—but newer evidence shows that lanes as narrow as nine feet can still be safe for driving.

- Narrowing lanes and to widen sidewalks eases crossing for pedestrians and gives them more space to walk.
- Lanes can also be removed from serving traffic and designated for buses, trolleys, or other types of transit.
- Traffic lanes can be transformed into bicycle lanes.
- All street lanes can be narrowed together to create more room for non-auto uses.
- Vertical elements like trees or bollards further reduce the "optical width" of a narrowed street, thereby discouraging speeding.

4. Bulbs—Chockers—Neckdowns.

Interchangeable terms for sidewalk extensions in selected areas—such as at intersections or at mid-block—as opposed to a full sidewalk widening. The benefits:

- Provide a haven for pedestrians waiting to cross the street
- Shorten the crossing distance
- Define parking bays
- Deflect through traffic at a corner
- Function as entry points
- Provide space for amenities and enhancements (e.g. kiosks, trees, lighting)

5. Chicanes.

Sidewalk extensions that jog from one side of a street to the other to replicate such a circuitous route. The benefits:

- Narrow, curving roads encourage motorists to drive more slowly and carefully
- An undulating path interrupts any clear view ahead and compels drivers to slow down
- Chicanes can be formed using sculpture, plantings and parking to enhance the appearance and function of a street
- Diagonal parking and parallel parking can be alternated to create a chicane effect.
- Chicanes are best used on narrow roads, to prevents cars from swinging out to maintain their speed around the bends.

6. Roundabouts.

Large, raised, circular islands at the middle of major intersections, around which all oncoming vehicles must travel until reaching their destination street, where they then turn off. The benefits:

- Create a "calmed," steady flow of traffic
- Reduction in conflict points, which can lead to fewer accidents
- Traffic signals are not customarily required (although traffic control signs are prominent)
- Streets narrow as they approach the roundabout, and crosswalks are installed on these approaches—thereby slowing oncom-

ing vehicles and giving pedestrians a safe, obvious opportunity to cross

• Enhanced with fountains, sculpture or attractive landscaping, the island can serve as a striking gateway

• A sloping ramp around the perimeter of the raised island allows buses, trucks and other large vehicles to maneuver the continuous curve while still maintaining a lowered speed.

7. Traffic Circles.

Essentially "mini-roundabouts" designed for small intersections, often used to slow traffic from a wide street into a smaller local street. Traffic circles:

• Help to slow down traffic in neighborhoods and remind drivers that they must proceed carefully

• Help to sustain lowered vehicle speeds when they're used in a series

• Provide an opportunity for community activity in residential areas, where citizens can create plantings or add other enhancements

8. Raised Medians.

Elevated islands parallel to traffic lanes down the middle of the street, as on a boulevard. The benefits:

• Curtail vehicle space

• Provide a safe in-between refuge for pedestrians as they make their way across the street, split up a lengthy curb-to-curb distance (especially helpful for people who cannot move quickly)

• Provide ideal locations for trees, flowers, sculpture and other amenities

9. Tight Corner Curbs.

The longer the radius of a curve, the faster a vehicle can move around that curve—as many pedestrian witness when, in crossing at an intersection, they are confronted by a car whizzing around the corner seemingly out of nowhere. Reducing a corner radius to somewhere between one and twenty feet can:

• Inhibit the speed of turning vehicles

• Give pedestrians a better chance to see and be seen by approaching traffic

• Add sidewalk space, thereby shortening the distance to the other side of the street

10. Diverters.

These physical barriers redirect traffic heading for a certain street onto a different course, reducing vehicle overload on vulnerable (usually residential) streets overrun by through traffic looking for shortcuts.

• **Diagonal Diverters** traverse an entire intersection, actually creating two unconnected streets that each turn sharply away from one another.

• **Semi-Diverters** restrict traffic in one direction to prevent entrance to a street, while permitting traffic to pass through in the other direction.

• Although they effectively reduce traffic volume, diverters must be part of a comprehensive improvement scheme or else they can end up simply displacing congestion.

11. Road Humps, Speed Tables, and Cushions.

These devices reduce speed by introducing modest up-and-down changes in the level of the street, thereby requiring drivers to decelerate.

• **Road humps** (or "speed humps") are rounded mounds, approximately three inches high and 10 to 12 feet long. They effectively slow down traffic to 15–20 mph without making drivers uncomfortable. For optimum speed reduction, road humps need to be placed at frequent, designated intervals based on the street's dimensions, to minimize the tendency to accelerate between them. (Humps are not to be confused with the speed *bumps*, which are usually at least 5–6" high and less than three feet long.)

• **Speed tables** are road humps that are flat on top and sometimes slightly longer. They are the same width as the street and rise to meet the grade of the sidewalk, providing safe and comfortable crossings for walkers and wheelchairs (and greater access for snow clearance than road humps). One benefit of speed tables is that people cross at the point where drivers decrease speed.

• **Cushions** cover only part of the width of the street to allow passage for emergency vehicles, buses or other large vehicles, and bicycles; they are usually placed at varying intervals to respond to the need to channel the wheels of larger vehicles, while still providing hurdles wide enough to slow standard-sized vehicles.

• It is important to highlight road humps, speed tables and cushions with clear markings to alert approaching drivers. This can be accomplished by: painting words and symbols directly on the street; changing the texture of the street surface; or using signage (the word "Bump" instead of "Hump" is a standard approach thought to effectively put drivers on the alert).

12. Rumble Strips and Other Surface Treatments

• **The rumble strip** provides visual and aural cues to alert drivers to areas that require special care (shopping centers, freeways undergoing construction work, schools, entrances to residential neighborhoods). Materials like granite and concrete are roughened by being broken into raised lines or patterns, and placed in strips across roadways, usually in a series. Drivers can lessen the vibration and the abrasive sound they create by slowing down.

• **Changes in pavement color and texture** (such as bricks or Belgian blocks), used in interesting and visually attractive ways, can also have the effect of rumble strips. These paving treatments also: delineate and create awareness of a pedestrian crosswalk or haven; make a street appear narrower than it is to deter speeding; define a street from a sidewalk or a parking lane.

Before Traffic Calming: Major Considerations

The "starter set" of traffic-calming tools outlined above can be effective in a variety of ways. However, each tool has its own specific applications, and not every one fits every single circumstance. Some tools are more effective if used in combination with each other, or with alternative transportation approaches like bicycles, buses or light rail. The right use hinges on existing conditions along a street and the desired outcomes. The following is a sampler of issues that need to be considered when making traffic calming choices.

• Do emergency and service vehicles use the area? Do school buses?
• Is there a problem with through traffic?
• What are the surrounding uses? Residential? Commercial? Retail? Cultural? Entertainment? Civic? Educational? Other?
• Who are the users? Are there many elderly or disabled people or children?
• What kinds of activities are going on in the vicinity or are planned to go on?
• Are there plans for improving the area? If so, how?
• What kinds of streets are being looked at? What is the ideal speed desired?
• Is transit service available? If so, where and what kind?
• Where is drainage needed?

Transit and Traffic Calming

Transit can be an efficient, more economical and less polluting alternative to the automobile—but transit alone doesn't necessarily make a place more livable. People still need to cross streets safely to reach a train station, bus stop, or other transit hub. And they need a pleasant and direct walking route along the way. This is where traffic calming comes in.

Traffic calming measures can make the trip to the transit station more walkable and convenient, while providing space for amenities to make the trip more pleasant. Although traffic calming and transit seem to be natural partners, sometimes their goals can conflict. When a traffic-calming strategy performs its job well, it may interfere with the efficient movement of a transit vehicle, or even its comfort, as when speed humps create a bumpy ride on buses. Certain strategies can maintain the benefits of traffic calming while allowing transit to function effectively:

Cushions enable buses to pass smoothly over an area, yet still slow smaller vehicles. Bus "bumpouts" or "nubs" allow buses to pick up passengers without having to move out of the traffic lane. They extend across a parking lane to meet the traffic lane (and the bus that is in it), giving passengers a safe and accessible approach, while also saving travel time. Nubs can be built to line up with both the front and rear doors of a standard bus, and can accommodate amenities like bus shelters, benches, telephones and waste receptacles.

By and large though, as long as they are coordinated to meet the needs of a specific street environment and its surrounding community, traffic calming and transit can work together to provide the comfortable, convenient and safe connections that enhance a place and promote a positive experience there. Two considerations to make are: How does transit relate to sites where traffic-calming improvements are needed? How can transit and traffic calming reinforce one another in order to help people get from place to place without driving?

Liabilities

Transportation agencies often believe they could be sued by drivers (not pedestrians) who might have a collision if design standards that give cars unencumbered, speedy passage are not followed. However, the most serious (and fatal) collisions are caused by high speeds. Traffic calming creates a set of checks and balances that compel those at the wheel to drive slowly and carefully, making streets safer for both drivers and pedestrians.

In practice, liability is a murky area, subject to interpretations that can conflict from one jurisdiction to another. In New Jersey, for example, the Borough of Belmar was sued by Monmouth County for trying to make a street safer to cross. The street, Belmar's Ocean Avenue, is usually clogged with vehicles that rarely abide the 25 mph speed limit. Throngs of summer tourists cross Ocean Avenue to get to the beach, and on average, there is a fatal pedestrian/vehicular accident every two years—a rate that prompted the Mayor and his borough to take action.

EDITORS' NOTE

The following information is provided about this best practice case study to facilitate future research.

Name: City of Hilden
Population: 54,736 (2012)
Region: Mettmann District
Province/State: State of North Rhine—Westphalia
Country: Germany
Official Name: Federal Republic of Germany
City Website: http://www.hilden.de/

The City of Hilden's traffic calming efforts started in 1992 with a municipal government shift in transport from vehicles to cycles and public transit. The municipal government limited vehicle speeds on public streets to 18.5 miles per hour throughout the city's built up areas. Currently one-fourth of all trips taken by citizens in the city are done by using their bicycles. This lower speed limit made citizens feel safer walking and using their bicycles throughout the city on public roadways. They became a model for other cities throughout Germany and cities in other countries throughout Europe.

Chapter 30

Hong Kong, China, Other Cities, Develop Transit Systems that Serve Mixed-Use Areas

Dae-Hong Minn

Modern satellite cities are beginning to dot the landscape throughout Asia, from South Korean suburbs linked to Seoul by bullet train, to China's newly emerging inland "eco-cities." In a region where youth culture and traditional values simultaneously clash and coexist, new communities are emerging far from the traditional coastal cities, linked by a weblike network of high-speed and local trains and subways.

Mass transit is the new paradigm for these emerging markets, and the train has fully trumped the car as the mode of transportation around which to design new cities. Since so much of the architecture in today's Asia is unfolding far from traditional city centers, the associated mass transit components not only shape, but also define these essentially 21st-century destinations.

With more than 60 percent of the world's population, Asia's rapid population growth is driving the construction of new communities that connect to traditional urban centers primarily by trains. The planning of these new communities, while influenced by culture, climate, and regulations, is ultimately shaped more by transit than by any other single factor. Rising populations, rapidly growing traffic congestion, and the desire for a green and sustainable planet have made transit-oriented designs popular throughout the world. These designs do not work everywhere, but they are essential to nearly all rapidly expanding urban centers in Asia's emerging markets.

In established areas like Tokyo or Hong Kong, elaborate transit systems have long served as the central nervous system of the urban fabric. But designers of new urban communities in Asia—both new communities and new mixed-use developments within well-established cities—are challenged to move beyond subway stops, and create urban community identities that are shaped by factors much more profound than the name of their transit stations.

In Tokyo, private rail companies are now leveraging options with real estate developments, maximizing their infrastructure to include housing, shopping, and entertainment. Tama New Town, for example, is a new development with plans to hold more than 360,000 people in 21 residential areas on the rail lines serving the area. Tama Centre, the largest station, has been designed to encompass office towers, a shopping plaza, and residential areas.

Originally published as "Transit-Oriented Design in the New Asia," *Urban Land*, Vol. 68, No. 1 (January 2009), by the Urban Land Institute, Washington, D.C. Copyright, the Urban Land Institute, all rights reserved. Reprinted with permission.

In Hong Kong, the Admiralty station houses five-star hotels, an upscale shopping center, and several housing projects. The components of the Admiralty station are designed to be an integral part of the fabric of Hong Kong, and although centered on the transit station, they are connected to, rather than distinct from (as has been the case many times in the past), the surrounding neighborhood.

The Asan Baebang mixed-use complex is a master-planned community outside Seoul currently under construction, designed to accommodate 25,000 residents. One of South Korea's new high-speed train lines will serve the development—one stop and 25 minutes from central Seoul. The train station is also there, while construction of the buildings is just beginning.

In addition to residential space, split between condos and rentals, Asan Baebang will have office and retail components. The pedestrian traffic flow in Asan was designed to take advantage of the Cheonan Stream that runs through the development; the flow of pedestrians from the high-speed train station at one end toward the department store at the other end mimics the flow of the water, and juxtaposes the calm of nature with the modern retail concourse. The project is large enough to become a destination for people coming from Seoul, and the high-speed connection will facilitate two-way traffic.

Other countries in Asia also are embracing transit-oriented development. This is most evident in China, which currently is building more than 5,000 miles (8,046.72 km) of new high-speed train lines and 35 Metro systems for its booming cities. As recently as 1997, only three cities in mainland China had subway systems—Beijing, Tianjian, and Shanghai. Now, the number of cities is set to increase along with China's urban population.

In Guangzhou, plans are underway for a new form of mass transit known as bus rapid transit (BRT), which provides a Metro-like infrastructure for a fraction of the time and cost. The first phase of Guangzhou's BRT is expected to be in operation later this year. Seoul, Beijing, and Jakarta have all implemented BRT in the last five years. In a turn-about trend, this innovative transit idea has even trickled back to the United States where Chicago's Mayor Richard Daley has considered BRT routes based on his experience with this form of transit in Asian cities he has visited.

Unlike the slow swell of migration experienced in the Western world since the late 19th century, countries like China, Japan, and South Korea have seen their urban populations explode in just a few short decades. Reports from the United Nations and the World Resources Institute estimate that in 1950, 17 percent (232 million) of Asia's population lived in urban areas. In 2005, urban populations reached 40 percent (1,562 million), and by 2030, urban populations are estimated to increase to more than 70 percent. This presents unique planning challenges, particularly in a country like South Korea where the mountainous terrain makes it nearly impossible to create contiguous suburban communities like those in the West.

In many Asian countries, government-controlled zoning principles in the 1960s led to regimented growth of downtown areas with no naturally occurring central business district. Instead of a growing downtown circle, office buildings were placed along a single street, extending for miles. In Seoul, for example, single-use zones came about in part because zoning codes did not develop over a long span of time; in a rapidly changing world, there was little time to try new strategies, abandon what did not work, and adopt what did work. Similar dynamics also have occurred in other emerging Asian markets. Building codes honor the tradition of privacy and require that residential towers be set back from the street and substantially apart from each other; the city of Seoul spent several decades building residential-only or commercial-only projects. Today, that mindset has been scrapped in favor of master-planned themed communities offering a range of uses designed to create 24/7 environments.

For example, one design for a Seoul-area community, named Gwang-Myeong, includes a mixed-use complex anchored by a transit station. The commercial components all include entertainment and retail focused exclusively on music and arts. The community was designed to create a vibrant 24/7 district with a unique identity and with a density that would ensure around-the-clock activity.

As the city expands outward, it is taking to heart the lessons Western cities have learned in regard to urban sprawl. Seoul has built a bullet train–based mass transit system, and its communities are designed around this mass transit, rather than around the expressways.

The Eunpyeong mixed-use development (EPPF), a proposed satellite district on the outskirts of Seoul served by the extensive train system, is part of the current flurry of development. The plan calls for a highly programmed eight-story retail and entertainment complex; sculptural in form and festive in use, the bow-shaped building will appear to float above ground to allow the landscape of the two neighboring mountains to flow through. At night, this monolithic glass volume, designed to give the district a distinctive identity, glows as a showcase of light. Restaurants, cafes, and other retailers abound, intertwining the retail complex with the 24/7 transit hub.

Train lines that are weaving a web pattern across China's interior are creating new opportunities for retail centers at intersections that did not exist until recently. But as quickly as retailers multiply, shoppers demand consolidation and a single location where they can conduct as much shopping in one place as possible. In short, one-stop-shopping is coming to Asia.

One way this is being addressed is by transforming industrial or distressed sections of older cities into modern shopping enclaves. Dongnam Distribution Center, for example, embodies this trend. Born out of a redevelopment project envisioned by the mayor of Seoul, Dongnam will house tens of thousands of small vendors that were set up along the river, enabling shoppers to arrive via subway and buy whatever they need in a central location. Meanwhile, the vacated space along the river will be replaced by a new rail line that will help spur further growth. At Dongnam, the presence of thousands of shopkeepers is expected to create a destination for consumers.

Shopping and entertainment, of course, must be tailored to the social preferences of the target audience and are less subject to public sector control. These social preferences vary from city to city and country to country throughout Asia. In Korea, the social habits of Koreans strongly affect transit-oriented development. For example, Koreans often are more actively social during the week than on weekends—which are reserved for family—joining friends after work before heading home much later in the evening. As a result, a destination in Korea must have a variety of attractions available throughout the week: sports, health and wellness facilities, and cultural attractions. Reflecting this trend, transit developments need to be built in conjunction with a project that has a multitude of such attractions.

The cities of 21st-century Asia are evolving quickly, as they must to serve a rapidly growing population. Fortunately for that population, the governments and the architects they work with have come to understand the importance of transit-oriented design.

Editors' Note

The following information is provided about this best practice case study to facilitate future research.

Name: City of Hong Kong
Population: 7,184,000 (2013)
Region: South Coast
Province/State: Special Administrative Region

Country: China
Official Name: People's Republic of China
City Website: http://www.gov.hk/

Chapter 31

Istanbul, Turkey, Other Cities, Mitigate Climate Change through Public Transit Options

Guenter Karl

Urban planning has become increasingly important since, in 2007, 50 percent of the global population is considered to be living in urbn areas. Urban planning has a direct impact on climate change because well-planned cities provide a better foundation for sustainable development than do unplanned cities. Urban areas are major emitters of greenhouse gasses (GHG), therefore having a significant impact on climate change. As expressed in the Habitat Agenda under the Global Plan of Action: Strategies for Implementation, UN-HABITAT believes that in order to deal with climate change effectively urban development through proper urban planning is the key. The Agenda, adopted by all member states of the UN, states Habitat's commitment to sustainable energy use and sustainable transport, key issues in climate change mitigation as well as key elements of urban planning. As a result of this mandate, UN-HABITAT must work with Habitat Agenda partners to use urban planning and development as a mitigation measure for climate change.

Besides the overall umbrella entry point of urban planning and development, there are four other entry points to deal with sustainable urban development. These are transportation, home and office buildings, industrial production and poverty reduction. Each of these entry points are major causes of greenhouse gases and therefore climate change. If each entry point is well planned they can each greatly impact on climate change mitigation.

Transportation offers huge opportunities for advancement. Encouraging carpooling and the use of energy-efficient vehicles through incentives/disincentives (ex: offering parking lots near office buildings to those who use these transport methods) is one strategy that will reduce GHG emissions. Mass and alternative transportation options are a second strategy that will reduce the reliance on personal vehicles. These options will also encourage people to move closer to the downtown area so they can have access to these opportunities, thus reducing the need for personal vehicles and reducing travel times.

Encouraging people to move away from areas outside the city, reduces the urban sprawl, increases the density in city centers thereby increasing the need for well planned

Originally published as "Climate Change Mitigation Through Urban Planning and Development," *United Nations Framework Convention on Climate Change* (October 2010), by the UN-Habitat, United Nations, Istanbul, Turkey. Reprinted with permission of the publisher.

construction and renovation of buildings in these areas. Buildings, both commercial and residential are another major cause of climate change. The use of legislation to create environmental standards that all new buildings must meet is one method of reducing the impact. Unfortunately it is the older buildings that are the major cause of emissions therefore it is necessary to create incentives for renovating and upgrading these buildings. Incentives could include encouraging the use of recycled building materials, the purchase of energy efficient appliances and technologies or offering free home/office energy audits.

Free energy audits and other such incentives also could be part of the solution for industry. Industrial production emits significant amount of GHGs and educating and informing industry where there are energy losses that could turn into gains is a viable option for mitigating climate change. This could include waste heat recovery that could be reused as a source of energy. Encouraging the use of energy efficient systems by showing the longer run financial benefits or through incentives can also induce industry to opt for sustainable business practices. Disincentives are another means of mitigating of climate change within the industrial sector, for example increasing chargers or fines for the use of unsustainable practices and for exceeding emission levels.

Poverty reduction is the final entry point into sustainable urban development under the umbrella of urban planning. As long as there is poverty, there is a percentage of the population that, no matter what incentives/disincentives are given, will not see the environment as a priority. They have no choice but to use the cheapest energy options, for example, which are usually the most environmentally harmful (ex: charcoal). Approaches that can be used to mitigation climate change within this percentage of the population include educational and training initiatives on the environment and sustainable urban development. Though they may

not have an option at that moment, as poverty is reduced, they will be better able to make the proper decisions. The major concern is the poverty itself and without its reduction, mitigation of climate change will never be realized. It is therefore imperative that Habitat Agenda partners continue their work on poverty reduction through the many mechanisms in place and by partnering with one another to develop new means of tackling the poverty reduction issue.

Developing countries are a stakeholder in climate change mitigation that needs special emphasis. Currently they are emitting 25 percent of the GHG emissions but receive as mush if not more of the implications as the developed countries. Therefore it is imperative that developing countries are included in the discussions and strategies on climate change as they will become increasingly important as they continue to develop and grow. This fact has not been fully recognized. With their resource limitations they are unable to take the necessary steps needed for mitigation. Developing countries need support in their efforts and to be given incentives to use sustainable technologies and practices during this high growth period. They have a unique opportunity, if they plan correctly, to avoid the mistakes made by the developed countries. The technology and information is available and if they are able to use these mechanisms, they will be able to develop sustainably from the outset and avoid having to restructure and rebuild in the future.

Government's role in climate change mitigation is different at different government levels. At the national level, they must create policies, incentives and disincentives that encourage sustainable urban development. They must also incorporate environmental education/training in all elements of the educational system, from primary school through to adult education programs (continuing education). The local level's role includes enforcing policies and regulations (ex:

restricting urban sprawl). It is local government who must set the future growth strategies through urban planning. They have the ability to create mass/alternative transportation systems.

The private sector must be involved in the mitigation of climate change as well. Though they must stay within the rules and regulations set by government, this is not their only role. They must continually research and create alternatives to the harmful technologies and products/services currently on the market. A profitable approach that the private sector should use is the creation of business opportunities that promote sustainable urban development and the use of technologies/products/services that reduce their impacts and save them money. Partnering with the public sector will make the transition to sustainable business practices much easier and more successful.

Youth are a percentage of the population, especially in the developing countries, therefore must be a major stakeholder in the mitigation of climate change. It is the youth that will be around as the effects of climate change are felt more significantly. Their role includes educating others on climate change and possible mitigation measures. They must pressure the private sector through their purchasing power, demanding that the private sector take notice of the impact the are having and take action to prevent this impact. They must also pressure the governments and the private sector through lobbying for greater environmental standards and measures. Finally, as they join the labor force, they can create sustainable businesses and encourage sustainable activities within their businesses/personal lives.

UN-HABITAT's roes include enabling the Habitat Agenda Partners to implement the mandate of the Habitat Agenda, adopted by 196 UN member countries, on sustainable energy use and transportation systems. UN-HABITAT is mandated to address the issue of climate change in the context of urban planning and development. However, it needs other Habitat Agenda Partners in order to achieve progress in that area, therefore its major role is catalyze partnerships with UNFCCC, UNEP, local authorities, youth and other relevant stakeholders to mitigate climate change and encourage urban planning.

Well-planned cities are an efficient use of space and energy. They cluster large groups of people together, reducing the need for transportation and infrastructure to provide the basic services that the population requires. All stakeholders have roles they can play to encourage the activities within the four entry points: transportation, home/office buildings, industrial production and poverty reduction. Some of these roles include the creation of incentives/disincentives, education and training on climate change mitigation strategies and the research, creation and promotion of new technologies that improve the environment. Many technological solutions however, are available for climate change mitigation, especially in developed countries. The problem is that these technologies are not being used on a wide enough scale to generate a significant impact. These technologies need to become affordable and practical in order to receive widespread application. Developing countries must be given special emphasis. They must be given the opportunity to use these technological solutions and the lessons learned from the past and must be supported in their efforts by developed countries. Partnership among stakeholders is therefore a basis for the mitigation of climate change. UN-HABITAT is prepared to pay special attention to this issue and encourages Habitat Agenda partners to approach them with ideas for partnering on the sustainable urban development and urban planning aspects of the climate change issue.

Editors' Note

The following information is provided about this best practice case study to facilitate future research.

Name: Istanbul Metropolitan Municipality
Population: 13,854,740 (2012)
Region: Marmara Region
Province/State: Istanbul Province
Country: Turkey
Official Name: Republic of Turkey
City Website: http://www.ibb.gov.tr/

Istanbul's metropolitan municipal population is 14.1 million citizens, making it the largest city in Turkey, the second largest city in the Middle East, and the third largest city in the world. The city's trans-portation system includes a bus rapid transit network, a light-rail rapid transit system, traditional trains, funicular railways, trams, and maritime transit services (e.g., sea buses and ferryboats).

In 1996, the United Nations Conference on Human Settlements was held in Istanbul, at which time the concept of sustainable development was endorsed. In 2010, the United Nations held their UN-Habitat and Climate Change Mitigation Workshop in Istanbul. This article represents a speech that was presented at this conference.

The UN-Habitat's website (http://www.unhabitat.org/) has additional information concerning the best practices for sustainable transportation options being used in cities located in countries throughout the world.

Chapter 32

London, England, Other Cities, Redesign Their Roadways and Spaces for People

Project for Public Spaces

"Lighter, Quicker, Cheaper" (LQC) describes a local development strategy that has produced some of the world's most successful public spaces—one that is lower risk and lower cost, capitalizing on the creative energy of the community to efficiently generate new uses and revenue for places in transition. It's a phrase we borrowed from Eric Reynolds at Urban Space Management.

LQC can take many forms, requiring varying degrees of time, money, and effort, and the spectrum of interventions should be seen as an iterative means to build lasting change. We often start with **Amenities and Public Art,** followed by **Event and Intervention Projects**, which lead to **Light Development** strategies for long-term change. By championing use over design and capital-intensive construction, LQC interventions strike a balance between providing comfortable spaces for people to enjoy while generating the revenue necessary for maintenance and management.

PPS is working to support communities to create great destinations through the LQC process. Our demonstration projects draw upon local assets and people to transform underutilized urban spaces into exciting laboratories that reward citizens with authentic places and provide a boost to areas in need. These projects provide a powerful means of translating stakeholder visioning into physical reality.

PPS Can Help Implement a Wide Range of Low-cost, High-impact Interventions:

LQC Amenities and Public Art

Ranging from flexible seating to book and game kiosks, amenities provide a low-cost means to quickly inject new layers of comfort and activity. Similarly, rotating public art, particularly if it is interactive, can quickly transform a space and provide a unique means for encouraging return visitation.

• San Francisco's Cannery Row combines flexible, adaptive reuse with in-depth management and programming to become a great public destination.
• Temporary public art creates a changing identity for a space that compels return visits.
• The redesign of Bryant Park, one of

Originally published as "Lighter, Quicker, Cheaper: Transform Your Public Spaces Now," *Resources—Great Public Places* (February 2012), by the Project for Public Spaces, New York, New York. Reprinted with permission of the publisher.

PPS's first projects, has resulted in one of the most-used urban parks in the world. It is the flexible amenities that allow the space to evolve and draw visitors again and again.

LQC Events and Intervention Projects

Events provide a creative platform to build momentum, showcase local talent and build new partnerships. These events can evolve into ongoing interventions that provide experimental means of testing the community vision and adapting design and programming based upon user observation and evaluations.

• Streets and sidewalks compose approximately 80 percent of a city's public space. Temporary street closures enable communities to envision new possibilities for these often overlooked assets.
• Reclaimed materials for reclaimed spaces: Shipping pallets create a potluck dinner table under a raised freeway in Brooklyn, N.Y.
• Creative partnerships: Working with a local landscape store, a temporary park can be created in the middle of the street at no cost.

LQC Light Development

As an alternative to capital-intensive construction, adaptive reuse and temporary structures enable significant transformation with relatively minimal cost. LQC Light Development can transform underutilized spaces and a district's identity, as well as attract more partners for long-term transformation. Existing buildings can be given a facelift; sheds, shipping containers and tensile structures can enable creative new uses.

• Brooklyn's Pier 1 Pop-Up Park served as an interim low-cost, multiuse destination until a more capital-intensive park was created.
• Rather than redeveloping, Britain's Camden Lock painted facades and transformed the ground floors of historic buildings to create a unique attraction.
• Granville Island, one of Canada's biggest tourist draws, is also cherished by locals for the authenticity preserved through low-cost of adaptive reuse of former industrial structures.

Approach

Identifying Opportunities

PPS works with local stakeholders (often including city staff) to begin building capacity and excitement. Together we identify the potential opportunities, partners, and talent. We help you establish a local task force to shepherd the campaign and implementation.

Action Plan

A short-term action plan becomes a road map for the local task force to use. It often includes resources like amenities, suggested events and event layouts, and can include quick studies for various types of markets.

A medium and long-term strategic plan translates the short-term interventions into a more mature vision and becomes a guiding framework for future development and investment. It also becomes a tool to attract additional partners. These plans could encompass:

• Detailed building and space programs for the medium and long term ("interwhile" uses)
• Concept drawings and layouts for all key spaces
• Tenanting and management strategies
• Future development steps
• Precedents and benchmarks

- Guidelines for public and private space design and management

EDITORS' NOTE

The following information is provided about this best practice case study to facilitate future research.

Name: City of London
Population: 8,308,369 (2012)

Region: Southeastern
Province/State: England
Country: Great Britain
Official Name: United Kingdom of Great Britain and Northern Ireland
City Website: http://www.london.gov.uk/

The Project for Public Spaces' website (http://www.pps.org/) has additional information concerning the best practices for placemaking being used to improve neighborhoods in cities throughout the world.

Chapter 33

Lund, Sweden, Implements Sustainable Transportation Programs for Its Citizens

Christian Ryden

In July 2011, Lund Municipality was awarded recognition as Sweden's most environmentally sustainable city. An area of sustainability in which Lund is especially strong is transportation. The municipality of Lund has a highly developed environmentally adapted transport plan (abbreviated to LundaMaTs) that has been extended to develop the transport system to encompass environmental, economical, and social sustainability (abbreviated to LundaMaTs II). The plan represents a long-term effort to reduce car travel and increase the proportion who walk, cycle, or travel by public transport.

Pedestrians

Pedestrian traffic in a small city like Lund is especially significant. That is, with the right infrastructure, most trips could be made on foot as most things are within walking distance. Most transport demands can be met by walking. The city has already closed several streets and squares to car traffic, and several more are limited to bus traffic during certain parts of the day. Lund is already an attractive pedestrian environment, but project proposals for further improvement include a pedestrian traffic plan, improved accessibility for the disabled, an increased number of safe outdoor environments.

Bicycle Infrastructure

Lund is already one of Europe's foremost cycling cities. The municipality has made efforts to improve cycling infrastructure to make cycling appealing. Further plans include additional bicycle infrastructure improvements, bicycle traffic safety campaigns, and working with private and public actors to develop new ways to increase cycling. In Lund, 43 percent of all trips are made by bicycle. There are 5000 bike parking spaces in the town, including a multistory facility at the central train station, and 160 km of bicycle paths. There has been no increase in car usage for the past 10 years, and the city has ambitions of decreasing car use.

Originally published as "Lund, Sweden: An Ambitious City of Ideas and Innovation," *ICLEI Case Studies–EcoMobility* (October 2011), by ICLEI–Local Governments for Sustainability, Bonn, Germany. Reprinted with permission of the publisher.

DECREASING CAR USE AND INCREASING TRANSPORT SAFETY

Statistics of kilometers driven by car annually, per inhabitant were measured. In 2010 the figure was 2 percent lower than the previous year, meaning that motorists in Lund slightly decreased their car use. Measured by the lowest mileage by car per capita is Lund in 5th place in Sweden, just behind Stockholm which ranks 4th. Alternatives to private automobiles are plentiful, thus making it quite easy to travel without a car. In addition to the options of cycling and walking, there is an accessible bus system that connects approximately 400 bus stops with 11 bus lines. The bus fleet is run on compressed natural gas, with a few smaller buses using diesel fuel.

Plans of introducing a tram network are currently underway, to allow for faster public transport with a greater passenger capacity. Lund is also well connected to nearby Malmö, Sweden's third largest city, by train, bus, and bicycle path. Decreasing car use is also part of an effort to increase road safety, a measurement in which Lund ranks highly. Despite already being reputed as a city with high mobility safety, Lund has a vision of zero deaths and injuries from traffic. In the past 10 years, the city has halved the number of deaths and injuries from traffic accidents.

Using Technology to Encourage Reevaluation of Modal Choice

A new internet service is now available to people who wish to review their everyday travel choices. The online application allows people to compare different vehicles based on cost, time, environmental impact, and physical enrichment. The map uses a service known as the Open Street Map, a wiki map, where users constantly contribute by updating the content to improve its accuracy. Over time, the map becomes more and more refined.

Plans for Continuing and Increasing EcoMobility

While Lund is already an outstanding example in many respects, the city continues to strive for higher levels of excellence in the field of sustainable transportation. These efforts are exemplified in the LundaMaTs II plan, which takes a broad approach and incorporates innovative interdisciplinary perspectives. The six areas within which concrete measures are organized: urban planning, pedestrian traffic, bicycle traffic, public transport, road transport, and commercial transport. Projects included in the action plan are: a pedestrian traffic plan, physical accessibility, coordinated goods transport, intelligent transport systems, and dozens more. These projects are intended as steps to reach the conditions that must exist (management, planning, implementation, follow up and cooperation) to meet the plan's vision and targets for sustainable transportation.

CITIZEN AWARENESS AND INVOLVEMENT

As a university city with a high proportion of young people, youth involvement is often directed at environmental issues, with students organizing awareness-raising campaigns, or working with the city government to improve local sustainability. Lund is also home to a number of high tech companies and manufacturers, whose attention to sustainability can have a great impact.

The City of Lund is located in southern Sweden and has a population of approximately 82,800 people. It is one of the oldest cities in present-day Sweden, founded around the year 990. It is also home to Lund University, one of Scandinavia's largest institutions for education and research. The city has a density of 3,215 inhabitants per km squared and covers a total area of 25.75 kilometers squared.

EDITORS' NOTE

The following information is provided about this best practice case study to facilitate future research.

Name: Lund Municipality
Population: 82,800 (2010)
Region: Southern
Province/State: Province of Scania
Country: Sweden
Official Name: Kingdom of Sweden
City Website: http://www.lund.se/

Chapter 34

Manchester, England, Converts a Street for Cars into a Walkway for People

Lawrence Houstoun

Urban public spaces are parks and plazas within walking distance of major concentrations of people, leisure places that can be reached on foot or by bike or public transit. They can be destinations where people go to have fun or they can be urban linear parks that take people somewhere else. Urban public spaces in America are as old as Savannah's colonial public squares. In the 21st century, the unprecedented expansion of populations in and near downtowns has triggered the generation of new and more popular urban spaces in communities large and small.

Within the past 50 years, the composition and number of urban open space users have changed greatly. As demand and preferences change, so have park design and responsibilities for care and financing, along with expectations about users. This article is about changes in urban open spaces and leading ideas for expanding and adapting this essential amenity.

Today, more are being created, they are closer to their beneficiaries, they offer greater benefits to nearby properties, and they reflect greater concern about the quality of urban life. Importantly, they display civic imagination at its best.

Once upon a time, the U.S. government published decennial list of national parks and recreation plans along with surveys asking Americans, "What do you most enjoy doing in your leisure time?" In the 1930s, the highest-ranked activity was driving for pleasure. Curiously, that was number one when cars were much less numerous than today, were less comfortable, and took a greater share of family budgets.

By the 1970s, the plan and its survey were terminated. In the traffic-plagued, postwar world, fewer people thought of driving as recreation. Before the national plan concept was dropped, it became apparent that the plan's context was essentially suburban. The Department of the Interior refused to include urban recreation in the national plan. Why bother with cities?

They were losing population by the millions, especially among those most likely to use the state and federal parks. Of the dozen or so such facilities in Allegheny County, Pennsylvania, for example, only one large park had direct access by public transportation from Pittsburgh, the region's urban center. Attention was focused on the big and remote parks, not the ones closest to people.

Since the U.S. government effectively denied that local governments needed or de-

Originally published as "Secondhand Parks: New Opportunities for Urban Public Spaces," *Public Management*, Vol. 94, No. 2 (March 2012), by the International City/County Management Association, Washington, D.C. Reprinted with permission of the publisher.

served parks and recreation, both supply and demand for urban open spaces have changed markedly. Here are nine of the changes that are shaping urban open spaces today:

New Residents

First has been the change in local government populations. Locality centers are drawing residents in unprecedented numbers, households that can afford to live almost anywhere. They include all ages. As a generalization, people aren't moving to communities for employment opportunities; many of them have had a net job loss. The new migration is largely amenity driven. There are more amenities per square mile in metropolitan centers than elsewhere in their regions.

New Places

Urban public spaces are cropping up in new places as civic leaders see the opportunities for leisure where manufacturing, commerce, and transportation had long dominated. Reusing municipal streets has been successful in Manchester, England, where a new street was created in order make it into a pedestrian way. Another such street was created on one of New York City's busiest streets. So crowded by cars was Broadway at Times Square that the intersection was considered obsolete.

Boston built a linear pedestrian way over a subway tunnel and a destination park over a reconstructed parking garage. Hartford has created an elevated park over a rail line and a highway, one that that connects the commercial center with the Connecticut River. Earlier, San Francisco created pocket parks by replacing one or two parking spaces in some blocks with small leisure places.

In Arlington County, Virginia, athletic fields have been created out of a former PCB-filled brownfield. Inserted between a major highway and active CSX tracks and beneath the flight path of planes leaving Reagan National Airport, in an all but forgotten dump, the county park has already seen soccer competitions. Nearby Marymount University has shared some of the acquisition and development costs and will use the park as its home field for lacrosse and soccer games. The area of the worst lead contamination is beneath the small, paved parking lot.

New Sponsors

Entities other than general governments have become the creators, designers, and maintainers of urban public spaces. At one time people looked exclusively to governments to fulfill these responsibilities, but today the largest and best financed of the business improvement districts (BIDs) are seeing the creation or re-creation of parks as important elements of their overall economic missions. Real estate interests have paid to restore such parks as New York's Bryant Park, capturing the value added to nearby buildings as bait for higher office rentals.

New Tests for Success

In decades past, success was measured by such tests as "Are they cheap to maintain?" Today, public spaces are being examined in terms of their benefits to residents, to visitors, and to real estate values. Are they well used?

Success is measured by numbers of users. If urban public spaces are crowded, they are successful. People are not satisfied with mere space fillers, those vacuous, tax-exempt places where the public cost of security and maintenance far exceeds their civic benefits. In pursuit of low-cost maintenance, many localities simply poured concrete and installed inhospitable benches that seemed to attract only panhandlers.

Urban public spaces enrich host communities, serving as rarely acknowledged economic assets. *City Beautiful*, a 2008 report published by the Federal Reserve Bank of Philadelphia, described a study of 250 metropolitan areas that found that the extent of amenities present, including parks, produced the third-highest rates of growth. Convenience of parks and golf courses were among the 15 factors studied. The report urged officials to invest more in recreational capital as the digital age has produced new priorities for selecting residence and work locations.

New Reuse Opportunities

Just as new concentrations of amenities attract newcomers to downtown, changing economic purposes have made redundant and reusable land and structures available to accommodate increased population and expanded leisure facilities. The decaying waterfront in Wilmington, Delaware, has been transformed into a mixed-use complex with an active theater company, farmers market, restaurants, minor league baseball stadium, and a river-edge walkway. Washington D.C.'s Anacostia River sports a handsome new water-edge park in a segment of the river earlier considered useless and virtually poisonous.

New Opportunities

Two major forces contributed to the urban real estate revolution benefiting urban centers. First, the commercial centers of U.S. cities were grossly overbuilt a century ago for today's retail markets and are obsolete for today's office requirements. Retail stores were replaced by vacant lots. With dwindling demand for small-office space and much shopping moved to out-of-town locations, land

prices crashed in downtowns. Yet arts and cultural institutions kept alive by public and private subsidies continued to draw culture patrons to eating and drinking establishments.

Second, tastes change. Old is in. Suburban life palled. Downtown property had become inexpensive, and New York's success with converting attractive older office towers into popular residential units stimulated conversions elsewhere. About the only asset missing was readily accessible leisure space, and urban centers began to overcome that deficiency.

New Values

Decades of fear of crime had dampened enthusiasm for living and visiting downtowns. This concern has since passed in all but a few commercial centers. Five years ago, a survey of those who newly moved into central Philadelphia listed the neighborhood's absence of crime, second only to walking to work, as the two principal appeals of inner-city living.

Newcomers found that handsome town houses and apartment towers were appealing and affordable. Suddenly central cities bloomed with strollers and pets and new restaurants and swanky town houses. Demand has spread to additional blocks and long-dormant neighborhoods. Once marked by widespread blight, downtowns have become the metropolitan centers of places to have fun. The Rose Fitzgerald Kennedy Greenway in downtown Boston is an economic generator, attracting hordes of tourists and residents to its varied attractions, even in winter.

New Appreciation for Communities

In the scramble for park financing, more costs are being shared with nonprofit corporations, developers, and other businesses.

Owners of substantial structures are paying for air rights to build along side of or above New York's High Line, and BIDs are recreating, maintaining, and programming long-neglected parks in Philadelphia and elsewhere. The increasingly shared financing with nongovernmental entities may also produce more shared responsibility for open space governance.

A mixed board of directors—local officials and assessed property owners—illustrates a decision-making structure that is a promising improvement over one composed of only government or only residents. Although BIDs are not entirely composed of leisure facilities, the public-private successes of more than 1,000 BIDs are impressive. Most BIDs are authorized to finance urban open spaces.

New Places for Urban Spaces

Probably the most remarkable new urban space in America is Manhattan's High Line, an abandoned, elevated freight line that served the Meatpacking District for a half century. Traveling at approximately the third-story level, the High Line made it possible to make pickups and deliveries by rail at the sides of warehouse-style structures.

In one instance, the tracks passed entirely through a building, adding interest to what has become a national attraction, an elevated and landscaped linear park. Confirming what scores of real estate studies have shown, the elevated park has stimulated billions in private investment in a district previously known as a neighborhood eyesore. On a sunny Saturday in late November, the place is mobbed.

Central Philadelphia sits between two rivers. At the westerly one, the Schuylkill, a linear park shares space with an active freight line. Along the Schuylkill, the first of several planned segments of an urban linear park has been cleaned, landscaped, and expanded, linking residential centers to 25 miles of trails to Norristown and Valley Forge.

The trail follows CSX on the city side and overlooks the new 25-acre recreation space between the river and the University of Pennsylvania, a reuse of land long occupied by rail yards serving U.S. mail trains. Plans call for pedestrian bridges linking the east and west sides of the Schuylkill and at least one segment to be cantilevered over the river to permit people to pass uninterrupted around a still-active factory. The responsible nonprofit corporation, Schuylkill Banks, encourages fishing and conducts boat tours among various historic points of interest along the shore.

On the east side, a former shipping pier has been converted to a half-acre park complete with grassy slopes, trees, and seating for public presentations and river watching. The Race Street Pier Park is an early phase of a seven-mile linear park.

Can We Capture More of this Resource?

The supply of abandoned or undesirable urban land seems inexhaustible at the metropolitan centers. When rail transportation was an essential resource, for example, rail lines converged at the centers. Much of that redundancy remains unused.

Similarly, there is little evidence that the residential appeal of these centers will diminish as it is principally appealing to the three-quarters of American households who are without children and even some who have them. The National Association of Realtors released a study of householders suggesting a rosy future for inner-city living. Its 2011 survey reported, for example, that people want a park within a three-minute walk. That's not a prescription for a low-density, suburban lifestyle.

Mixed uses are especially important for successful parks. The late urbanist Jane Jacobs, upon studying a park that was particularly popular, observed that users were continually coming and going—early morning dog walkers, then businesspeople walking to work, then mothers tending children, then sunbathers, and so on.

She noted that mixed uses produced a constant flow of users, the ultimate test and unlikely where a park attracts only baby tenders or office workers. Jacobs wrote that the greatest influence on park use is the number and variety of potential users in the surrounding blocks, much more so than what is in the park.

Philadelphia has begun a process that other towns and cities would do well to watch. A complete inventory of land potentially converted to urban open space (from concrete playgrounds) has been completed for the entire community, and the city has set bold, yet attainable goals that all residents should have a park within a half-mile walk of their homes.

Maps in Philadelphia's 2010 report show where this standard is met and where it is not. Although much work has been accomplished in center city, some large opportunities exist despite the existing density. An elevated, abandoned rail line, for example, remains un-used and is highly suitable for conversion to open space.

Urban public spaces attract and retain populations. They help support local growth, and living is healthful and stimulating. Parks make better neighbors than all that wasted land we've inherited. This may be a golden age in terms of the accessibility, utility, and popularity of urban public spaces. Business and governments should treat these amenities as investments in economic development and antidotes to sprawl.

Walkable has replaced driveable among the baby-boomer and millennial generations in selecting residential locations, wrote Charles B. Leinberger in the November 25, 2011, *New York Times* opinion piece, "The Death of the Fringe Suburb." Conversion of secondhand land to urban public spaces is a wise course for this century.

Editors' Note

The following information is provided about this best practice case study to facilitate future search.

Name: City of Manchester
Population: 503,000 (2011)
Region: Northwest England
Province/State: England
Country: Britain
Official Name: United Kingdom of Great Britain and Northern Ireland
City Website: http://www.manchester.gov.uk/

Chapter 35

Mexico City, Mexico, Includes Transit and Mobility Goals in Its Green Plan

Silvia Marchesi

The transportation and mobility components of Mexico City's *Plan Verde* (Green Plan) agenda, designed to lead the city towards a state of EcoMobility, was launched in 2007. The Plan is based on a multi-component strategy to reduce traffic congestion and reduce greenhouse gas (GHG) emissions. The strategy has resulted in a set of programs to improve and expand public transportation systems, as well as offer more cycling and walking options. Citizens are being educated about the importance of sustainable mobility's role in fostering a healthier, more mobile, and safer city. The Green Plan emphasizes local action, in particular, through initiatives such as the *Hoy No Circula* (Today Don't Drive) and *Muevete en Bici* (Get on your Bike) programs. Mexico City's leadership under Mayor Marcelo Ebrard, who also serves as Chair of the World Mayors Council on Climate Change, was developed in consultation with multilateral organizations, NGOs, scientists, academic experts and the private sector as well as enjoying strong citizen support.

The Importance of a Green Transportation Plan

Pollution levels pose serious health risks in Mexico City. Until a few years ago, ecological experts estimated that spending a day in Mexico City was equivalent to smoking about 40 cigarettes. The city's physical geography also contributes to the problem; the lower atmospheric oxygen levels at Mexico City's altitude (around 2,200 m above sea level) causes incomplete fuel combustion in engines—this translates to higher carbon monoxide emissions and other compounds. Intense sunlight and heat exacerbate the problem by transforming volatile organic compounds and nitrogen oxides into smog.

The Green Plan is responding to these challenges with an integrated approach wherein results are already apparent: The city's ozone level exceeded the Mexican national standard (0,100 parts per million) for 333 days in 1990, while in 2009, the number of days declined to 180.

Originally published as "Mexico City, Mexico: Mexico City's Green Plan–EcoMobility in Motion," *ICLEI Case Studies*, No. 120 (November 2010), by ICLEI–Local Governments for Sustainability, Bonn, Germany. Reprinted with permission of the publisher.

As more individuals choose green modes of transportation, global GHG emissions, local traffic congestion and air pollution will be reduced. Other important achievements might include a decrease in traffic fatalities and more lively streets and neighborhoods. Reforming car-oriented cultures is a major challenge for cities around the world. There are many reasons for this, including infrastructure planning that caters to the automobile, socio-economic developments (i.e. social status related to car ownership and the growth of a middle class who can afford a car) and insufficient alternative modes of transportation.

The City Context

Mexico City is North America's largest metropolis as well as the financial, political and cultural capital of Mexico. The entire metropolitan region has around 21 million inhabitants while the Federal District has 8.8 million inhabitants.

Transportation is an integral part of life in Mexico City as well as a serious logistical issue. Millions of city residents commute to and from work an average of 2.5 hours a day. The city operates around 28,000 microbuses which are outdated with respect to environmental efficiency and safety. The number of cyclists is increasing, but Mexico City's car-centered culture still makes cycling a dangerous mode of transportation.

The federal and local governments are constantly monitoring environmental conditions in the city and have implemented several initiatives to reduce air pollution and decrease traffic congestion. Improving the city's public transportation system is a major priority since the system contributes to roughly half the city's total GHG emissions. Mexico City's efforts have been recognized internationally for sustainability achievements.

Mexico City's Green Plan: Moving Forward with a Sustainable Transportation Policy

The Green Plan is aiming to improve the efficiency of Mexico City's public transportation system and promote non-motorized means of transportation—essentially, Eco-Mobility—in order to reduce GHG emissions and vehicle congestion on roads. Offering more environmentally-friendly transportation options to citizens is a major component of the Plan.

Improvements to the city's public transportation system focus on two key areas: Subway expansion and bus route expansion. The plan proposes to add a 12th line to Mexico City's subway system which is already one of the biggest underground systems in the world. According to a Line 12 feasibility study, estimated demand for the additional line is greater than 367,000 passengers per day on working days.

With respect to buses, the Plan calls for three additional bus corridors to be added to two pre-existing transport channels. Mexico City's Metrobus system provides rapid service using bus-only road lanes. Metrobus has enjoyed success since its 2005 launch and the same bus program has been implemented in other cities. In addition, the Plan advises replacing the city's old, polluting microbuses, with larger, eco-efficient vehicles.

Almost 50 percent of Mexico City's private school students arrive to school each day by car. These cars comprise 25 percent of the vehicles circulating in the city. In response, the Plan introduced the "compulsory pupils transport" program (*Programa de Transporte Escolar,* PROTE) to lower the number of private vehicles on Mexico City's streets and encourage students to travel by foot, bicycle or public transportation.

The Plan also asks for improvements to

the city's walking and cycling conditions. The "pedestrianization" of the city's historical centers and of some of its neighborhoods began in 2010. Cycling-friendly infrastructure was introduced by increasing the length and number of bike lanes—an endeavor called *Programa de Corredores de Movilidad No Motorizada* (Non-Motorized Lanes Program) which also includes an educational program, *Muevete en Bici* (Get on your Bike).

On certain Sundays part of the Paseo de la Reforma, the biggest city centre street, is blocked to cars in order to provide space for recreational activities among pedestrians and cyclists. The Plan also introduced a bicycle sharing system located in strategic places downtown; *Ecobici* (EcoBike), was launched at the beginning of 2010 and allows people to borrow bicycles for short periods at an affordable price. Bikes can be returned to one of 85 stations in the city center. The stations are usually situated close to public transportation stops to allow functional interchange between different means of transportation.

The road component of the Plan has already made a significant progress with *Hoy No Circula* (Today Don't Drive). The program aims to relieve traffic congestion and improve air quality by prohibiting a segment of automobile traffic one day a week. The Plan extended the *Hoy No Circula* program to Saturday (*Hoy No Circula Sabatino*).

The Plan also aims to improve existing road infrastructure, for example, with road adjustments in order to solve 350 conflicts point in the city or the introduction of intelligent traffic lights along the main street.

Results and Impacts of the Project in the Community

Results are already apparent in all five areas of the Plan only three years into its implementation:

- **Improvements in the quality and availability of public transportation:**

The Metrobus currently has two different lines and shuttles about 473,000 passengers daily, 15 percent of whom indicated they previously commuted by car. As a result, Mexico City's carbon dioxide emissions have decreased by 80,000 tons annually. The bus system has been extended by 50km and a third bus corridor is now under construction. The goal is to build five corridors by 2012, in addition to constructing a 12th subway line—a process that began in 2008. Mexico City has replaced roughly 470 unsafe, polluting microbuses with 128 long buses that use cleaner diesel technology.

- **Lowering the number of vehicles in circulation:**

The Programa de Transporte Escolar started through a rule that prohibited parents from bringing their children to school by car. It was launched in 2009 in only a few private schools, with new ones added gradually: As of September 2010, 21 schools are now involved. The program met several obstacles during its implementation, however, for reasons related to safety and cost.

- **Promoting non-motorized means of transportation:**

Mexico City's bicycle lanes have been extended by 31km and the Sunday *Muevete en Bici* program has become popular among citizens. *Ecobici,* the city's bicycle rental program, registered 4,000 users within its first three months of operation. There have been an estimated 50,000 bicycle trips taken in the city using *Ecobici* bikes.

- **Speeding up road mobility:**

The *Hoy No Circula Sabatino* program cut roughly 960 tons of pollutants (mix of hydrocarbons, carbon monoxides, nitrogen oxides) each Saturday, and reduced the daily average number (excluding Sundays) of cars on Mexico City's roads by 342,000.

- **Fortifying a New Road Culture Respectful for Bikes and Pedestrians:**

Mexico City's traffic code was adjusted in 2009 to improve safety conditions for pedestrians and cyclists. Two main factors contributed to the success of the Green Plan's transportation component: Improvement of the public transportation system—including its level of eco-efficiency—and initiatives promoting cycling and walking.

Lessons Learned

Megacities such as Mexico City require well-connected and fully integrated public transportation systems to support citizens' quality of life. Introducing a Metrobus system, microbus replacements, and a subway expansion all contribute to lowering GHG emissions and traffic congestion.

The *Ecobici* program **diversified the public transportation system** and widened its accessibility by situating bicycle stations close to bus and subway stops. Public transportation and bicycles are both considered to be affordable in Mexico City—an important consideration, as over 60 percent of Mexico City's Federal District residents are considered "poor" or "moderately poor." *Muevete en Bici* Sundays are very popular because they offer citizens the benefit of car-free days as well as social and cultural opportunities

Another relevant aspect is the 15-year length of the Plan. **Mid-term frameworks allow more precise goal-setting** for environmental issues wherein processes are usually slow and gradual, for example, broad behavior changes or big adjustments to infrastructure. The Green Plan allows for long-term strategizing with a holistic view to policy making and resource planning.

Some of the Plan's programs did not achieve intended results. It is important to underline, though, that the Green Plan is an ambitious document, whose goals would even be considered a challenge among richer and smaller cities. Improvements to infrastructure, while already showing positive results, are not advancing on schedule.

The *Programa Transporte Escolar* (PROTE) met with considerable resistance from families and schools. Some possible reasons for this program's limited success are: It was only aimed at private schools and not public schools and there was a lack of incentive—students were required to pay for public transportation without being offered compensation. The program was also written and launched without stakeholder involvement and was implemented as an ordinance. Also, the program did not have a public education component—an important element at the core of the Green Plan.

Planning and public participation are crucial ingredients to the success of a city's eco-transportation plan. Careful consideration about available resources as well as context help to form realistic plans wherein challenging goals motivate stakeholders. Public participation builds support for activities, helps educate wider audiences and facilitates useful information exchange about local conditions.

Replication

The Green Plan's potential for replication consists of the following aspects:

- Adopting an integrated strategy, with a holistic approach that considers infrastructure and its inter-linkages, as well as the social significance of transportation in the local context. The Plan concentrates on infrastructure improvements as well as on awareness raising and education.
- Long-term commitments which allow a city to plan a detailed initiative over several years.
- Well-defined goals with specific targets, even if targets are incorporated into a broader policy framework.

Decades of car-oriented strategies make it difficult to shift toward more ecomobile transportation patterns. This is why the Green Plan is an important and inspiring document: It indicates the potential for major environmental initiatives to be adopted by other megacities around the world.

EDITORS' NOTE

The following information is provided about this best practice case study to facilitate future research.

Name: Mexico City
Population: 8,851,080 (2010)
Region: Southern
Province/State: Federal District
Country: Mexico
Official Name: United Mexican States
City Website: http://www.df.gob.mx/

The Transportation Section in Mexico City's Green Plan includes a 15-year timeframe (2007 to 2022). This plan integrates EcoMobility principles like enhancing the public infrastructure for cyclists and pedestrians, and constructing new public transportation systems.

The "Acknowledgements" section of the case study listed Emma Wadland as the editor, and Guilherme Johnston, Nuno Quental and Richard Simpson as contributors to this study.

Chapter 36

Monrovia, Liberia, Other Cities, Promote Non-Motorized Transportation Options

Luuk Eickmans *and* Imelda Nasei

Functioning transportation networks are a key element for cities and towns across the globe and are a precondition for economic activity and social participation. In addition to its importance as an urban service in terms of moving people and goods, the transport infrastructure and service sector itself is a significant generator of wealth and employment. However, the economic and social benefits of urban transport are frequently accompanied by negative side effects such as congestion, social exclusion, accidents, air pollution and energy consumption.

Since the mid–20th century, the negative side-effects of urban transportation have become particularly apparent in the metropolitan areas of developed countries. Rising car traffic volumes are increasingly causing loss of economic productivity, environmental degradation and affect overall quality of life in cities. In developing countries, rapid urbanization and motorization in combination with insufficient investment in infrastructure have led to similar problems, often exacerbated by urban poverty and social exclusion. In the face of a rising global population, continuing urbanization and the emergence of megacities, there is heightened urgency to apply solutions in the urban transport sector that contribute to sustainable urban development and to provide a comprehensive response to the issue of global warming.

As the United Nations agency for housing and urban development, UN-HABITAT promotes policies and models to achieve sustainable urban transportation systems across the globe. Set against the overall mission of the organization to promote socially, environmentally and economically sustainable human settlements development, the practical work places particular emphasis on promoting effective answers to the challenges of the rapid urbanization process in developing countries and the needs of the urban poor. At the same time, urban transport policy all over the world has to substantially contribute to solutions addressing global warming. The central task is to encourage transport policies and investments that contribute to improved urban productivity, living and working conditions for urban residents by catering for their mobility needs in an economically efficient, environmentally sustainable and socially inclusive manner.

Originally published as "People and Mobility: Promoting Non-Motorized Transport Options and Compact Cities as Complements to Public Transport," *Sustainable Mobility for African Cities Conference* (October 2010), by the UN-Habitat. Reprinted with permission of the publisher.

To work towards sustainable urban transport systems, five key thematic areas can be identified (i) Linking transportation to urban planning to reduce motorized trips, (ii) Non-motorized transport infrastructure, (iii) Public transport systems (iv) Car traffic demand management and (v) Vehicle and fuel technologies and efficiency.

The Expert Group Meeting on "Sustainable Mobility for Africa Cities: Promoting Non-Motorized Transport Options and Compact Cities as Complements to Public Transport" brought together representatives from key agencies, institutions and other stakeholders involved in urban transport issues in the region. At the center of the discussion was the current state of non-motorized transport infrastructure and public transport systems in West Africa. Effective practices and policies enhancing the finance and application of non-motorized and improved public transport systems in West African cities were addressed. Participants discussed in interactive sessions, the way forward on working towards healthier and safer modes of travelling accompanied by increased mobility.

Program Objectives

The discussions held during the meeting explored how models and approaches have been successfully implemented to promote non-motorized and public transport in West African cities. Best practices served as input on how similar approaches can be transferred and applied widely.

The objectives of the Meeting were as follows:

• The development of an understanding of the current status, key issues, challenges and opportunities for sustainable urban transport systems in West Africa, including non-motorized transport and public transport.

• The development of a network of key stakeholders active in developing sustainable urban transport systems in West African cities and beyond. The network should build a basis for future exchange on non-motorized and public transport best practices, problem solving mechanisms and partnerships in the promotion of sustainable urban transport systems.

• The development of a broad agreement on an operational plan for the promotion and financing of sustainable urban transport mechanisms in West Africa. The operational plan should serve as a basis on the way forward for the promotion and financing of sustainable transport mechanisms in West African urban areas.

The Expert Group Meeting took place at Hotel Meridien on Thursday 7th of October 2010. The meeting was attended by development organizations (including GIZ, UN-HABITAT and I-CE), civil society organizations involved in bicycle advocacy from around Africa and government officials.

This report covers the process and general debate of the Expert Group Meeting on Sustainable Mobility for African Cities in Dakar, Senegal, following the 1st UATP Congress on African Public Transport. The Expert Group meeting was jointly organized by UN-HABITAT, the African Bicycle Network, and the GIZ.

The Presentations and Debates

The Expert Group Meeting was organized in three sessions. The first session of the meeting drew upon presentations providing an overview on policy initiatives promoting sustainable transport systems, the second session focused on country experiences whereas the closing session gave room for a panel discussion on the way forward on the promotion of sustainable transport in African cities.

As a curtain raiser the program started with the release of the video: "Cycling with Honourable People" (Copyright 2010 © African Bicycle Network http://www.you

tube.com/watch?v=hG01RtuJ8JE) a video made by the African Bicycle Network on the cycling culture in Burkina Faso.

Effective Strategies for Sustainable Urban Transport. Policy Options for National and Local Governments

Christian Schlosser, Chief, Urban Transport Section, UN-HABITAT, Kenya
UN-HABITAT's Urban Transport Section focuses among others, on enhancing access to mobility for the urban poor in the context of sustainable urbanization.

The world currently experiences a variance in urban growth. In the North, almost half of the cities decline in population size. The South, however, faces a situation where almost half of the cities are growing very fast. Cities in the developing world grow ten times faster than cities in the North. Motorized transport will grow rapidly in the developing countries resulting in a huge demand for oil and fossil energy.

Here, low-income residents are excluded from access to high quality, safe and healthy urban transport options. Traffic congestion in urban areas leads to increased fuel consumption and loss of productive time. The road safety situation in many cities is currently a more serious issue than crime.

Working towards sustainable urban mobility UN-HABITAT focuses on five key areas of intervention: linking transportation to urban planning to reduce motorized trips, promoting non-motorized transport infrastructure, promoting public transport systems and services, car traffic demand management/parking and vehicle and fuel technologies and efficiency.

In the face of rising motorization, models for sustainable transport in developed and developing countries will only be successful if they surpass the mainstream by providing higher quality of life, energy savings and economic efficiency and opportunities.

ISSUES OF DEBATE

The adherent discussion centered on the key areas of intervention for the promotion of non-motorized transport infrastructure.

Participants pointed out that the promotion of bicycle use consists of a complex set of parameters, including technical know-how of planners, behavior of road users, infrastructure, etc. Unfortunately, in Africa the issue of the status of bicycle users is an additional component affecting the use of bicycles. Bicycles are often referred to as the "poor man's" mode of transport.

Participants agreed on a need for campaigning for the improvement of (the image of) bicycle use in Africa. Successful campaigning for bicycle use should include all aspects indicated:

INFRASTRUCTURE

Well-trained planners in the field of bicycle infrastructure designs are of crucial importance. City planners in Africa have been trained to plan and design cities for cars, hardly taking non-motorized transport into consideration.

RECOGNITION OF BENEFITS OF BICYCLES

Detailed information on the benefits of non-motorized transport is limited, making research in this field important.

Furthermore, awareness creation seems crucial to gain recognition of the benefits of cycling. Participants are in the opinion that people tend to stick to car use since they are not aware of alternatives.

The message that needs to be carried on should not be anti-car, but rather pro-cycling and pro other non-motorized transport means.

Manchester can serve as a best practice

for a behavior change, where the attitude of road users and planners shifted from pro- car to pro-non-motorized transport.

ROAD SAFETY

Capacity building and education of road users in regard to road safety is essential, especially with regards to bicycle use. In Kisumu, Kenya for example, there are about 21,000 boda boda (a two-wheeled bicycle taxi) riders on the road plus an enormous number of matatus, buses and other road users. Due to limited space available on the roads this creates a conflict situation between all road users.

STATUS

The image of bicycle use in Africa needs to be improved urgently. Cycling should not be looked down upon as an activity only conducted because limited financial resources do not allow the use of public or private transport means.

The situation is similar in China, where the negative image of bicycling (the use of bicycles is associated with poverty) has led to an increase of cars (owning a car means wealth). Bringing the people (especially the wealthier people) back to cycling is very challenging.

Civil society organizations play an important role in transforming the perception of bicycle use in Africa into a more positive picture. These organizations are campaigning for bicycle use and equip governments as well as decision and policy makers with knowledge and experiences on the benefits of bicycle use. It is time to join hands to lobby for non-motorized transport and document and disseminate experiences and best practices.

Sustainable Transport: A Sourcebook for Policy-makers in Developing Cities

Michael Engelskirchen, Transport Advisor, GIZ

The German International Cooperation has five focus areas of work within the field of transport. These key areas are: sustainable urban transport, transport policy and infrastructure management, poverty and transport, climate and transport as well as energy efficiency in the transport sector.

Transport is unique as the only development sector that worsens as incomes rise. While sanitation, health, education and employment tend to improve through economic development, traffic congestion tends to worsen.

The problems that unplanned traffic causes are manifold. Limited road space blocked by cars and inefficient use of urban road space lead to traffic jams. Polluted air exposes dwellers to emissions and contributes to climate change. Excessive car dependence makes roads unsafe and disadvantages vulnerable road users.

The major causes for the current transport situation in many developing countries are a lack of appropriate tools with decision makers to evaluate transport projects, a lack of appropriate capacity in municipal staff, a lack of access to international/national best practices and improper skills in formulating a coherent urban transport policy.

To improve the situation of urban mobility in developing countries, GIZ is working with a three-legged approach: (1) Implementing projects—facilitating changes, (2) Sharing experiences and best practices—changes in transport policy and (3) Developing and disseminating resources—increase capacity of staff.

One major delay to the improvement of urban transport in the developing world is the lack of dissemination. While there are good practices within a number of local and regional governments, it is often difficult to spread these solutions to other cities and regions. To facilitate the dissemination of knowledge, GIZ launched the Sourcebook for Sustainable Urban Transport Policy. Consisting of more than 27 modules which can be retrieved separately as PDF's at www.sutp. org, it is aimed directly at decision makers. The modules are available in English and a growing number of other languages such as French, Spanish and Chinese. The source-book provides a comprehensive insight into sustainable transport ranging from institutional questions and land use planning to transit and NMT options as well as questions of financing and environmental impacts. In order to maximize its impact on decision makers, practical examples of successful projects are given. Furthermore, a non-technical language and attractive layout should facilitate the dissemination of knowledge. The different modules of the Sourcebook can also easily be integrated into short term training courses and capacity building.

ISSUES OF DEBATE

Participants suggested that the source-book which has been developed for the Asian continent should be modified to suit the African setting. The input from local organizations will be important when implementing this modification. Furthermore, it is essential to strategies the dissemination of the useful inputs provided by the Sourcebook.

Although experiences with the GIZ Sourcebook in Asia provided successful with policy makers; in Africa a revised version may be needed to suit the local setting.

A major contributor to the successful implementation of the sourcebook is training, since capacity building is of crucial importance in the field of policy makers working on urban mobility. Furthermore, the Sourcebook should be made available to universities to integrate the information into the curricula. The Cycling Academic Network (CAN) for instance is supervising PhD students on non-motorized transport curricula and could be encouraged to use the source-books literature.

Non-Motorized Transport. The Ghana Experience in the Past, Present and Future

Magnus Qurshie, Director, Centre for Cycling Expertise (CCE), Ghana

The key message of the third presentation was that the use of bicycles will increase once the appropriate infrastructure is in place. Like most low- and middle-income countries of the world, cycling plays an essential role in urban transport in Ghana. In the Northern part of Ghana cycling is the pre-dominant mode of transport. In the recent past, cities and communities grew in Ghana, farmlands were relocated, homes and businesses that could be reached by bike or foot became far apart. Mobility and urban sprawl became an issue. In the wake of Ghana's development road engineering was vehicle-oriented rather than being people-oriented approach. By then, many road infrastructure designs lacked facilities for NMT.

The Centre for Cycling Expertise, mandated to promote and support non-motorized transport (NMT) has been at the forefront in the fight for NMT facility provision on Ghana's roads. This "fight" started with informal negotiations with Project Managers and contractors during construction to add cycle lanes and walkways.

A major achievement in Ghana is that NMT has become a part of the policy document "National Transport Policy." Besides constant lobbying with policy makers, trainings for engineers and planners (including students) are conducted to incorporate non-motorized transport into the agenda. Profound statistics and research materials are essential to make a statement when lobbying.

Most cities in Ghana do have a transport policy, but they do not have a bicycle master plan. This is perceived as gap and thus CCE is offering cycling inclusive master plans, being a guide to multi annual infrastructure implementation.

Political will and financial constraints are not the only challenges for enhancing non-motorized infrastructure designs, training and sensitization are also essential. Organizing bicycle awareness caravans with middle and upper class people will help to raise the awareness for the importance of bicycling.

ISSUES OF DEBATE

An important component for the implementation of non-motorized transport infrastructure is to lobby cities to implement awareness raising activities. This can be done through arguments for non-motorized transport infrastructure backed-up with statistics and research material on the importance and benefits of non-motorized transport. Once the stakeholders responsible for urban transport in a city have been convinced by the importance of NMT infrastructure it becomes essential to provide professional advice. Furthermore, a frequent consultation among the stakeholders should be promoted in order to continuously prepare and plan for infrastructure development.

The Monrovia Transport Authority

Senwan T Wiah, Manrovia Transport Authority, Liberia

The Monrovia Transit Authority (MTA) is a public transit entity, established in 1979 to provide reliable, efficient and safe transportation services. But, as a result of the Liberian civil war, the premises of the MTA were completely vandalized and sat desolate and dormant for over 20 years. However, in the year 2007 a team has been put in place to resuscitate the only transit system in the country, so as to have the MTA resume providing trans-

port services. Most of those who utilize its services are the poorest of the poor.

Technically, the viability of MTA is a crucial issue as the national government strives in its quest to reduce poverty. The team drew up and put into motion a three-year plan to put some form of organized but affordable urban transit system into operations. With limited financial empowerment and therefore used buses donated by the Spanish government, the system was able to press some 12-city transit buses into service operations in two months. To date, MTA transports approximately 300,000 persons monthly throughout Monrovia and its suburb.

To achieve this success it was necessary to educate and convince role models to advocate with policymakers and politicians. Talking and illustration proved to be more convincing than reading material. The costs of bus transit system compared to costs of private cars were shown to policymakers for instance.

The Transport Authority recommended the "4E Process" when lobbying for public or non-motorized transport designs:

- Educate Government and Political Leaders
- Educate Policy and Decision Makers
- Educate and train your consumers/population
- Educate stakeholders like businesses people and consultants (foreign and local)
- Currently the agency is working on stabilizing the bus system and increasing the number of buses on the routes.

ISSUES OF DEBATE

The Monrovia Transport Authority has achieved great accomplishments in the past, continuous lobbying and promotion among policy makers are crucial to create a high level of awareness of the project. Dissemination of successful initiatives like the Monrovia

Transport Authority activities is important for lobby purposes to further support the implementation of sustainable transport projects with an integrated non-motorized transport setting.

Cooperating with influential people (in the case of Liberia the president) has proved to be very important in order to ensure a successful transformation of the transit system.

The Potential of Non-Motorized Transport in Bus Rapid Transit

Patrick Kayemba, Director, First African Bicycle Information Organization (FABIO)

FABIO's mission is to promote active transport for improved quality of life through networking, advocacy, bicycle accessibility, capacity building and awareness creation.

The organization believes that non-motorized transport is an essential component when planning for Bus Rapid Transit Systems. BRT systems alone will not solve congestion problems; the design needs to incorporate non-motorized transport.

The current transport situation in Kampala, the capital city of Uganda, shows a melting pot of road users. Motorized and non-motorized modes of transport share the same road without them being designed for a mixed use. Integrating infrastructure for non-motorized transport is important in order to protect vulnerable groups. Achieving a planning environment that caters for the needs of non-motorized transport participants requires advocacy and lobby work.

In Uganda, the country where the First African Bicycle Information Organization is based, the lobby and advocacy activities are undertaken using a dual approach: bottom up and top down. The bottom up approach implements working with the communities to provide access to income generating activities, education and health care through bicycle interventions and dissemination and showcasing at governmental (politicians) level. With support from GIZ, ITDP, I-CE, UN-HABITAT, Cycling out of Poverty, etc., pilot and demonstration projects are created, which benefit the targeted communities. However, the top down approach is equally important and implemented by engaging policy makers in cycling promotion and by organizing the first African PABIN network as well as exposure visits.

FABIO is continually influencing the BRT process planned for the city of Kampala as a member of the national BRT technical committee to integrate non-motorized transport into the planning process. The continued transfer of expertise and knowledge through North-South (I-CE, ITDP, etc.) and South-South (ABN, exchange visit with Peñalosa, etc.) cooperation is a key tool to keep on and improving lobbying for non-motorized transport solutions.

ISSUES OF DEBATE

A major challenge that was encountered in the preparation for a BRT system in Kampala was how to cope with job losses of current transport providers. In the case of Monrovia this challenge was addressed by utilizing an open market approach. This resulted in a healthy competition which eventually increased the quality of transport.

In Kampala the challenge will be addressed by integrating the transport operators in the development of the plans. And at the same time business case studies are conducted and shared with the operators to inform about the business opportunities that will be created through the implementation of a Bus Rapid Transit System.

Seville—The transformation into a Cycling City and the Velo-City Congress 2011

Matthias Nuessgen, Velo-City Seville 2011, Spain

The upcoming Velo-City Conference 2011, the world's largest cycle planning conference will be held in Seville, Spain. Seville has been undergoing a make over in the last few years and transformed into a Cycling City. The planning principals when transforming Seville into a cycle city were connectivity, continuity, no steps and bidirectional. Connectivity implies the capacity of the network to connect multiple destinations whereas continuity stands for the fact that the network is never interrupted, especially not in intersections. The bike lanes should not have steps in their transitions from the walkway to the pavement. Having a bidirectional system generates a sense of company to the users and the impression of a bigger number of cyclists to others.

Seville is proud to host the next Velo-City which will take its historical relation to focus on South and North America and its geographic location to focus on Africa and the Mediterranean.

The main thematic focus areas are: health (the bicycle as a healthy mode of transport), education (towards the change of mobility habits), efficiency of public investments (regarding sustainable transport) and economic impact and employment creation (the social component of the cycling industry). All topics listed will be examined from a social and technical point of view.

ISSUES OF DEBATE

Recommendation from the participants to the organizing committee of Velo-City 2011 was to have a diverse mix of participants at Velo-City 2011, avoiding having a similar audience over again. Suggestions were made to invite three key groups to Velo-City: (1) Civil Society Organizations, (2) policy/decision makers and (3) engineers. This could facilitate the dissemination of best practices across the whole spectrum of non-motorized transport.

Closing Comments

Non-motorized transport and compact cities complementing public transport systems are essential components when planning for sustainable transport solutions. Most trips in African cities are still undertaken by non-motorized transport. Consequently, interventions in the transport sector should seek to maintain the modal share of non-motorized transport while improving quality and safety for pedestrians and cyclists.

Successful initiatives improving the quality of non-motorized transport infrastructure are on the rise and case studies presented during this one-day event provide insights in achievements accomplished so far. Nevertheless, awareness raising and lobbying for the benefits of implementing non-motorized transport design needs to continue, as repeatedly outlined during the meeting.

The meeting was perceived as a fruitful event with diverse input of presentations, discussions and corridor chats. Because of the ambitious program and the extensive discussions, two presentations (from I-CE and BEN South Africa) had to be cancelled.

The meeting location was intended to draw people from the UATP Congress of African Public Transport that was going on simultaneously. Yet, most of the participants of the Expert Group Meeting were from the non-motorized transport lobby and advocacy groups. This shows the need to identify a strategy to motivate public transport stakeholders to attend to non-motorized transport interests and recognize the added value of combining the two. Keeping these experiences in mind for upcoming events like Velo-City 2011, it shows that an interesting program is not sufficient to draw attention beyond non-motorized transport lobby and advocacy groups. More effort is necessary to create a bigger interest among policy makers and public transport officials.

It is time to "join hands" to lobby for non-motorized transport to create a more sustainable mobility path. The documentation and dissemination of best practices at conferences like Velo-City are essential. Lobbying with policy makers needs to continue while statements placed on NMT benefits need to be enforced by accurate research material and statistics. Furthermore, the involvement of civil society organizations in campaigning for an increased use of bicycles needs to continue and increase. These organizations should forward their knowledge and experiences regarding non-motorized transport.

The participants appreciated the positive atmosphere of the event and acknowledged the interesting inputs that were given by the contributors. The participants from ABN also expressed their thanks to UN-HABITAT for providing an international stage for their cause.

EDITORS' NOTE

The following information is provided about this best practice case study to facilitate future research.

Name: City of Monrovia
Population: 970,824 (2008)
Region: Northwest
Province/State: Greater Monrovia District
Country: Liberia
Official Name: Republic of Liberia
City Website: None

The UN-Habitat's website (http://www.unhabitat.org) has additional information concerning the best practices for sustainable transportation options being used in cities located in countries throughout the world.

Their website also lists an overview of the speakers and panelists that participated in this program titled "Sustainable Mobility for African Cities," which was held in Dakar, Senegal. This forum was co-sponsored by the Urban Transport Section of UN-Habitat, located in Nairobi, Kenya, and the African Bicycle Network, which is located in Kisumu, Kenya.

Chapter 37

Montreal, Canada, Other Cities, Have Some of the Finest Streets in the World

Project for Public Spaces

A central part of PPS's work is helping communities get the most out of their streets, both as transportation links for all modes of commuters and as vital places for people to enjoy. That's why we showcase many of the world's best streets in our website's **Great Public Spaces** listings, which begins with people's nominations of their favorite public spaces—streets, parks, squares, markets, buildings and others.

The world's finest streets are listed below in nine (9) categories. The top five (5) streets in each category are shown below listed by the city and country that the streets in each category are listed in. The website of the Project for Public Spaces, shown below under Editor's Notes, lists other streets in each of these categories.

Boulevards

Montreal, Canada: Boulevard Saint Laurent

Why It Works: Affectionately known as "The Main," it bisects Montreal down the middle, linking affluent residential neighborhoods to the north with the garment district,

Little Italy, the Plateau district, Chinatown, Vieus (Old) Montreal, and the seaport. Fourteen distinct nationalities call The Main theirs. There are people walking about 24 hours a day, and enjoying the sights and smells of the various cultures that call this street home. It is trendy, eclectic, nostalgic and packed during summer festivals. Summertime is when The Main is closed to traffic in the Plateau neighborhood as festivals take over the street.

More Great Boulevards:

Avenida de Mayo
  Buenos Aires, Argentina
Kungsportsavenyn
  Göteborg, Sweden
Passeig de Gracia
  Barcelona, Spain
Avinguda de Gaudí
  Barcelona, Spain
Las Vegas Boulevard/The Strip
  Las Vegas, NV, USA

Commercial Streets

London, England: Camden High Road
Why It Works: Camden Town throngs

Originally published as "Touring the World's Finest Streets," *References—Great Public Places* (December 2013), by the Project for Public Spaces, New York, New York. Reprinted with permission of the publisher.

with locals, shoppers and tourists, no matter what the time or day of the week. Full of independent shops and markets, the streets are intertwined and pedestrian friendly, lined with old unique buildings, each one different from the next. Each street fosters new and unique experiences. Dozens of train and transit lines come here, with the main underground tube station right in the center of things. There is no dominating age group, race or gender, and if you wanted to meet people from every corner of the world in one day, Camden Town would be the place to do so.

More Great Commercial Streets:

Devon Street
Chicago, IL, USA
Venice Beach
Venice, CA, USA
Elmwood Avenue, District
Buffalo, NY, USA
St. Mark's Place
New York, NY, USA
The Loop
University City, MO, USA

Iconic Streets

Barcelona, Spain: Las Ramblas
Why It Works: A tremendous variety of eateries, shops, markets, and cultural institutions can be found here, along with a huge number of pedestrians and people-watchers. About 1.5 kilometers long, Las Ramblas is really a sequence of three pedestrian-oriented street/boulevards. Its central pedestrian promenade is unique in many respects, not the least being a clear aesthetic quality created by its pleasant proportions, relative to adjacent development. Landscaping and ample seating are two other big strengths. A mix of activities promotes diverse image and flexible character; Las Ramblas is universally seen as Barcelona's most characteristic, most important, and best street. A huge number of different enterprises are in operation here—traditional retail, spe-

cialized vending, kiosk sales, markets and exchanges, fairs and exhibitions, shoe-shining, eateries and pubs, music and much more. There are also a number of museums and cultural institutions.

More Great Iconic Streets:

Psirri
Athens, Greece
Passeig, De Gracia
Barcelona, Spain
Las Vegas Boulevard/The Strip
Las Vegas, NV, USA
Champs-Elysees
Paris, France
Rua Augusta
Lisbon, Portugal

Pedestrian Streets

Glasgow, Scotland: Buchanan Street
Why It Works: With richly ornamented Victorian and Edwardian commercial buildings as a backdrop, Buchanan Street is Glasgow's grandest promenade and the true heart of the city. Along its length you'll find numerous small shops, two shopping arcades, two major shopping centers, a museum and library, and a design center. There are regular displays of street theatre and a monthly farmers market. In 2003 it was voted Scotland's favorite street in a BBC/CABE poll. In summer 2004 it was awarded a Congress for New Urbanism award for excellence. Glaswegians are renowned for their friendliness and sense of humor. Buchanan Street epitomizes this and is a very convivial place. It is the city's main promenade where people meet up to shop or socialize. The ratio of locals to tourists is well balanced.

More Great Pedestrian Streets:

Wall Street, Asheville
Asheville, NC, USA
Strøget District
Copenhagen, Denmark

Cat Street
   Tokyo, Japan
Lincoln Road
   Miami Beach, FL, USA
Locust Walk
   Philadelphia, PA, USA

Main Streets

Madison, Wisconsin: State Street
Why It Works: This main street is the meeting place and social center of Madison, connecting the University of Wisconsin campus and the Madison Capitol. It is vibrant and busy at all time of the day, week and year. The street is designed to be comfortable and accessible for all modes of transportation: pedestrian and bikes, trolley, bus and auto traffic. It is closed down for street fairs and other events, welcoming all ages and ethnic groups. It is an example of a wonderful "college town" main street that connects to the larger community and invites the community into the college's public life. The shops and restaurants transition from student-oriented to more community-oriented as one approaches the Capitol. A farmers market surrounds the Capitol at the end of the street.
   More Great Main Streets:

West Main Street, Sackets Harbor
   Sackets Harbor, NY, USA
Alleg Street
   Borås, Sweden
Sainte-Catherine Street
   Montreal, QC, Canada
President Clinton Avenue
   Little Rock, AR, USA
Art Street
   Taichung County, Taiwan

Market Streets

Paris, France: Rue Mouffetard
Why It Works: Rue Mouffetard is a remnant of an old Roman road. Some buildings date from the 12th century, and many have distinct histories. In one sense, this street represents the history of Paris. The market of Rue Mouffetard fills every morning as people come to do their daily shopping. Its vitality is reminiscent of a scene from the Middle Ages. After the market closes, restaurants open up, offering a wide variety of ethnic foods as well as traditional French food at cafes and creperies. Colorful images of local produce, quaint Parisian shops, and diverse crowds along with the constant chatter of market buyers and sellers create a wonderful and long-lasting impression. The minimal vehicle traffic and the presence of shop vendors add to the feeling of safety and comfort for pedestrians.
   More Great Market Streets:

St. Mark's Place
   New York, NY, USA
Rue des Rosiers
   Paris, France
Rue de Buci
   Paris, France
Rue Montorgueil
   Paris, France

Transit Streets

Zurich, Switzerland: Bahnhofstrasse
Why It Works: Bahnhofstrasse, which connects the main train station with the lakefront, is Zurich's most famous and exclusive retail district. Individual retailers and high-end department stores sit side by side with art galleries, hotels, restaurants, renowned confectioners and Swiss bank headquarters, all of which draw a diverse crowd of locals and tourists alike. The real secret behind Bahnhofstrasse's commercial success, and enduring appeal for the pedestrian. However, is likely its seamless integration of different transit modes, and the street's hyper accessibility. Numerous tram lines service the Bahn-

hofstrasse, most of which interface at either end with rail, ferry, or bus. Private vehicles are prohibited for most of its length, while signaling and careful paving treatment ease their integration with bicyclists and pedestrians where permitted. Because of this restricted automobile access, the many pedestrian-only, cobblestone alleyways that lead onto the street, and the leisurely pace of window shoppers that stroll its sidewalks, Bahnhofstrasse feels largely like a comfortable, pedestrian boulevard.

More Great Transit Streets:

Istiklal Caddesi
  Istanbul, Turkey
Kungsportsavenyn
  Göteborg, Sweden
  Bourke Street
  Melbourne, Australia

Waterfront Streets

Melbourne, Australia: Acland Street
Why It Works: Acland Street has an intimate scale that brings pedestrians into close contact with its many cafes and street musicians, giving it the air of a bustling, linear party. Outdoor tables are prominent, and are often situated at the edge of the sidewalk, channeling passers by through cafes rather than around them; in this way pedestrians are integrated into the cafe scene, and are allowed a closer look at the wares displayed in the numerous bakery windows. Festive touches include a bold, checkerboard patterned sidewalk with decorative tile insets. Acland Street is a place of leisure. People go there to relax, socialize, and enjoy good food and music.

More Great Waterfront Streets:

West Main Street, Sackets Harbor
  Sackets Harbor, NY, USA
Nyhavn
  Copenhagen, Denmark

Venice Beach
  Venice, CA, USA
River Walk
  San Antonio, TX, USA

Residential Streets

Budapest, Hungary: Toth Arpad Setany
Why It Works: This wonderful spot for a promenade acts as a gathering place for locals and visitors who appreciate the beautiful architecture, trees, benches, fountains, and an incredible vista. The street as a whole is greater than the sum of its parts—but its parts are impressive: the architecture is historic and harmonious; mature trees make a shady canopy; a wide walkway follows along a spectacular view; old-fashioned streetlights and benches line the street. At one end of the street is Budapest's palace, which is a major destination for visitors. Go up any side street and there is a quiet restaurant, cafe, or shop. The street is a favorite place to walk or jog on a sunny day to enjoy a breath-taking looking out at the hills behind Budapest.

More Great Residential Streets:

Fenway
  Boston, MA, USA
The Fan District
  Richmond, VA, USA
Washington Square Park, NYC
  New York, NY, USA
The Village of Arts and Humanities
  North Philadelphia, PA, USA
Berkeley Hills
  Berkeley, CA, USA

The projects in each of the categories were nominated and/or contributed by the Project for Public Spaces.

EDITORS' NOTE

The following information is provided about this best practice case study to facilitate future research.

Name: City of Montreal
Population: 1,649,519 (2011)
Region: Southeast
Province/State: Province of Quebec
Country: Canada
Official Name: Same
City Website: http://www.montreal.gouv.qc.ca/

The Project for Public Spaces' website (http://www.pps.org/) has additional information concerning the best practices for placemaking being used to improve neighborhoods in cities throughout the world.

Chapter 38

Münster, Germany, Is Known as the Bicycle Capital of Germany

Hana Peters *and* Santhosh Kodukula

Münster is a city name that is synony-mous with bicycling in Germany. With ap-proximately 296,000 inhabitants and a cycling modal share of nearly 38 percent, Münster is often referred to as the bicycle capital of Ger-many. The modal split for residents for the year 2011 showed a high proportion of nearly 64 percent of trips attributed to the Environ-mental Network of pedestrian, bicycle, and public transit. Urban development has been promoted with the objectives of saving re-sources and ensuring environmental compat-ibility for decades to come. The evolved city structure—a compact and lively center, attrac-tive district centers, and a virtually ideal green system—ultimately provides the ideal precon-ditions to this end, and demonstrates a firm commitment to the future. There are also many universities in Münster with outstand-ing international reputations, accommodating approximately 50,000 students. The city also hosts several headquarters of innovative cen-ters in the fields of research and technology transfer.

The City of Münster takes an inte-grated and very citizen-oriented approach to urban development. In terms of mobility, this means that it makes efforts to accommo-date a variety of modes of transport, with a structure and urban design that shape and impact the transport patterns. In contrast to Münster's compact urban design, large, sprawled cities have longer routes to consider when developing new and improved trans-port options. Providing for cycling and pub-lic transport in large cities is cumbersome and costly when compared to their more compact counterparts. Since it is relatively dense, Münster is therefore able to fulfill two envi-ronmental objectives: reducing emissions and protecting open countryside.

On a typical workday, approximately 1.43 million journeys take place within the city's transport network. Residents account for around 1.06 million of these trips, with visi-tors from out of town accounting for the ap-proximately remaining 371,000. The 2007 modal split was 10.4 percent public transport, 15.6 percent pedestrians, 36.3 percent car, and the highest, 37.6 percent for bicycles. The driv-ing goal is to reach a 50 percent modal share for cycling within the next 10 to 20 years.

Role of Cycling

Cycling can help reduce pollution and traffic congestion. Bicycles have low energy

Originally published as "Munster, Germany: Cycling and Transport—The Way Forward," *ICLEI Case Studies*, No. 158 (August 2013), by ICLEI–Local Governments for Sustainability, Bonn, Germany. Reprinted with permission of the publisher.

consumption and bring health to their users. They can also provide quick, affordable access to parts of cities that are more difficult to reach by public transportation, or large vehicles. In many cases, trips made by car are short enough to be substituted by bicycle. Making cycling and walking easy makes a city people-friendly rather than car-friendly.

Bicycle traffic is the embodiment of Münster's transport system. Bicycle traffic is a tradition both in the city and the Münsterland region. Since the 1950s, Münster has promoted cycling by means of planning and consistent implementation. And this strategy has always been based on a sound overall concept, rather than single measures: the success of an urban cycling concept depends largely on the design of an integrated system.

Bicycle traffic in Münster is divided into a core network that runs primarily in conjunction with the main roads (for the most part on dedicated cycling lanes), and an ancillary network characterized by routes removed from the roads, either along agricultural paths or as dedicated cycling lanes.

Attractive walking routes, together with open and inviting building facades that are designed at a human-scale height make the urban space of Münster feel more accessible for pedestrians and cyclists. Better signs and way-finding for cyclists and pedestrians also make it a more desirable place to pass through or access by these modes. These measures also serve to make public transport more accessible, as it allows non-motorized transport users to navigate their way to the nearest bus stop.

Bike Parking Facilities

Germany's largest bike parking station is situated close to Münster's central train station. It provides 3,300 places. In addition, it offers every imaginable service: a repair shop, a bike washing bay and rental outlet, lockers,

and much more. Because of its great success (all the places are used), a second one will be built at the opposite end of the railway station. This will further encourage travelers to cycle to and from public transport.

Circular Promenade

The city has a primary network for cyclists in the form a circular promenade encircling the old town, which helps distribute bicycle traffic and which serves as a connecting link between the bicycle tracks along the main artery roads and the unobstructed thoroughfare through the old town. Additionally, all residential areas are 30 km/hr. zones, thus promoting safety for cyclists when they share the streets with cars, even in the areas when there are the separated priority lanes for bikes. Sign posting for bicycle traffic along 245km of the network adds to the ease of use and links the network to neighborhoods and public transport.

To further assist with way-finding, a bicycle city map is available in shops throughout the city.

Infrastructure—Upgrading & Maintenance

Within the realm of cycling, Münster is currently focusing especially on the upgrade and maintenance of bicycle traffic infrastructure, road safety, and information services. This includes good provisions for cycling infrastructure at early stages of development in new residential areas. Within the context of the EcoMobility Alliance, Münster aims to increase cycling in the city by up to 50 percent and gain perspectives on implementing and increasing other modes of eco-mobility. Identifying and taking advantage of synergies between eco-mobile modes such as bicycling and public transport is one approach. This will not only encourage regional travelers who must cover distances that exceed an easy cycling range to bike to a bus stop and take the bus to their destination (or vice versa), but will also increase the overall convenience of each mode independently.

Cycling & Public Transport in Münster

Public transport is the core of a transport system in any city. Public transport that is arranged in networks is more efficient than a single corridor arrangement. Ideally, pedestrian and bicycle networks should feed into the public transport system, forming a synchronized intermodal whole. Münster exemplifies this ideal through local and regional bus transport complementing its ever-growing network of cycle lanes.

Local public bus transport in Münster is based on a city bus system, and a regional bus system (called ÖPNV). The former consists of a total of 19 lines running at approximately 20-minute intervals, or less than 10 minutes on the major traffic arteries during peak hours, and covers the entire city area, including the more removed outer-lying districts, connecting all of those areas with the city center. The regional bus system covers both the rail line connections and the transport links with the surrounding region. Also noteworthy, are the express bus lines that provide high-quality transport in areas further removed from rail line connections.

Münster prioritizes very early implantation of cycling provisions and public transport in new residential areas. Having good cycling and public transport infrastructure early on means that residents are provided with viable alternatives to the car right from the start. Consequently, they can adopt sustainable transport behaviors as soon as they move in, rather than having to change

existing habits, which is usually much more difficult.

In order to persuade commuters in Münster to consider public transport, the so-called "Public transport promotion programme" was set up and developed by the city council in 1993. This includes improving the speed and reliability of buses through mechanisms such as bus priority lanes, and measures to increase passenger comfort. Furthermore, bike & ride and park & ride facilities have been implemented at all rail stations and key bus stops.

Citizens in the Loop

The city of Münster makes a conscious effort to inform citizens and visitors about choosing an environmentally and climate-friendly mode of transport. For this purpose, the "Mobilé" mobility center was set up together with the communal transportation company, Stadtwerke Münster. Here customers are provided with information on the best travel options, as well as on potential alternatives. The mobility services also include providing information on road and rail traffic in the region, reduced tariffs for commuters and students, buses and trains that can all be used within the integrated public transport system, and traffic education, and thus create greater awareness of the environmentally friendly transport choices available at a very early stage.

Lessons: By Foot, on Wheels

Cities aspiring to be more like Münster in terms of transport would be advised to start by accommodating both cyclists and pedestrians. In order to do so, they need to complete the public space network by linking up pedestrian routes, and by making bike lanes continuous and coherent. Reformatting existing roads to accommodate bike lanes is a crucial first step for increasing bicycle ridership. In many cases, multi-lane roads can spare a lane to be separated for cyclists, or street parking can be reduced to accommodate one. Bike lanes that are physically separated from car traffic are often safer, especially on streets with a thoroughfare speed of over 30km/hr. For rapid planning purposes, the lanes can be initially indicated by street signs and painted road markings; and the physical barrier to cars swerving into the lane can be implemented afterwards to improve quality.

Furthermore, beyond appropriate lanes and roads, installing proper bike parking facilities at various destinations is a quick and effective way of encouraging uptake of cycling. Such techniques do not require overhauling existing transport infrastructure, but rather merely adapting it to be more accommodating of sustainable modes.

When cyclists are prioritized in a city, and when this approach is combined with an effective public transport system, cycling and public transport become more viable options than driving. Cycling becomes the optimal choice for short trips, as does combining cycling with a bus ride for longer journeys.

Münster in the EcoMobility Alliance

Münster was among the first cities to participate in the EcoMobility Alliance, helping pioneer the project of knowledge sharing among advanced cities. Münster hosted the second EcoMobility Alliance city workshop in 2013, during which cities and expert partners gathered in Münster to focus on how the city can further its efforts to be bicycle friendly and harmonize its ambitious cycling goals with other forms of EcoMobility.

The City of Münster shared the city's methods of bicycle traffic promotion and explained the city's process of planning of the bike path system, as well as future ambitions for incorporating e-bicycles. Participants discussed traffic safety solutions, with special emphasis on bicycle safety, and explored how bicycle use can help increase public transport ridership at both city and regional levels.

Münster's case example and the analyses of guest experts offered practical as well as visual tools for anyone who wants to know and understand the kind of infrastructure and planning that needs to be put in place to create a bicycle-friendly city.

EDITORS' NOTE

The following information is provided about this best practice case study to facilitate future research.

Name: City of Münster
Population: 296,599 (2012)
Region: Northwestern
Province/State: State of North Rhine-Westphalia
Country: Germany
Official Name: Federal Republic of Germany
City Website: http://www.muenster.de/

The "Acknowledgements" section of the case study listed Heiner Bruns and Dietmar Konig, city of Münster, as contributors to this study.

Chapter 39

Nagano, Japan, Other Cities, Manage Traffic with Technology

Committee on Intelligent Transport

Modern life demands growing mobility. This mobility is increasingly provided by private cars, but the very freedom that cars offer is severely reduced by chronic traffic congestion. Our cities have responded to this crisis with policies that try to reconcile our insatiable demand for increased mobility with the need to reduce traffic jams, protect the environment, and ensure safety. But further efforts are clearly needed.

Intelligent transportation systems (ITS) can help by applying communications and information technology to the problem. Whether offering real-time information about traffic conditions, online information for journey planning, or even cars that drive themselves, these systems increase safety and reduce travel times.

The following is an overview of current types of intelligent transportation systems and some suggestions for what they might achieve in the future.

Keeping Things Moving: Traffic Management Systems

Advanced traffic management systems ensure that networks of roadways are used to their maximum capacity. These computerized systems, commonplace all over the world, coordinate traffic signals to minimize delays, control the rate of traffic merging onto expressways, and detect accidents and vehicle breakdowns.

Such systems can be combined to solve complex traffic problems, as was done in Nagano, Japan, during the 1998 Olympic Games. Nagano's infrastructure was underdeveloped. Congestion already occurred daily and was expected to worsen with the influx of visitors. Snowy conditions were also likely.

Sensors were installed along Nagano's main arteries. The system collected and processed information about congestion, travel times, and traffic regulations. This information was provided to drivers via information boards posted along roads, telephones, faxes, and the Internet.

Infrared beacons were installed in the vehicles carrying athletes and officials. Optimum routes and travel times were calculated for official vehicles, based on their positions as broadcast by the infrared beacons, and supplied to the drivers. In addition, traffic signals were programmed to give official cars priority. The system succeeded, ensuring safe and

Originally published as "Fighting Traffic with Technology," *The Futurist*, Vol. 34, No. 5 (September–October 2000), by the World Future Society, Bethesda, Maryland. Reprinted with permission of the publisher.

efficient operation of official vehicles and providing accurate traffic information to other drivers.

Knowledge Is Power: Traveler Information Systems

Uncertainty is one of the major problems that drivers face. Smart travelers use information to make better decisions about their travel plans. Transportation authorities have been collecting traffic data for many years, but they have seldom shared it with the public. Advanced traveler information systems aim to plug this gap. When more information is available to travelers, they will adjust their time, route, or mode of travel to their own advantage, improving conditions overall.

Growing congestion: The hours of traffic delay per driver since 1982 has more than doubled in very large urban areas, quadrupled in large and medium urban areas, and quintupled in small urban areas.

Simple traveler information systems include radio traffic reports and "localcasts" in the vicinity of special locations such as congested airports. More advanced applications include traffic congestion maps and information accessible over the Internet; in-vehicle navigation systems that provide maps, traffic flow information, and directions; and traffic information broadcast to personal communication devices (pagers, smart watches, cellular telephones, etc.).

More-detailed information that could be regularly broadcast in the future includes predicted journey times, weather conditions, Yellow Page services, parking, and park-and-ride information. Such information could encourage drivers to leave their cars at a park-and-ride site and continue the trip by public transport.

Electronic variable message signs, electronic kiosks, and cable television broadcasts are already deployed in many metropolitan areas and will soon appear in dozens more. A radio channel is being launched in Europe to provide traffic information in the user's own language. Personal information services, such as Trafficmaster (United Kingdom) or Visionaute (France) already enable subscribers to avoid unnecessary delays by avoiding congestion.

Automatic systems that detect accidents or traffic jams and broadcast warnings to variable roadside signs or in-vehicle devices can greatly improve safety. For example, Los Angeles's "Smart Corridor" project uses an array of cameras and other devices to monitor traffic flow on the Santa Monica Freeway. When an accident or heavy congestion occurs, controllers in the traffic center steer motorists off the freeway onto alternate routes by means of variable message signs. Detoured drivers are guided through parallel city routes and back to the freeway with the help of special "trailblazer" signs.

High-Tech Directions

Finding your way in an unfamiliar city using only a printed map is becoming more and more difficult because of traffic congestion. Vehicle navigation systems using the satellite-based Global Positioning System and CD-ROM digital maps are intelligent answers to this problem, but these systems don't take the real-time traffic situation into account.

In a number of cities, especially in Japan, travelers are able to routinely enter a destination into a system that will then calculate the optimum route based on current traffic conditions. The system gives the driver directions either through visual diagrams on a screen or by synthetic voice. In some cases, drivers also have the option of seeing the current picture of traffic congestion displayed on an electronic map and choosing their own routes accordingly.

Such advanced systems will require enough traffic sensors in the road to collect and distribute reliable and timely traffic information. They will also need better wireless connections to quickly handle the data moving between the car's computer and the system's central computer.

When the Car Becomes the Driver

Advanced vehicle control systems actively aid the driver in the task of driving. Vehicle manufacturers and suppliers see a large potential market for these products. Governments encourage these technologies because they improve safety and enhance road capacity.

Technologies already available include antilock brakes, traction control, and skid control. Emerging technologies include adaptive cruise control, driver drowsiness detectors, infrared night vision systems, and lane warning sensors.

Further in the future are automatic collision avoidance systems, which will relieve the driver of some or all control of the vehicle. These will be similar to autopilot systems in airplanes. Fully automated highways will require not only in-vehicle controls, but also in-highway equipment that will guide vehicles to their destinations.

Much work has been done on systems that enhance the vision of drivers in poor weather. This can be done through infrared or other video techniques to provide an image of the road ahead, shown to the driver in a display superimposed over the normal view through the windshield.

Wireless communication In cars: This Mercedes-Benz S55 experimental model is equipped with a wireless connection that could allow drivers to access a traveler information system, thereby avoiding traffic jams.

Driver assistance such as intelligent cruise controls are beginning to arrive on the market. These detect when the driver's vehicle is following another vehicle too closely and either warn the driver or automatically slow the vehicle to maintain a safe distance. Other systems can detect vehicles straying out of their lane and again warn the driver or guide the vehicle automatically back into the middle of the lane.

Some accidents result from drivers falling asleep at the wheel. Systems are now available to detect drowsiness and sound an alert to wake the driver. Similar systems can detect an imminent collision and deploy crash restraints such as air bags. Other devices actively under development will detect potential collisions and warn the driver or possibly take action automatically.

Collision avoidance systems are intermediate steps toward the more distant goal of complete vehicle automation, a concept that has been successfully demonstrated in Japan, Europe, and the United States in recent years.

Managing Emergencies

Travelers want to feel that they are in secure environments where help is immediately at hand when needed. In the case of serious injury or accident, the speed with which skilled first aid can be rendered to victims has a major impact on the medical outcome. Thus, any system that shortens the time before help arrives will save lives.

Such systems are being implemented by private organizations or consortia in Europe and the United States. They require the combination of vehicle location, as with a Global Positioning System, and wireless communication. Emergency notification can be initiated manually—by the driver pushing a panic button—or automatically—through the air bag triggering mechanism, for example. The automatic notification of emergencies, sometimes known as Mayday services, is very important in remote rural areas outside the reach of cellular telephones.

Pay As You Go

Electronic toll collection systems are installed at many toll plazas, enabling drivers to pay tolls automatically without cash and without stopping at a toll station. These systems reduce delays and prevent fraud and toll avoidance.

Simple systems are now commonplace around the world. These systems use an electronic tag, which is detected each time the vehicle passes a toll plaza. The driver is then sent a bill, or the toll can be automatically deducted from a prepaid account.

More-advanced systems, which allow transactions at expressway speeds, are used in Toronto on Highway 407. The Melbourne city link road in Australia uses a similar system. Both of these roads offer only electronic toll facilities.

Electronic tolling has worked well in Oslo, Norway. Threatened with chronic congestion, the city asked drivers to use an electronic tolling system. Since 1990, drivers must pay a toll to enter Oslo's beltway. Drivers can stop to pay with cash at a conventional tollbooth, or—in the case of the 73 percent who hold a prepaid ticket—enter the beltway without stopping if their car is equipped with an electronic tag. The windshield-mounted tag contains a driver ID and account information and sends this information via two-way radio communication to a roadside beacon. The tag is checked against a database, and, if the account is not valid, the vehicle is photographed and the driver fined.

Electronic tolling improves driver convenience and reduces labor costs to road operators. Even the non-equipped vehicles benefit, since the lines in the manually operated lanes at the toll plaza also get shorter, reducing the time delay in toll payment.

Improving Public Transport

More-efficient public transportation is crucial to reducing congestion, and intelligent systems can be applied here as well.

For example, the "5T" system helps buses run on time in Turin, Italy. On board each bus is a location system that identifies its position (to the nearest five meters) and reports automatically to a central control room. If the bus is behind schedule, the control center changes the timing of traffic signals ahead of the vehicle. This public transport priority system has improved bus travel time by 14 percent with no adverse effect on private traffic.

In Paris, a smart card makes the buses and Metro easier to use. The card is prepaid and can be reloaded at vending points at bus and Metro stations. The card communicates with the on-vehicle ticket machine or the ticket gate just by its proximity; it does not have to be placed in a slot, making it very convenient.

Putting It All Together

Transportation professionals need to be aware of the benefits offered by this new technology and the challenges in making it work. Governments around the world are implementing intelligent transportation systems, and they are finding that their efforts require considerable cooperation among many agencies and organizations.

Many different stakeholders are involved. Transportation professionals need to build alliances with public transport operators, private sector information service providers, city planning authorities, banks, electronic payment system providers, and, not least, the general traveling public.

The overriding purpose of intelligent transportation systems is to save cost, time, and lives, and this objective is common to all regions of the world.

EDITORS' NOTE

The following information is provided about this best practice case study to facilitate future research.

Name: City of Nagano
Population: 387,146 (2011)
Region: Chubu Region
Province/State: Nagano Prefecture
Country: Japan
Official Name: State of Japan
City Website: http://www.city.nagano.nagano.jp/

This article draws upon the *ITS Handbook 2000: Recommendations from the World Road Association (PIARC)* by the PIARC Committee on Intelligent Transport, edited by Kan Chen and John C. Miles.

The World Road Association (PIARC) is a worldwide association for exchanging knowledge and techniques about roads and transportation. Copies of the book can be obtained by contacting Artech House, 685 Canton Street, Norwood, Massachusetts 02062. Telephone 1–800–225–9977; Website www.artech house.com. (Or order online from www.wfs.org/specials.htm.)

A French version of the book can be obtained by contacting PIARC at La Grande Arche, paroi Nord, Niveau 8, 92055 LA DEFENSE, Cedex, France. Telephone 33–1479–68121; Website www.piarc.org; e-mail piarc@wanadoo.fr.

Chapter 40

Paris, France, Reduces Traffic and Pollution by Promoting the Use of Bicycles

Bertrand Delanoe

Vélib' is a large-scale public bicycle sharing system in Paris, France. Launched on 15 July 2007, the system has expanded to encompasses around 18,000 bicycles and 1,200 bicycle stations, located across Paris and in some surrounding municipalities, with an estimated ridership of 100,000 people per day in average.

Since December 2011, Vélib' has been complemented by Autolib', an electric car sharing scheme operating on similar principles. Vélib' is operated as a concession by the French advertising corporation JCDecaux. As of 2013, Vélib' is the world's third-largest bikesharing program, after the 90,000-bicycle system in Wuhan, China, and the 61,000-bicycle system in Hangzhou, China.

The initiative was proposed by Paris mayor and French Socialist Party member Bertrand Delanoë. The system was launched on 15 July 2007, following Lyon's Vélo'v success and the pioneering 1974 scheme in La Rochelle. 7,000 bicycles were initially introduced to the city, distributed among 750 automated rental stations, with fifteen or more bicycle parking slots each. The following year, the initiative was enlarged to some 16,000 bicycles and 1,200 rental stations, with roughly one station every 300 meters (980 ft.) throughout the city center, making Vélib' the second most extensive system of its kind in the world, surpassed only by the Hangzhou Public Bicycle Program in China.

Bicycle Hire System

How does it work? What is the underlying principle?

Vélib' is a self-service bicycle hire system. Cycle racks have been set up all over the city to allow subscribers to the system to take a bicycle from a rack close to their point of departure and to leave it at the rack closest to their destination. They borrow the bicycle for the trip and then they return it.

Where can you find a bicycle?

At a fixed point, there will be 8/10 cycle racks within a radius of 300 m in each 20 districts of Paris. The number of cycle racks will be strengthened near places generating traffic (railway stations, shopping districts, etc.).

The website will provide a map of the cycle racks, with the availability of bicycles in real time: www.velib.paris.fr

Originally published as "Velib: The Public Bicycle of Paris," *City of Paris Website* (May 2013), by the City of Paris, District of Paris, France.

167

How many cycle racks?

- 750 on July 15
- 1,000 in early September
- 1,451 by the end of 2007

How many bicycles?

- 10,648 bicycles on July 15
- 14,197 in early September
- 20,600 by the end of 2007.

Where are the cycle racks positioned?

The cycle racks will be placed either on the road (in the place of parking spaces) or on the pavement, depending on the local situation.

What are the opening hours?

It is an automatic system that works 24 hours a day, 7 days a week.

May I keep my bicycle for several days? Keep it at home?

The idea behind self-service bicycle hire is to travel from one point of the city to another on the basis of an intermodal transport strategy (travel using several different means of transport to optimize the journey and traveling time). For long term-use, there already exist bicycle hire specialists with whom JCDecaux has no intention to compete. This is why the longer subscribers keep the bicycle, the more they pay.

As there will be more than 20,000 bicycles throughout the city, subscribers are always sure to find one quickly at a cycle rack. It is in the subscribers' interest to keep the bicycle only for the time they need it and to return it to a cycle rack as soon as they have completed their journey. They then merely take another bicycle when they need one again.

Acquiring a Bicycle

How much does it cost?

The cost can be broken down into two elements: the cost of the subscription, and the cost directly linked to the amount of time the bicycle is used.

- The cost of the subscription depends on its length: €1 for 1 day, €5 for 7 days and €29 for the year.
- As far as the cost of each journey is concerned, the first half-hour is always free, irrespective of the type of subscription. The second half-hour costs €1, the 3rd half-hour costs €3 and subsequent half-hours cost €4.

How can you subscribe?

How to subscribe depends on the length of the subscription:

- For a subscription for one year, simply send a subscription form to Vélib,' along with a check for the deposit or permission to debit sums directly from your account. This form can be downloaded from the Internet (www.velib.paris.fr) or can be found in the information leaflets available in the district town halls, the Paris post offices, from baker's shops and newsagent's/tobacconist's partnering the scheme, as well as from the RATP (Paris metro) ticket offices as of June 13.
- For short-term subscriptions (1 or 7 days), users merely need a credit card as soon as the service is up and running (mid–July). They insert their card directly into the terminals at the cycle racks; the procedure will be extremely simple; users merely follow the instructions displayed on the screen.

Can you borrow a Vélib' with your "carte Orange" season ticket?

It is possible to register a Vélib' subscription on a *Pass Navigo* season ticket either for a long-term subscription (simply give the *Pass Navigo* number when registering); or for a short-term subscription, by following the instructions when taking out the subscription.

What is the deposit used for? When is it debited?

The deposit is for a total of €150. For the long-term subscription, the deposit takes the form of a check or a direct debit authorization (valid for one year), both of which remain un-cashed.

For the short-term subscription, the deposit is paid in the form of a pre-authorization to debit the amount directly from a bank account (this remains un-cashed).

As in all rental services, the deposit is used to protect the rental company from the risk of bicycle theft. It may be cashed if the General Terms governing Access and Use of Vélib' are not respected, notably in the event of failure to return the bicycle within a period of 24 hours.

What do you do if you lose your subscription card?

First of all, call Vélib' at 01 30 79 79 30 to inform them that you have lost your card; your account will be frozen temporarily to ensure that nobody else can use your card.

A new card will be sent to the subscriber as rapidly as possible.

Do you need insurance?

All general household insurance policies also cover civil liability risks related to a bicycle trip.

The Bicycles

Where are the bicycles manufactured? By whom?

The bicycles are a JCDecaux design and are manufactured by the Cycles Lapierre company in their factory in Hungary (for reasons of production capacity).

Why are different sizes of bicycle not available?

The principal idea of the service is the ability to take a bicycle from any cycle rack in the city and to return it to any other. If several different sizes were available, the fluidity of the service would be compromised because it would be impossible to guarantee that all the different sizes are available at each cycle rack. This is why it was decided to adopt a universal, unisex model, with an adjustable saddle suitable for all users taller than 1m 50.

Why don't you provide a helmet?

As it is an automatic system, with no human intervention at the moment of rental and return, it was not possible to plan for the supply of accessories. What is more, it is not compulsory to wear a helmet and whether to do so is up to individual users to decide.

Is it possible to attach a child carrier?

No. The bicycle has been designed in such a way that it is not possible to attach a child carrier or carry someone on the back. This decision was made for safety reasons: for users not familiar with carrying a child on a bicycle, the additional weight could cause them to lose their balance and fall down.

Why are the Vélib' bicycles so heavy?

A Vélib' weighs 22kg whereas a similarly equipped bicycle sold in a shop weighs only 18kg. The additional weight is due to the choice of materials used, which must be extremely strong to withstand intensive use.

The Vélib' are used much more than standard bicycles because they are ridden 24 hours a day, 7 days a week and are subject to considerable stress. To ensure that users enjoy access to bicycles in a good state of repair, the bicycles must be robust. The weight also guarantees their stability. A standard bicycle covers about 200 kilometers per year whereas the Vélib' will cover at least 50 kilometers per day, or 18 250 kilometers per year.

How much does it cost to manufacture the bicycle?

The bicycle costs more to make than a bicycle sold in a shop because of the specific manufacturing process (strength of materials, heavy duty components, etc.).

Using the Bicycle Service

When will we be able to use the Vélib'?

Starting in mid–July 2007, 24 hours a day, 7 days a week.

Who can use the service?

Everyone aged 14 or more. Between the ages of 14 and 18, users much also have permission from their legal guardian (to be sent along with the subscription form).

What clothes should you wear? What type of shoes?

The bicycle is very easy to use; they may be ridden by men and women wearing ordinary clothes.

General Information about the Bicycle Service

Is there a website?

Yes, this public bicycle system does have an official website! It is located at the end of this chapter for readers to reference for additional information.

Impact of Bicycles on the Environment

How is the availability of the bicycles regulated? How do the maintenance technicians travel?

The availability of the bicycles is regulated using clean vehicles powered by bio-fuel. The maintenance technicians will travel on bicycles powered by additional electric motors.

Upkeep of the Bicycles is Eco-Friendly

How are the bicycles kept clean?

The vehicles, bicycles and cycle racks are washed using rainwater, making it possible to avoid the use of detergents in their upkeep.

"Pure" water boasts a natural cleansing property. The anti-graffiti product used is also eco-friendly.

Recycling

Is the bicycle recyclable?

99 percent of the bicycle can be recycled. JCDecaux has created channels dedicated to the recycling of used bicycle tires; this is a "first" in France.

Cycling in Paris

How many cycle paths are there?

370km of cycle paths already exist; the map of these paths can be obtained from the paris.fr website, in the "bike paths" section.

How many accidents occur?

The number of bicycles used in Paris is growing constantly while the number of bicycle accidents is remaining stable.

Where the Revenues Go

Where does the money earned on the self-service bicycle system go?

Revenues from subscriptions and from bicycle hire charges are paid to the Paris town hall. However, JCDecaux will be able to benefit from a profit-sharing scheme based on the quality and efficiency of the service. The amount of the profit sharing is capped at 12 percent of the sum of annual advertising revenues and annual bicycle hire revenues.

The Jobs Created

How many jobs have been created related to this initiative?

400 people will be recruited to take charge of the installation and smooth working of the 20,600 bicycles in Paris. This cor-

responds to 285 jobs on a full-time equivalent basis.

What type of jobs?

The jobs, based in Puteaux and Paris, correspond to different profiles:

• **Maintenance Technician:** he or she is responsible for operations related to washing, upkeep and general maintenance of the cycle racks and bicycles with a concern for the quality of the work carried out.

Desired profile: Experience in a maintenance activity and knowledge of spare parts, cleaning products and tools.

• **Regulation Officer:** he or she is responsible for transferring the bicycles from one cycle rack to another to ensure the best possible distribution of bicycles between the racks.

Desired profile: Experience desired in a professional activity related to operations in an urban environment.

• **Mechanic:** he or she carried out upkeep and preventive maintenance work and repairs on the bicycles in a workshop.

Desired profile: Technical school certificate as a mechanic—Initial experience in a comparable activity.

• **"Terminals" Technician:** he or she is responsible for the upkeep and maintenance of the electronic terminals located at the cycle racks allowing users to borrow and return the bicycles.

Expected profile: Knowledge of electromechanical or electrical engineering essential (technical school certificate or vocational training certificate in electromechanical engineering or equivalent). Initial experience in a mobile position is an additional advantage.

• **Upkeep Officer:** he or she is responsible for the upkeep of the cycle racks.

Desired profile: An eye for detail, autonomy, rigor, responsiveness and excellent inter-personal skills; heavy goods vehicle driving license.

• **Storekeeper:** he or she is responsible for managing arrivals/departures using the SAP software, for the reception, control, handling and inventorying of equipment, the preparation of sites and in-house orders, the verification of stocks and inventories, and the upkeep of the store and its surrounding area.

Expected profile: Knowledge of inventory management essential and the use of SAP and electronic office software (Excel) desirable, physically capable to moving heavy loads, a license as a fort-lift truck operator would be an advantage.

• **Subscription Administrator:** he or she takes charge of Vélib' subscription files and provides prompt and precise answers to all requests for information.

Desired profile: At ease in inter-personal relations and on the telephone, sense of customer relations, rigor, reliability and autonomy.

Bicycle Training

What is the "Cycloschool"?

The "Cycloschool" is the training course specially set up by JCDecaux to provide employees with the specific information they need for the bicycle rental.

EDITORS' NOTE

The following information is provided about this best practice case study to facilitate future research.

Name: City of Paris
Population: 2,243,833 (2009)
Region: Northern
Province/State: District of Paris
Country: France
Official Name: French Republic
City Website: http://www.paris.fr/

Chapter 41

Rome, Italy, Other Cities, Have Some of the Best Train Systems in the World

Center for New Urbanism

Smart transportation is green, and there are a number of beneficial forms of green transportation that support and enhance walkable urbanism. These green transportation options make our lives easier, reduce congestion, reduce our dependence on cars & foreign oil, are safer & less costly, and help save the planet:

Trains—Modern High-Speed trains like the Eurostar, the French TGV, & the Japanese Bullet train; Regional trains; Monorails; Light rail; Trams; Trolleys; & People-movers. Clean electric trains are a major form of daily transportation all across Europe, and are the single most powerful transportation choice that can solve serious mobility, environmental, economic, health, and social problems on a global scale.

Bicycles—A major form of daily transportation in many countries.

Bicycles are the most sustainable form of transport, are the least expensive to use, are pollution-free, take up the smallest amount of space for riding and parking, and provide daily exercise for riders.

Towns and cities have to be made bicycle-friendly to encourage their wide use.

Scooters—Electric and push types are heavily used in urban areas as daily transportation.

Rollerblades—Used in urban areas by many as daily transportation.

Walking—An often forgotten way to get around because so many places have been made hostile to pedestrians. Still the preferred choice in dense urban areas.

State-of-the-art *Fast Trains* are in operation all around the world. Some of the most state-of-the-art high-speed train systems can be found in the following major cities and countries:

- France
- Germany
- London
- Japan
- Paris
- Rome
- Tokyo

America is addicted to oil, because for many decades the political leaders have put all our money exclusively into roads and airports. This has perpetuated and increased our car and oil addiction. This left no money for building train systems, which are the green transportation choice that would reduce our car and oil addiction, help solve climate change, environmental problems, and safety and mobility issues.

In Europe, they spend their transporta-

Originally published as "Green Transportation Alternatives," *Creating Livable Sustainable Communities* (July 2013), by the Center for New Urbanism, Alexandria, Virginia. Reprinted with permission of the publisher.

tion money building first-class train systems at all scales, from national high-speed networks down to streetcar trams on city streets. They have been doing this for years, and now have state-of-the-art train networks reaching many thousands of miles.

American political leaders need our help to get America off oil. We need to help them understand the need to build a national high-speed rail system.

Here is our plan to help kick our oil and car addiction:

The New Train Plan

This is a plan for America to take a leadership role in building the world's greatest, state-of-the-art, high-speed train network. This will be a coast-to-coast system connecting every major city together with Eurostar level trains that travel at 200+ miles per hour. (These trains are already in regular daily use all across Europe and Japan).

Investing in a nationwide, high-speed train network solves many problems all at once. A new train system provides the best solution for improving mobility, stimulating the economy, reducing dependence on foreign oil, saving lives, reversing global warming, and cleaning up the environment. A high-speed train network will free up huge bottlenecks in our transportation systems, encourage travel and commerce of all forms, and would create millions of jobs with one of the largest public works construction projects in American history.

A nationwide train system will solve the problems facing both the airline and automobile industries at the same time. Furthermore, it will cost a great deal less than fixing either industry. A new train network will significantly increase mobility in a safe, clean, fast, and efficient way. This will make it easy and pleasurable to travel nationwide in a seamless system of fast and sleek trains.

A new train system promotes many different goals for improving society. Trains are the most effective way to encourage smart growth, urban revitalization, and the creation of livable, walkable communities. They are a sustainable form of transportation that strengthens and stabilizes our economy, can help break our dependence on foreign oil, and stem the transfer of our countries' wealth to the increasingly unstable Middle East. A high quality train system is a long-term, community-building investment that benefits many. It is the smart transportation solution for our society today, and well into the future. High-speed trains are a major form of daily transportation all across Europe, many of them making a profit for their operators, while providing safe, moderately priced transportation for the public.

3 Level System

The new train system would be planned to become the primary American transportation network for carrying passengers as well as light cargo. The train system's customers would consist of the following:

• A large percentage of current and past airline customers looking for alternatives to flying
• A significant percent of automobile drivers seeking alternatives to congested roads
• Projected growth of both drivers and flyers encouraged by the affordability, safety, and convenience of trains.

The new train system would be made up of an extensive network of connecting train lines in a 3-tiered, seamless system as follows:

1. THE NATIONAL SYSTEM

This level of trains would serve as the national fast system now covered by airplanes. It would consist of super high-speed train lines connecting central cities together into a web of train lines across the nation. The trains operating at this level would be state-of-the-art Eurostar TGV type trains that regularly travel at 200–300 mph. These trains would offer a wide range of services making it convenient for business and leisure travelers. These would include the full range of seat configurations, lounge and dining cars, sleeper cars, and business cars with internet connections, and various business and retail services.

2. The Regional System

This level of trains would serve as the medium-speed regional system linking the high-speed trains to the many regional destinations. They would connect to all the smaller cities and towns within each region. This system would be comparable to the Washington, D.C. Metro system in speed, range, and level of service. These trains would be top quality, medium speed trains capable of traveling at speeds of up to 125 mph.

3. The Local System

This level of trains would serve as the local collector system connecting to the regional trains. It would have stops in all neighborhoods and central gathering places, as well as employment centers, retail locations, and sports & recreation facilities within each community. These trains would be standard quality, light rail and modern streetcar-type trains, and would operate along the streets.

For more information about trains as a major form of daily transportation in the U.S., and how they can solve our growing congestion nightmare on our highways and runways, visit the website of the Center for Design Excellence (http://www.urbandesign.org/, and click on the menu item titled "New Deal 2009" to read more about the *New Deal National Rail Plan*.

Editors' Note

The following information is provided about this best practice case study to facilitate future research.

Name: City of Rome
Population: 2,645,907 (2013)
Region: Lazio Administrative Region
Province/State: Province of Rome
Country: Italy
Official Name: Italian Republic
City Website: http://www.commune.roma.it/

The Center for New Urbanism's website (http://newurbanism.org/) has additional information on international transportation initiatives being undertaken in cities throughout the world.

Chapter 42

Songdo, South Korea, Other Cities, Connect Their Waterfront Areas to Public Transit

Paul Lukez

Transit-Oriented Developments (TODs) are becoming increasingly attractive to the real estate/development market as energy costs rise and global warming threatens the natural environment. Integrating multi-use projects with strong public transit networks decreases demands on auto-centric mobility, while improving air quality and the quality of life. TODs typically are found along existing or newly constructed public transit lines located outside urban cores. Sited on the periphery of cities, they often function as semi-autonomous communities, while at other times they are entwined within an already established metropolis.

Until recently, though, contemporarily developed TODs—not cities or towns—have rarely been located along waterfronts. Transit-oriented waterfront developments present special challenges for the construction approval process, given the unique, often sensitive, site ecologies. These challenges, however, are offset by the higher values that are generated where landscape is leveraged as an attractive and ever-more valuable amenity. Transit-oriented water front developments can help meet the needs of expanding me-

tropolises, providing amenity-rich communities that are connected to larger urban regions through public transportation. Within this framework, a site's sensitive ecology is sustained and land along its waterfront is used.

Barcelona, Spain, for example, extends its inner harbor developments along the coastline to TOD developments northeast of the city proper. Songdo City, an island in the Yellow Sea west of Seoul, South Korea, built entirely on fill, illustrates how new, "manufactured" waterfronts can drive development and design decisions, especially when these waterfronts are fully integrated with infrastructure and transit networks. [Songdo City was a winner of the 2008 ULI/*Financial Times* Sustainable Cities Awards]. False Creek, located in Vancouver, British Columbia, shows how industry-dominated waterfronts can be transformed and revitalized, building on the strengths of an industrial waterfront's unique characteristics. Revere Beach in Massachusetts is an example of how a historic waterfront site, scarred by damaging development trends, can be repaired and revitalized by intertwining new and adjacent developments.

Originally published as "Connecting Waterfront to Transit," *Urban Land*, Vol. 68, No. 1 (January 2009), by the Urban Land Institute, Washington, D.C. Copyright, the Urban Land Institute, all rights reserved. Reprinted with permission.

Barcelona, Spain

The redevelopment of contiguous sites along the length of Barcelona's waterfront has yielded beaches, pedestrian promenades, restaurants, shops, entertainment venues and three TODs along its length: the inner harbor, the Olympics Village and the recently developed Forum-Diagonal Mar District.

The inner harbor, once separated from the city by warehouses, factories and railroad tracks, is now a hub of commercial, recreational and cultural activities, such as the Barcelona Maritime Museum, the Aquarium of Barcelona and the IMAX Port Vell Theater. Adjacent neighborhoods have benefited as housing and commercial developments continue to thrive.

The 1992 Olympics was an important catalyst for the development of Barcelona's waterfront. In preparation for the Olympics, railroad tracks were relocated and warehouses were torn down, opening up the city to the sea. The urban design by Martorell Bohigias Mackay (MBM) Arquitectes of Barcelona provides a strongly defined "wet" square or port with more than 670 moorings. In addition, more than 2500 housing units, as well as hospitality, recreational and commercial venues, line the waterfront and its landscaped Litoral Park. Two iconic towers—the Hotel Arts, designed by Bruce Graham and Frank O. Gehry and owned by Ritz Carlton Hotels; and Mapfre Office Tower, a 40-floor office tower designed by Inigo Ortiz & Enrique Leon Arquitectos and owned by the Mapfre insurance company—rise above the new waterfront development.

The Olympics Village is served by two bus lines, a subway, two trains and Barcelona's network of bicycle rental centers, all of which help ease the demands on infrastructure that typically accompany new developments. A pedestrian promenade travels from Port Vell and the inner harbor past the Olympics Village down the almost three-mile

(4.8km) stretch of new beaches and waterfront developments.

At the terminus of this stretch is a 50-acre: "20.24ha" site developed for Forum Barcelona 2004 and anchored by Herzog & de Meuron's triangular Forum building. Like the Olympics, Forum Barcelona 2004 has generated new growth along the waterfront such as Diagonal Mar, a mixed-use housing, entertainment and shopping district. Diagonal Mar, which intersects with the boulevard Via Diagonal, provides 160,000sqm of residential space, 57,000sqm of hotel space, as well as 240 shops, a market and a movie theatre. A sewer plant is integrated into the landscape of a 35-arce "14.16ha" park adjoining Diagonal Mar that includes three lakes, footpaths, sports facilities and a children's play area.

New bike routes, created as part of Forum Barcelona 2004, extend to Diagonal Mar and link residents and visitors of the waterfront development to Barcelona's larger bicycle network. Public transportation to the area is provided by 10 bus lines and three subway stops, which link the site to major points throughout Barcelona. Diagonal Mar demonstrates how a continuous stretch of waterfront can be punctuated with transit-oriented nodes strung together by parks and amenities.

Songdo City, South Korea

When it is completed in 2014, Songdo City will be one of the world's first master-planned cities designed on sustainable design principles as an international business district. Initiated by the Korean Government, the US$35 billion project is located on a newly created artificial 1,500-arce "607.04ha" island strategically located in the Yellow Sea, 40km west of Seoul. It is expected to relieve development pressure from Seoul, while serving as an economic catalyst for Korea's economy. As an international business hub, it is directly tethered to Incheon Airport by a

11.9km bridge, shortening the typical 60-plus-minute trip to 15 minutes. Because of the island's compact design, the waterfront plays an important part in the design of the new transit-oriented community.

Every building in Songdo is expected to be LEED (Leadership in Energy and Environmental Design) certified and the U.S. Green Building Council has accepted the city as a pilot in its LEED for Neighborhood Development (LEED-ND) rating criteria.

To attain its goal of being a community-oriented sustainable city, Songdo will incorporate an expansive network of open public spaces with business and cultural amenities connected to multimodal public transit. Plans for Songdo include a 100-acre (40.5-ha) park (Central Park) a golf village; an international school; an international hospital; an "ecotarium"; a museum; office towers; residential towers; and retail, restaurant and entertainment venues.

As an international business district, Songdo's infrastructure must be able to accommodate up to 300,000 people per day, of which approximately 240,000 will be commuters from the mainland. The high volume of commuters required an extensive and fully integrated multimodal public transportation network.

A seawater canal links the city to the waterfront, as it provides ubiquitous waterfront access throughout the city. The main artery of the canal runs east and west across the island through Central Park, and smaller branches extend north and south into residential and business districts. Water taxis travel along Songdo's canal network with stops at the Cultural Centre, city hall and city museums; water taxis also run along the north and south branches of the canal, providing access to business and residential districts. The seawater in the canals never freezes, allowing the water taxis to run year-round. The network of canals and its interaction with Songdo's other public transportation systems help reinforce the relationship between the city and its waterfront.

The water-based transit network is linked to the subway line (and its three stops) and the mainland beyond. The subway stops are located so they can service all buildings within a half-mile walk. In addition, there are numerous pedestrian and bicycle-friendly paths as well as bike storage and rental facilities throughout the city. Electric cars can also be leased for short terms.

Approximately 40 percent of the island's total area is designated as open space. The main waterfront promenade curves from the island's southwest corner to its most northeast point, providing views of the city and landscape along its path. The promenade is bisected by the Cultural Centre, whose supporting public spaces are set perpendicular to the promenade and cut into the city's fabric, linking the waterfront to a park that is centrally located on the island and in the heart of the downtown area.

At the eastern end of the island, an estuary lines the island's waterfront. A bike path follows the waterfront park as part of its loop through the island's green spaces. As a master-planned international business district that is simultaneously sustainable, community oriented and transit oriented, Songdo City aims to become an international paragon of sustainable urban design.

Vancouver, British Columbia

Within the past 30 years, False Creek, an inlet running through Vancouver, has been transformed from an industry-dominated urban waterfront into a sustainable, transit-oriented waterfront community. Vancouver officials stopped industrial production along False Creek in 1970 as part of an overall redevelopment strategy. By 1975, the Greater Vancouver Regional District developed a Livable Regions Strategy that mandated high-density housing, public open space and convenient access to public transportation. Located along the creek are South False Creek, a residential development, and Granville Island, a community gathering place.

In accordance with the guidelines set forth by the Livable Regions Strategy, South False Creek has a residential density of 45 units per acre (110 units per ha). Buildings are interspersed with doughnut-shaped enclaves that provide a transition from the city's public realm to the residential private realm. Each residential unit is allotted only one parking space, road widths are regulated to prevent heavy traffic and increase pedestrianism, and sidewalk curbs are rounded to encourage the use of bicycles. A bus line—developed with subsidies from the original residents of South False Creek—runs directly to the development from downtown Vancouver, and trolleys provide convenient access to the SkyTrain, an elevated rail system that has multiple stops along the False Creek waterfront. The adjoining Charleson Park connects South False Creek to the waterfront and continues to provide a gathering place in the middle of downtown Vancouver.

Granville Island, located along False Creek's south shore, was conceived as a combination of public parks and recreational facilities that would complement the residential units of South False Creek. Before 1970, the combination of automobile traffic and factory pollution had made Granville Island an undesirable and largely avoided place. (The factories on Granville Island manufactured parts and industrial machinery/equipment that served the forest, mining, construction and shipping sectors.) The revitalization effort, however, has made Granville Island more publicly accessible. It now is home to public markets, artists' studios, theatre companies, an art institute, a hotel, shops and restaurants, many of which occupy Granville's original factories.

Because it is located beneath the Granville Bridge and is difficult to reach, the island has implemented a multimodal approach to public transportation. Two buses, which run approximately every 20 minutes, take visitors near the foot of the bridge; other bus routes have stops within easy walking distance of the island. Water transport is also available with the Aquabus and the False Creek ferries, both of which make trips regularly around False Creek and have stops on Granville Island. The Cyquabus, a bike-friendly version of the Aquabus, has bike racks on board and multiple bike racks are conveniently located throughout the island. A bicycle and pedestrian pathway runs past Granville Island along the south shore of False Creek and maintains the connection between the island and South False Creek.

South False Creek and Granville Island offer examples of how high-density housing, public space, recreational amenities and public transportation can be combined to turn industry-dominated waterfronts into sustainable urban communities.

Revere, Massachusetts

Revere Beach, located in Revere, Massachusetts, an inner-ring suburb that is 11.3km north of Boston, is the site of a new US$500 million multi-use development. Once known as the "Coney Island" of Boston, Revere Beach is a coastal landmark that has provided both employment and entertainment to Boston area residents since it opened as America's first public beach in 1896. It began to deteriorate as a tourist destination in the 1950s, however, and as fewer and fewer people visited the amusements along Revere Beach Boulevard, the area fell into decline.

Located in the interstitial region between the city of Boston and its inner suburbs, Revere Beach is positioned to appeal to both urban and suburban populations. The town is located five to 10 minutes from Logan

Airport and downtown Boston on the Blue Line, part of Boston's subway network. As both a waterfront development and an edge city connected to a metropolis by public transportation, Revere Beach is considered well suited for a transit-oriented waterfront development.

The new development—known as Waterfront Square—when completed will include a boutique hotel, residential towers, office buildings, restaurants, retail stores, and entertainment and cultural venues. An elevated outdoor plaza will be built above the renovated Wonderland Subway Station, and a pedestrian bridge will extend over Revere Beach Boulevard to link Waterfront Square directly to the Revere Beach Reservation.

Transit-oriented waterfront developments present new growth opportunities for cities looking to increase their develop-ment—without expanding their ecological footprint. To be successful, these waterfront developments need to balance economic and ecological parameters. Revitalization of decaying districts and restoration of landscape can generate value for both the site and the city. Connectivity through multimodal transit systems can ensure access and economic vitality, while helping enhance quality-of-life options for residents.

EDITORS' NOTE

The following information is provided about this best practice case study to facilitate future research.

Name: Songdo City
Population: 252,000 (2013)
Region: Northwest
Province/State: Seoul National Capital Area
Country: South Korea
Official Name: Republic of Korea
City Website: http://www.songdo.com/

Chapter 43

Strasbourg, France, Now Focuses on Non-Vehicular Types of Transportation

Ben Adler

Strasbourg, France, where the European parliament meets, is a thoroughly modern regional capital of Western Europe. Its downtown is filled with department stores, teenagers of any ethnicity sporting a European style that takes a lot of inspiration from their American counterparts of five years ago, and shwarma shops competing with McDonald's for their attention. But walk around Strasbourg's charming medieval city center and you will see that one thing is virtually unchanged from its medieval origins: the absence of automobiles.

This is not, however, an uninterrupted history. In fact, it is the direct result of actions recently taken by Strasbourg's government—ones that should inspire comparably sized older American cities, from Buffalo to St. Louis. Just like most American cities, the car's midcentury domination had largely forced public transportation out of Strasbourg. The once-extensive tram lines fell into disrepair, and the last one was taken out of service in 1960. But by 1989 traffic and parking had become major headaches for residents and for businesses in the dense warren of downtown streets. Rather than see retail flee to suburban malls, as it did in America, the city decided to take action.

This being France, where the entire political spectrum is to America's left, the conservatives running for city council in 1989 actually favored building a subway. But the socialists, led by Catherine Trautmann and Roland Ries, wanted to build a new tram. Conservatives and local business owners objected, arguing that a tram would take precious lanes away from cars. But that was exactly the point: to transform streets from hectic, unpleasant gasoline alleys into vibrant, multi-use communal spaces. "The tram means that you change the city," explains Jonathan Naas, transportation policy coordinator for Roland Ries, who is now mayor. By creating a buffer from the cars, he says, "You create places to walk, outdoor cafes to sit outside."

The socialists won in 1989, and Ries oversaw the development of tram lines. Initially there was only one, launched in 1994; now there are five. "In the beginning it was very hard," says Naas. "Business owners said people won't come to the center—it will be 'death city.' But it's exactly the opposite. It changed people. Shopping is now different. Before there was cars, noise, pollution."

The city center is an oval-shaped island, connected to the land by bridges on every

Originally published as "The French Revolution: How Strasbourg Gave Up the Car (and Why Midsized American Cities Can Too)," *Next American City*, Issue 25 (Winter 2009), by the Next City, Philadelphia, Pennsylvania. Reprinted with permission of the publisher.

side. Many, but not all, of the narrow medieval streets on the island have been closed to cars. Some of Strasbourg's most attractive, vibrant public squares, such as Place Kleber, were actually once choked by traffic. The different elements are complementary: The pedestrianizing of downtown streets followed tram construction because multiple tram crossings made driving downtown impractical. Bicycle lanes were constructed beginning in 1981 and have been continually expanded; there are now more than 100 kilometers of bike lanes around the city, and it's faster to bike than to drive through the city during business hours.

Most important, the system has been built and expanded with an understanding of the commuter's psychology. Once people are in their cars, they would prefer to drive all the way to their destination rather than switch modes. So the city has created powerful incentives for suburbanites to switch from their car to the tram: Parking is provided at suburban tram stations, free with a tram ticket that covers everyone in the car (also incentivizing car-pooling). Conversely, parking is prohibitively expensive at the lots downtown. As a compromise with the business community, parking garages were constructed in the center city, but they are elegantly tucked away below ground, and are not even full.

In keeping with this approach, the city intends to improve integration between the suburban commuter trains, which enter the main station just a few tram stops from the heart of town, and the local tram system. One might expect that to be enough to get people out of their cars. But, Naas explains, if you live, say, a 30-minute drive from central Strasbourg, and you must drive to the train station and park, wait for a train, walk through the train station to the tram stop, wait for the tram and then walk from the tram to your final destination, it may take an extra 10 minutes door to door. So to improve

ridership on the commuter trains they are building "train-tram," a suburban commuter train that can move seamlessly onto the tram tracks once in the city. No transferring for suburbanites will mean less hassle, less time and, hopefully, more riders.

A "Culture of Mobility"

The environmental benefits of Strasbourg's transportation policies have been obvious: Thirty percent fewer cars now enter Strasbourg each day than in 1990. Less obvious is the economic impact, but it is quite real as well.

Strasbourg's economic history is not unlike that of similarly sized American cities. Its location on the Rhine made it a natural fit for shipping and heavy industry, but those jobs are departing for cheaper wages in Eastern Europe. But unlike many postindustrial cities, Strasbourg is alive and well. If your business depends on trucking, all this public transport has not helped you. But it has been good for restaurants, retail and other tourism-related businesses such as hotels. "For service businesses it is clearly in their interest," says Bruno Grandjean, program manager for Vehicules du Futur, a Strasbourg-area nonprofit focused on sustainable transportation. Indeed, Grandjean's organization itself is evidence of the postindustrial economic opportunities created by Strasbourg's transportation transformation. They could have located anywhere when they launched four years ago. They chose Strasbourg because, Grandjean says, "there is a strong culture of mobility here in Strasbourg."

A case in point would be Vehicules du Futur's effort to create public cars that can be used like a bike-share program. The electric cars, which will carry up to six passengers and be wheelchair accessible, will be recharged at stations around the city. The hope is to make living without a car a viable option for residents of both the city center and the urban periphery. Currently, tram and bus lines on the hub-and-spoke system bring residents of peripheral neighborhoods to and from the center, but not as much around the periphery for, say, shopping or visiting friends. But with the car-share program they can drive around for those errands or, say, to the tram station. The cars will be built by LOHR, a manufacturer of trams and car carriers just outside of Strasbourg. Ultimately, Grandjean hopes, the car-share program will enable suburbanites to buy fewer cars and therefore drive less. "We know we have solutions for cities, and that we won't for rural areas for a long time," declares Grandjean. "The battle is for the suburban areas." Another example of the economic activity fueled by Strasbourg's transit shifts is Auto'trement, a car-sharing business founded nine years ago as a private-public partnership. Auto'trement is essentially the same as Zipcar, in that it rents cars on an hourly basis, although there are some slight differences in its pricing model. Initially supported by government subsidies, it is now a self-sufficient organization with several employees working out of its quirky little office overlooking a tram line in the city center. According to founder Jean-Baptiste Schmider, approximately 25 percent of the 1,600 members in the Strasbourg urban community gave up their car thanks to the program, and an additional 25 percent did not buy one because of it. That's 800 cars that have been kept off the road.

Cutting-edge Reality

Perhaps Strasbourg is such a hub of forward-thinking transportation enterprises because its evolution represents more than a few mere policy changes. Strasbourg leads a transportation revolution that is happening—fitfully—the world over. The revolution is the development of a fast-paced modern metropolis that does not require car ownership, a development befitting not only concerns about climate change and rising oil prices, but also the developed world's shift from an industrial economy to a service and knowledge economy. "The future isn't selling cars," says Schmider. "It's selling mobility solutions."

"Cars are expensive and spend 95 percent of their lives parked," Grandjean notes. "That is not optimal utilization."

Bigger cities such as New York, London and Paris have attracted attention for their own participation in this movement, with programs ranging from congestion pricing to bicycle sharing. Perhaps cities like Detroit, Buffalo and Cleveland should recognize that the era of an industrial economy predicated on people building cars, televisions and toaster ovens for each other in developed countries is over. Perhaps the federal government, instead of (or at least in addition to) delaying the inevitable with automaker bailouts, should focus on competing for global knowledge-sector business and tourism. Are the rich Chinese corporate titans of the 21st century going to want to put offices and take vacations in Phoenix, where they will have to rent a car and navigate an incoherent network of highways, when they could go to a European city like Strasbourg?

The Obama administration, with its emphasis on high-speed rail, reconnecting public housing to surrounding neighborhoods, and its smaller emphasis on mass transit, seems to have some grasp of this transformation. In May transportation secretary Ray LaHood visited Strasbourg and received presentations from the city government and from LOHR. But the dollar amounts being appropriated for these programs in the U.S. still pale in comparison to the subsidies for highway construction and auto-making.

Endeavors like the Vehicles du Futur public-car project—there is a much larger version planned for Paris—do have skeptics, even among green transport advocates. "The potential problem is the lack of reliability, because you cannot book online," says Schmider of Auto'trement. "It could work, but it's too early. Maybe in 10 years it will work when other cars are forbidden in the city center, or there are high tolls like in London."

Ask a random sample of Strasbourg residents what they think of the trams and bike lanes, and you are likely to find, as I did, complete and uniform approval. Whether old, like Richard Baron Schmidt, 63, a lifelong resident of Strasbourg, or young, like drama student Margot Becker, anyone old enough to remember the former system thinks the trams are an improvement. "Before the trams, coming downtown was difficult because of parking," says Schmidt. "Now it is easier and cheaper."

The only complaint about the trams seems to be that they make noise. But trams in other cities need not have that problem. In the years since the tram was started in Strasbourg, LOHR, whose massive campus sits in the cornfields (and next to a train station) just outside city limits, has developed a virtually silent tram. Rather than running steel on steel like a train, they put wheels encased in rubber on a single track. This makes for not only a quieter system, but one that is cheaper to build and cheaper to maintain. Other cities, as near as central France's 140,000-person Clement-Ferrand and as far as Shanghai, have purchased trams from LOHR.

The applicability to America, where high-speed rail has received appropriations from Congress, is admittedly questionable. Carlessness in Strasbourg grew out of, and reinforced, existing economic and structural realities."

An American Dream

Some might attribute this phenomenon entirely to a cultural difference, arguing that the French will take advantage of bike paths and trains but Americans will not. But the Strasbourgers I interviewed, whether politicians, pedestrians or businesspeople, all told me that the French, like Americans, have an emotional attachment to their automobiles, and that it is ultimately a political choice to encourage or discourage driving. Absent the incentive structure set up by Strasbourg, the French will take the path of least resistance—a car, whenever possible—just like Americans. "When you are in your car, you feel at home. You will not change that for free," says Olivier Hauchard, a consultant for LOHR who has lived in Strasbourg for more than 20 years. "It is not cultural. It is only a political decision."

"We had meetings around the city and three things came up," recalls Alain Jund, a member of Parliament who works on transportation policy. "One, there are too many cars in public places. Two, 'I don't have a place to park my car.' And three, we need public transportation. There was a contradiction. As politicians we had to make choices."

One particular cultural difference does matter: environmentalism. Hauchard says that in France, "Young people talk every day about pollution." Indeed, many of the people I chatted with, whether in their office or in the park where I found them drinking beer in midday, brought up the environmental impact of driving. Public concern about global warming, and understanding about the link between driving and emissions, has penetrated further in France than in America, which helps build public support for green transportation. Still, there are signs of a shift here at home: When I was in Leesburg, Va., a prototypical American exurb, their transportation office told me that in 2008, on user surveys on their commuter bus, people listed the environment as a reason for taking it (and ridership spiked, although that was primarily due to high gas prices).

The applicability to America, where

high-speed rail has recently been touted by the Obama administration and received appropriations from Congress, is admittedly questionable. Carlessness in Strasbourg grew out of, and reinforced, existing economic and structural realities. The sectors that benefit from the transportation links—hospitality, services and retail—fit with the city's natural advantages. Tourism was a natural growth area, thanks to the presence of the European parliament, the medieval center, the fact that it is a French city 10 minutes from Germany and fewer than three hours from Switzerland, Austria and Belgium. With a large university that specializes in science and engineering, it also made sense for Strasbourg to adopt transportation that appeals to students and young professionals. Bioengineering firms, which are increasingly able to locate anywhere, have been agglomerating in Strasbourg, and its high quality of life is one reason.

All of this is complementary with France's impressive nationwide transportation network. The high-speed TGV train has made it possible to go from Paris to Strasbourg in two hours and 20 minutes, for as little as 20 euros each way. That is half the previous travel time of a normal-speed train. So now shoppers at Strasbourg's famous Christmas festival can come in for day trips and hop on a tram from the train station to downtown. "Every part of Strasbourg is irrigated by the TGV effect from Paris," says Grandjean. The TGV effect from Paris helps Strasbourg because Paris is a center of wealth and economic activity. If you link two depressed areas by high-speed rail, as Grandjean himself points out, there may not be the same economic multiplier effect.

So this is not a model that could be imitated by midsized American cities that lack any of Strasbourg's advantages. Detroit, for example, might not see a lot of development in its decimated urban core just because the city builds a tram there. But what about cities with more similarities to Strasbourg? Buffalo has a rich architectural heritage, Olmsted parks, a major university, a nascent artist community and proximity to the Canadian border, Niagara Falls and Toronto. Could Buffalo, where the streets are often walkable but regional mass transit is limited, implement a creative class and tourism service economy development strategy through urban planning innovations like Strasbourg's?

Alas, Democratic Rep. Brian Higgins, who represents Buffalo, told me at the Revitalizing Older Cities conference that he thinks Buffalo's comparative advantage is its absence of traffic, and that should be reinforced, by continuing to accommodate cars and keeping density low. Such a strategy is shortsighted. Artists and other creative-class professionals are generally unenthusiastic about driving, and the era of cheap oil, as recent price shocks have demonstrated, may not last forever. And that's not even raising the moral considerations with regard to pollution and climate change. Whether any given city will realize the benefits that Strasbourg has if it adopts a similar transportation policy is obviously an unknown, but there is not a known example of such a policy causing massive depopulation, pollution, destruction of street life or economic decline in the way that its opposite—subsidizing driving through building highways—did to cities from Baltimore to St. Louis. Strasbourg, for its part, still has terrible traffic in its core—eliminating road capacity is hardly a recipe for reversing that—but now that one does not need to drive downtown, Strasbourgers are not prisoners to the traffic, and the streets are more pleasant.

One myth worth dispelling is that urbanists such as those who have revolutionized Strasbourg are as doctrinaire in their dedication to one mode of transportation as the car-huggers who built San Diego. That may be the stereotype of bicycle or tram advocates, but the facts on the ground do not bear it out. As Strasbourg expands the reach of its mass transit links, it takes a flexible approach embodied by the Vehicules du Futur project. They are going to build bus rapid transit for marginal areas, because it is cheaper than trams. Ronan Golias, Strasbourg's transportation chief, is described by colleagues as "a good engineer." The leaders of Strasbourg's smart growth strategy are pragmatists, not ideologues.

Today's visitor to Strasbourg would be as ignorant of the local history of traffic congestion and its discontents as a Vassar alum from Indiana would be of her new East Village block's history as an open-air drug market. Arrive at the train station and you can walk through its tall glass walls showcasing a park and the city beyond, or hop on a tram just a stop or two from the center of the city. When you arrive on the island that constitutes its medieval core—surrounded by a natural moat, it is now a UNESCO world heritage site—you will find a network of pedestrianized streets, and public squares with fountains. It would never occur to you that these tiny streets were once choked with cars, or that the fountains were once isolated by giant roads surrounding them. The only thing more absurd is the idea that anyone would rather have it that way.

EDITORS' NOTE

The following information is provided about this best practice case study to facilitate future research.

Name: City of Strasbourg
Population: 272,975 (2006)
Region: Northeast
Province/State: Alsace Region
Country: France
Official Name: French Republic
City Website: http://www.strasbourg.eu/

Reporting for this article was funded by a grant from the German Marshall Fund.

Chapter 44

Tokyo, Japan, Other Cities, Take Measures To Facilitate the Use of Gasoline-Free Cars

Jim Motavalli

Until recently, most people experienced clean-energy cars at auto shows, in the pages of magazines, or as image advertising—they weren't tangible. All that's changed now: You can actually see electric and plug-in hybrid vehicles on the street, picking up groceries with early adopters at the wheel, taking the kids to Little League, and—lo and behold—even charging up at public stations.

The basic types of clean-energy cars are as follows:

- **Battery electrics.** These cars have electric motors and battery packs, and no other means of propulsion. The range is generally 100 miles, but that's not likely to remain the standard for long. The Tesla Roadster can deliver 245 miles on a charge.
- **Plug-in hybrids.** The plug-in hybrid car acts like an electric car for the first 15 to 50 miles, but then can switch to an on-board internal-combustion engine that, in many cases, acts as a generator instead of directly driving the wheels. The Chevrolet Volt is an example of the plug-in hybrid, as is the Fisker Karma.
- **Hybrids.** Hybrids either use their electric motors as assists for the gas engine, or allow short bursts of electric-only driving. The Toyota Prius and Ford Fusion hybrids are examples of this car type.
- **Hydrogen fuel-cell cars.** The fuel cell, which produces electricity from hydrogen, replaces the battery pack. Hydrogen is the most abundant element in the universe; we'll never run out of it. The main challenge is not having enough hydrogen filling stations.

Nearly every major auto maker is planning new clean-energy models. Ford, for instance, intends to roll out five new models in 2012. Roland Berger Strategy Consultants forecasts that 10 percent of new cars globally will be electric by 2025, and the larger category that includes hybrids and plug-in hybrids will have grabbed 40 percent of the market by then. That would mean that half of new cars heading into showrooms around the world would be at least partly electric, but it's a pretty optimistic forecast—what ultimately rolls out depends to a great extent on what happens with gas prices.

Hydrogen fuel-cell cars should be ready for mass use in just a few more years. In addition, four car companies—Daimler, Toy-

Originally published as "The Road Ahead for Gasoline-Free Cars," *The Futurist*, Vol. 46, No. 2 (March–April 2012), by the World Future Society, Bethesda, Maryland. Reprinted with permission of the publisher.

ota, Honda, and Hyundai—plan to roll out tens of thousands of hydrogen-powered cars by 2015.

The near-term challenge is the lack of a hydrogen infrastructure. There are currently fewer than a hundred hydrogen stations in all the United States, and only a handful are public. Some entrepreneurs are attempting to change that. Tom Sullivan, the founder of Lumber Liquidators, has just started SunHydro, a private chain of hydrogen fueling stations along the U.S. east coast.

As it stands, though, the upcoming hydrogen-powered cars may end up being sold in Europe, South Korea, or Japan, where public commitments on hydrogen infrastructure are much stronger than in the United States. The U.S. government has had an on-again, off-again relationship with hydrogen-powered cars.

That's not to say that American consumers don't like electric cars. Demand is higher in the United States that anywhere else. But demand in China could surpass U.S. demand very quickly. China will likely become the world's largest electric-car market: It has put in place some of the world's best incentives for electric cars and quite a few manufacturers are lining up to sell them to Chinese buyers.

Demographics trends might also help the electric car market, as more people move to cities. Electrics will help fill the need for vehicles that can take people short distances at low speeds due to traffic and pedestrians. The obstacle for electric vehicles as "city cars" is the problem of charging them. In cities like New York, we're not likely to see on-street parking and charging units for electric vehicles.

What we will probably see are EV charging units in garages and buildings, but the rules and protocols have yet to be developed. Suppose you own a condo, and you want to install a charging station on the condo grounds. You have to bring in the condo as-

sociation on it, and it's going to slow things down. There need to be guidelines for apartment dwellers to charge electrics. Right now, that doesn't exist.

But smart meters do. A smart meter, installed on the side of your house, enables you, on your computer at work, to dial up software that shows you exactly how much juice each of your appliances is using, and allows you to shut some of them down remotely during peak power demand times.

Smart meters are a huge advance and are fortunately going mainstream at the same time that electric cars are hitting the road. The two can work together closely. When it's plugged in, your electric car is just another household load—and a pretty big one, sometimes doubling electricity consumption. If we get rally smart about this, we can create home networks that empower consumers to manage and reduce their power needs—and save money in the process. The smart home is finally coming to America, and it's making huge strides in Japan.

I visited Panasonic's Eco Ideas House in downtown Tokyo, and there was a plug-in hybrid Toyota Prius in the driveway. As I learned, the car and the house form a singularly green home energy management system. The house combines a five-kilowatt solar panel on the roof and a one-kilowatt hydrogen fuel cell in the backyard to generate electricity, and stationary five-kilowatt lithium-ion battery to store it. Holistic systems that use sophisticated power management electronics like this are all the rage in Japan, thanks to a combination of growing green consciousness, corporate commitment, and financial support from the government.

In Japan, Panasonic now sells home fuel cells that can supply 60 percent of a family's power needs. General Electric, in cooperation with a company called Plug Power, has planned to sell its own home fuel cells to Americans in the early 2000s. But without federal subsidies, the economics weren't there—the fuel cell would have produced electricity at a cost higher than that of grid power.

There are some good reasons to be optimistic for electric cars' future. At first, a fairly small percentage of people will buy electric and plug-in hybrid cars solely because they expect to save money on them. Most will be motivated by environmental concerns, but oil prices could certainly affect the popularity of electrics.

It is true that the automakers face major challenges to transitioning to electricity. But they are taking a chance with these new clean-energy cars. The revival of the electric car is now well under way, pushed forward by technological leaps, the imperatives of global warming, and the sobering prospect of peak oil. Electric cars are going to jumpstart our lives and do good things for the planet, too.

EDITORS' NOTE

The following information is provided about this best practice case study to facilitate future research.

Name: Tokyo Metropolis
Population: 13,185,502 (2011)
Region: Kanto Region
Province/State: Tokyo Prefecture
Country: Japan
Official Name: State of Japan
City Website: http://www.metro.tokyo.jp/

Chapter 45

Vancouver, Canada, Takes Measures to Increase EcoMobility Transport Methods

Michael Shiffer

Typical of most major metropolises, Vancouver has no freeways into or through its downtown area. In 1960, plans for a city freeway were rejected by an alliance of citizens and community leaders. Vancouver's urban development has since been focused on significantly reducing car use.

Shifting Vancouver Towards Sustainability

Growth in Vancouver's public transit ridership is exceeding all other major Canadian cities. Transit ridership has increased 52 percent for the Vancouver region over the last 10 years. The modes of transportation include buses, community shuttles, ferries, commuter rail, and an automated rapid transit system known as "SkyTrain."

Vancouver's bus service consists of trolleybuses, hybrid compressed natural gas (CNG), and conventional diesels that serve the entire city. The buses are in various sizes including small community shuttles, conventional and articulated. Some routes have dedicated lanes, which improves their efficiency.

Buses are bicycle and wheelchair accessible and run on renewable energy. The downtown streetcar links high-activity areas in the city with other transit modes. The SkyTrain, which consists of three lines of automated trains, is the world's longest automated light rapid transit system. The SkyTrain led to the development of multiple dense urban centers. The system runs mainly on hydroelectric energy, thus reducing its ecological footprint.

Cycling: Vancouver's Fastest Growing Transport Mode

Vancouver promotes biking as a safe, convenient, and healthy mode of transport. The city intends to integrate the bicycle network with the current transportation network to reduce traffic congestion. Vancouver has over 400 km of bike paths throughout the city. Nearly 60,000 trips (approximately 4 percent) are made every day on bicycle. In the downtown area and surrounding neighborhoods, this modal share is roughly 11 percent. Together, biking and walking account for nearly 50 percent of all downtown trips.

Originally published as "Vancouver, Canada: Increasing Intermodal EcoMobile Transport Methods," *ICLEI Cases Studies—EcoMobility* (October 2011), by ICLEI–Local Governments for Sustainability, Bonn, Germany. Reprinted with permission of the publisher.

More than 3,500 residents commute to work downtown by bicycle each day, an increase of 70 percent during the last decade. Half of all Vancouver residents commute less than five km to work and 80 percent commute less than 10 km. These short distances are ideal for biking. The Central Valley Greenway saw almost 2,000 cyclists per day were using this route within one month of its opening in 2009.

Walking: Vancouver's Top Priority

Seventeen percent of all trips taken in Vancouver are made by pedestrians. Still, the city plans to increase the modal share of walking by making streets easily accessible and safer for pedestrians. The city maintains more than 2,100 km of sidewalks and urges communities to make their sidewalk areas more appealing to walkers by decorating them and planting flowers. The city also maintains "greenways" for pedestrians and cyclists that connect parks, historic sites, communities, and retail areas along the waterfront and through nature sites. They provide alternative ways to travel through the city and create an enriched natural city experience. There are currently 90 km of greenways, with more being developed. The largest is Central Valley Greenway, a 25 km route in the city which links 11 SkyTrain stations, 23 bus routes, 16 bicycle routes, and 11 other greenways.

Fee Structure and Business Model

Vancouver has a ten-part goal of becoming the world's greenest city by 2020.

One of these goal areas involves transportation. In the last 15 years, the city's population increased 18 percent and commutes by 16 percent, but the number of daily vehicles entering the city continues to decline. There are two main goals of this initiative. The first is to achieve over half of all trips in the city by walking, bicycling, or public transport. The second of these goals is to reduce the average distance driven by vehicle per resident by 20 percent. To assist in meeting these goals, the city has allocated over $12 million (8.4 million €) per year for cycling paths and other transportation projects.

The City of Vancouver is one of Canada's main port cities. The city has a population of 640,000 people in an area of 115 km², while the metropolitan area has a population of 2.3 million people. This makes Vancouver the third metropolitan area in the country. Vancouver is one of Canada's largest industrial centers. Port activity generates much of Vancouver's GDP (gross domestic product). Mining and forest products are also a major part of Vancouver's economy. Furthermore, Vancouver has an ambitious plan to become one of the greenest cities in the world. Vancouver has been an ICLEI member since April 1993.

EDITORS' NOTE

The following information is provided about this best practice case study to facilitate future research.

Name: City of Vancouver
Population: 603,502 (2011)
Region: Southwestern Canada
Province/State: Province of British Columbia
Country: Canada
Official Name: Same
City Website: http://www.vancouver.ca/

Chapter 46

Victoria, Canada Takes Measures to Reduce Traffic by Promoting Their Solutions

Todd Litman

As more and more people around the world are able to afford their own cars, and daily traffic jams and pollution get worse in cities rich and poor, how do we find an easier way through the urban sprawl? Here the Victoria Transport Policy Institute in Vancouver, Canada, presents some of the latest thinking, and fresh ideas in urban transport planning.

Sustainability in urban transport is sometimes defined narrowly, focusing on a few impacts such as fossil fuel depletion and air pollution. But it is increasingly defined more broadly to include a variety of economic, social and environmental issues. For example, narrowly defined sustainability implies that sustainable transportation can be achieved by simply shifting to solar or nuclear-powered vehicles. But broadly defined sustainability requires additional transportation system changes and better planning, both to reduce accidents and provide non-drivers with improved transport options.

Conventional transport planning leaves specific problems assigned to agencies with narrowly defined responsibilities: Transportation agencies are primarily responsible for reducing traffic congestion problems, social agencies are responsible for helping disadvantaged people, and environmental agencies are responsible for reducing energy consumption and pollution.

This type of planning tends to be inefficient, because individual agencies often implement solutions to their problems which exacerbate other problems facing society. It also tends to undervalue solutions that provide modest but multiple benefits. For example, roadway widening may help reduce traffic congestion—but it indirectly increases vehicle travel, parking costs, consumer costs, accidents, fuel consumption and pollution emissions. Conversely, some energy conservation strategies, such as incentives for motorists to choose more fuel-efficient vehicles, may reduce total energy consumption, but because this reduces the per-kilometer cost of driving, it tends to increase per vehicle annual mileage, and so increases traffic congestion, parking costs, consumer costs and accidents.

In Victoria, we have identified a number of transportation planning reforms that help create more diverse and efficient transportation systems, which we call "Win-Win Transportation Solutions" because of their multiple benefits. These are cost-effective, technically feasible reforms that help solve

Originally published as "Tackling Those Traffic Jams—Win-Win Transportation Solutions," *World Urban Forum III—An Event on Urban Sustainability* (June 2006), by the UN-Habitat, United Nations, Vancouver, Canada. Reprinted with permission of the publisher.

transport problems by correcting existing market distortions that result in economically excessive vehicle travel. As a result, they help achieve a combination of economic, social and environmental planning objectives, including reduced traffic congestion, road and parking facility savings, consumer savings and choice, equity, safety and environmental protection.

A major barrier to more sustainable transportation is the perception that economic and environmental goals conflict. Some people oppose climate change emission reduction programs on the grounds that they reduce economic development. But *win-win solutions* can provide a combination of economic, social and environmental benefits.

Although individually their impacts may appear modest, typically affecting a small portion of total travel, their effects are cumulative. When all benefits and costs are considered, the solutions outlined here often turn out to be most cost effective solutions overall.

• *Least Cost Planning:* Least-cost planning, or Integrated Planning considers demand management solutions. It involves the public in developing and evaluating alternatives, such as using roadway expansion funding for transit improvements, rideshare programs or mobility management programs.

• *Parking Management:* Parking Management entails more efficient use of existing parking facilities—shared parking, flexible minimum parking requirements, and more direct user charges.

• *Commute Trip Reduction:* Commute Trip Reduction programs encourage people to reduce car trips. Typically they use a variety of incentives and support to reduce peak-period driving, including better cycling facilities and flexible working hours.

• *Transit Improvements:* There are many ways to improve public transit, including better vehicles and stations, more frequent service, reduced crowding, improved walking conditions to transit stations, and *HOV Priority* for High Occupant Vehicles (buses, vanpools and carpools) priority over general traffic, so public transit travel is faster and more efficient.

• *Walking and Cycling Improvements:* Walking and cycling travel can substitute for some motor vehicle trips. Communities with good walking and cycling conditions drive less and use transit more.

• *Smart Growth Land Use Policies:* "Smart Growth" land use policies encourage the development of more compact, mixed, walkable, transit-oriented communities, where residents drive less and rely more on alternative modes.

• *Traffic Calming and Management:* Traffic calming reduces speeds and volumes on specific roads. Typical strategies include traffic circles at intersections, raised crosswalks, and partial street closures to discourage short cut traffic through residential neighborhoods. This reduces car use, and increases road safety and creates a more pedestrian- and bicycle-friendly environment.

• *Road Pricing:* Road Pricing means that motorists pay directly for driving on a particular roadway or in a particular area. Transportation economists have long advocated road pricing as a way to fund transportation improvements and to reduce congestion problems.

• *Pay-As-You-Drive Pricing:* Pay-As-You-Drive (PAYD) pricing means that vehicle insurance premiums and other fees are based directly on how much the vehicle is driven. This provides a significant financial incentive to reduce driving, while making these charges more fair and affordable.

Many transportation problems are virtually unsolvable without such reforms. Many transportation planners recognize the potential benefits of these reforms, but they often treat them as measures of last resort, to be used to address specific congestion and air pollution problems where conventional solutions prove to be ineffective. Win-win solutions use the opposite approach—they apply market reforms whenever they are cost effective overall, taking into account all costs and benefits, and consider capacity expansion as a fallback if management strategies fail.

Most individual win-win strategies provide modest benefits, and so are not considered the best way to solve any particular problem. As a result, they are often overlooked, even if they are cost effective and could provide large benefits if implemented together.

EDITORS' NOTE

The following information is provided about this best practice case study to facilitate future research.

Name: City of Victoria
Population: 80,032 (2011)
Region: Southwestern Canada
Province/State: Province of British Columbia
Country: Canada
Official Name: Same
City Website: http://www.victoria.ca/

The UN-Habitat's website (http://www.unhabitat.org/) has additional information concerning the best practices for sustainable transportation options being used in cities located in countries throughout the world.

Chapter 47

The Benefits and Growth of Street Trees in Urban Places

Dan Burden

U.S Forest Service facts and figures and new traffic safety studies detail many urban street tree benefits. Once seen as highly problematic for many reasons, street trees are proving to be a great value to people living, working, shopping, socializing, walking and motoring in, around and through urban places.

For a planting cost of $250–600 (includes first 3 years of maintenance) a single street tree returns over $90,000 of direct benefits (not including aesthetic, social and natural) in the lifetime of the tree. Street trees (generally planted from 4 feet to 8 feet from curbs) provide many benefits to those streets they occupy. These trees provide so many benefits that they should always be considered as an urban area default street making feature. With new attentions being paid to global warming causes and impacts more is becoming known about negative environmental impacts of treeless urban streets. We are well on the way to recognizing the need for urban street trees to be preferred urban design, rather than luxury items tolerated by traffic engineering and budget conscious city administrators.

The many identified problems of street trees are overcome with care by designers. Generally street trees are placed each 15–30 feet. These trees are carefully positioned to allow adequate sight triangles at intersections and driveways, to not block street luminaries, not impact utility lines above or below ground. Street trees of various varieties are used in all climates, including high altitude, semi-arid and even arid urban places.

The science of street tree placement and maintenance is well known and observed in a growing number of communities (i.e. Chicago, Illinois; Sacramento, Davis, California; Eugene, Oregon; Seattle, Redmond, Olympia and Issaquah, Washington; Charlotte, N.C.; Keene, New Hampshire and Cambridge, Mass). Although care and maintenance of trees in urban places is a costly task, the value in returned benefits is so great that a sustainable community cannot be imagined without these important green features.

Properly Placed and Spaced Urban Street Trees Provide These Benefits:

Increased motorized traffic and pedestrian safety (contrary to engineering myths). See below article for details on mode safety

Originally published as "22 Benefits of Urban Street Trees," *Walkable Communities Resources—Articles* (November 2008), by the Walkable and Livable Communities Institute, Port Townsend, Washington. Reprinted with permission of the publisher.

enhancements. See especially the compilation of safety benefits detailed in, Safe Streets, Livable Streets, by Eric Dumbaugh Journal of the American Planning Association, Vol. 71, No. 3, Summer 2005. One such indication of increased safety with urban street trees is quoted from this document:

"Indeed, there is a growing body of evidence suggesting that the inclusion of trees and other streetscape features in the roadside environment may actually reduce crashes and injuries on urban roadways. Naderi (2003) examined the safety impacts of aesthetic streetscape enhancements placed along the roadside and medians of five arterial roadways in downtown Toronto. Using a quasi-experimental design, the author found that the inclusion of features such as trees and concrete planters along the roadside resulted in statistically significant reductions in the number of mid-block crashes along all five roadways, with the number of crashes decreasing from between 5 and 20 percent as a result of the streetscape improvements. While the cause for these reductions is not clear, the author suggests that the presence of a well defined roadside edge may be leading drivers to exercise greater caution."

1. Reduced and more appropriate urban traffic speeds. Urban street trees create vertical walls framing streets, providing a defined edge, helping motorists guide their movement and assess their speed (leading to overall speed reductions). Street safety comparisons show reductions of run-off-the-road crashes and overall crash severity when street tree sections are compared with equivalent treeless streets. (Texas A and M conducted simulation research which found people slow down while driving through a treed scape. These observations are also seen in the real world when following motorists along first a treed portion of a street, and then a non treed portion. Speed differentials of 3 mph to 15 mph are noted.

2. Create safer walking environments, by forming and framing visual walls and providing distinct edges to sidewalks so that motorists better distinguish between their environment and one shared with people. If a motorist were to significantly err in their urban driving task, street trees help deflect or fully stop the motorist from taking a human life.

3. Trees call for planting strips, which further separate motorists from one another, pedestrians, buildings and other urban fabric. This green area adds significantly to aesthetics and place making. Urban area medians with trees are safer than those without trees (R. Ewing, Caltrans Study, circa 2003). Medians reduce crashes by 50 percent or more.

4. Increased security. Trees create more pleasant walking environments, bringing about increased walking, talking, pride, care of place, association and therefore actual ownership and surveillance of homes, blocks, neighborhoods plazas, businesses and other civic spaces.

5. Improved business. Businesses on treescaped streets show 20 percent higher income streams, which is often the essential competitive edge needed for main street store success, versus competition from plaza discount store prices.

6. Less drainage infrastructure. Trees absorb the first 30 percent of most precipitation through their leaf system, allowing evaporation back into the atmosphere. This moisture never hits the ground. Another percentage (up to 30 percent) of precipitation is absorbed back into the ground and taken in and held onto by the root structure, then absorbed and then transpired back to the air. Some of this water also naturally percolates into the ground water and aquifer. Storm water runoff and flooding potential to urban properties is therefore reduced.

7. Rain, sun, heat and skin protection. For light or moderate rains, pedestrians find less need for rain protection. In cities with good tree coverage there is less need for chemical sun blocking agents. Temperature differentials of 5–15 degrees are felt when walking under tree canopied streets.

8. Reduced harm from tailpipe emissions. Automobile and truck exhaust is a major public health concern and contains significant pollutants, including carbon monoxide (CO), volatile organic compounds (VOC), nitrogen oxides (NOx), and particulate matter (PM). Tailpipe emissions are adding to asthma, ozone and other health impacts. Impacts are reduced significantly from proximity to trees.

9. Gas transformation efficiency. Trees in street proximity absorb 9 times more pollutants than more distant trees, converting harmful gasses back into oxygen and other useful and natural gasses.

10. Lower urban air temperatures. Asphalt and concrete streets and parking lots are known to increase urban temperatures 3–7 degrees. These temperature increases significantly impact energy costs to homeowners and consumers. A properly shaded neighborhood, mostly from urban street trees, can reduce energy bills for a household from 15–35 percent.

11. Lower Ozone. Increases in urban street temperatures that hover directly above asphalt where tailpipe emissions occur dramatically increase creation of harmful ozone and other gasses into more noxious substances impacting health of people, animals and surrounding agricultural lands.

12. Convert streets, parking and walls into more aesthetically pleasing environments. There are few streetmaking elements that do as much to soften wide, grey visual wastelands created by wide streets, parking lots and massive, but sometimes necessary blank walls than trees.

13. Soften and screen necessary street features such as utility poles, light poles and other needed street furniture. Trees are highly effective at screening those other vertical features to roadways that are needed for many safety and functional reasons.

14. Reduced blood pressure, improved overall emotional and psychological health. People are impacted by ugly or attractive environments where they spend time. Kathlene Wolf, Social Science Ph.D. University of Washington gave a presentation that said "the risk of treed streets was questionable compared to other types of accidents along with the increased benefit of trees on human behavior, health, pavement longevity, etc." She noted that trees have a calming and healing effect on ADHD adults and teens.

15. Time in travel perception. Other research and observations confirm that motorists perceive the time it takes to get through treed versus non-treed environments has a significant differential. A treeless environment trip is perceived to be longer than one that is treed (Walter Kulash, P.E.; speech circa 1994, Glatting Jackson).

16. Reduced road rage. Although this may at first seem a stretch, there is strong, compelling research that motorist road rage is less in green urban versus stark suburban areas. Trees and aesthetics, which are known to reduce blood pressure, may handle some of this calming effect.

17. Improved operations potential. When properly positioned and maintained, the backdrop of street trees allow those features that should be dominant to be better seen, such as vital traffic regulatory signs. The absence of a well-developed Greenscape allows the sickly grey mass of strip to dominate the visual world. At the same time, poorly placed signs, signals, or poorly maintained trees reduces this positive gain, and thus proper placement and maintenance must be rigidly adhered to.

18. Added value to adjacent homes, businesses and tax base. Realtor based estimates of street tree versus non street tree comparable streets relate a $15–25,000 increase in home or business value. This often adds to the base tax base and operations budgets of a city allowing for added street maintenance. Future economic analysis may determine that this is a break-even for city maintenance budgets.

19. Provides a lawn for a splash and spray zone, storage of snow, driveway elevation transition and more. Tree lawns are an essential part of the operational side of a street.

20. Filtering and screening agent. Softens and screens utility poles, light poles, on-street and off-street parking and other features creating visual pollution to the street.

21. Longer pavement life. Studies conducted in a variety of California environments show that the shade of urban street trees can add from 40–60 percent more life to costly asphalt. This factor is based on reduced daily heating and cooling (expansion/contraction) of asphalt. As peak oil pricing increases roadway overlays, this will become a significant cost reduction to maintaining a more affordable roadway system.

22. Connection to nature and the human senses. Urban street trees provide a canopy, root structure and setting for important insect and bacterial life below the surface; at grade for pets and romantic people to pause for what pets and romantic people pause for; they act as essential lofty environments for song birds, seeds, nuts, squirrels and other urban life. Indeed, street trees so well establish natural and comfortable urban life it is unlikely we will ever see any advertisement for any marketed urban product, including cars, to be featured without street trees making the ultimate dominant, bold visual statement about place.

Chapter 48

New Public Policies Link Transit Investments to Land Uses

Kate White

While focused on highways as the primary post–World War II transportation infrastructure investment, the Bay Area's dispersed 100 cities and nine counties simultaneously have recognized over the past several decades the need for more transit options to serve their growing populations. A plethora of transit agencies has evolved, today numbering more than 20, each with its own fare-collection system, operations technology, and schedules. The region is crippled by a lack of coordination among these agencies. Getting from point A to point B in the Bay Area region on transit is often a time-consuming and complex—if not impossible—feat. One effort to simplify transit use is the TransLink pass—being beta-tested by the regional Metropolitan Transportation Commission—which will allow customers to ride on multiple transit systems using only one card.

The system with the broadest reach is Bay Area Rapid Transit (BART) heavy rail, which opened its first segment in 1972. BART had the potential to provide new transit-centered neighborhood hubs linked throughout the region. However, originally only three counties bought into the system, and most of the stations have sat fallow as parking lots for decades because no clear cor-

responding land us plans were part of BART's expansion.

Addition to this challenge, regional planning is severely limited by California's legal land use structure, which gives home rule powers to each jurisdiction, putting land use control exclusively in the hands of each of the cities and counties. Most cities have chosen not to build higher-density development, resulting in an uncoordinated, haphazard land use pattern that forces most Bay Area residents to drive for the vast majority of their trips.

Ecological Urbanism

On October 17, 1989, when a magnitude 7.1 earthquake rumbled through the Bay Area, Mother Nature provided the opportunity for birth of a new movement, which the San Francisco Planning and Urban Research Association has termed *ecological urbanism*. Some freeways were destroyed by the earthquake, facilitating the knitting back together of entire San Francisco neighborhoods such as the Embarcadero and Hayes Valley. Trans-Form—founded in 1997 as the Transportation and Land Use Coalition—catalyzed co-

Originally published as "In Transition," *Urban Land*, Vol. 68, No. 9 (September 2009), by the Urban Land Institute, Washington, D.C. Copyright, the Urban Land Institute, all rights reserved. Reprinted with permission.

ordination of the many active organizations in the region to promote smart growth. TransForm has won billions of dollars in funding and passage of policies in the Bay Area in support of public transportation, smart growth, affordable housing, and bicycle and pedestrian safety. The coalition has received national funding from the likes of the Ford Foundation and is looked to as a model for other regional smart growth groups across the country.

One notable accomplishment conceived by TransForm and approved by the Bay Area's regional agencies in 2005 was a first-in-the-nation policy mandating that cities rezone areas around new transit stations to require housing before transit infrastructure could receive public dollars. This groundbreaking policy linking transit dollars to land use has refocused jurisdictions toward transit-oriented development (TOD). In addition to the incentive of transit dollars, regional agencies also are providing a growing pool of funds for neighborhood planning and, more recently, other infrastructure. This year, the pool of available funds for TOD planning grants available from the Metropolitan Transportation Commission to the Bay Area cities is expected to grow to over $60 million.

Dozens of cities have taken advantage of grants available from regional agencies for TOD planning and, in many cases, have subsequently partnered with ULI San Francisco to receive advice for ULI technical assistance panels. ULI San Francisco has brought private sector expertise to planning for 25 transit stations in the Bay Area, helping cities create both well-designed and economically feasible plans. The results of these technical assistance panels is shared at ULI San Francisco's annual TOD MarketPlace, which for the past four years has brought cities and developers together to share expertise in transit-oriented development.

The Bay Area's regional agencies also launched a voluntary program in 2007 to encourage cities to designate priority development and conservation areas, and have targeted these areas for infrastructure investment and other funding. Though the Bay Area regional agencies do not have as much land use authority as that granted some regional agencies, such as Portland's Metro, this incentive program is a way to nudge local jurisdictions in the direction of smart growth. And it has had some encouraging results: 50 cities in the Bay Area have designated 100 priority development areas within their jurisdictions. These efforts are consistent with the recently passed state Senate Bill 375, which calls for each California region to create a Sustainable Communities Strategy to help the state meet Governor Arnold Schwarzenegger's goals for reducing of carbon dioxide emissions. TransForm was instrumental in the passage of this statewide legislation.

TransForm also is engaged on a grassroots level with faith-based, neighborhood, social justice, and environmental groups to build a YIMBY—yes-in-my-backyard—constituency for smart growth. Called the Great Communities Collaborative, this effort targets transit-rich neighborhoods with significant potential for infill development.

Carpools and Car Sharing

In the 1990s period leading up to a TOD-focused regional policy, a number of local entrepreneurial alternatives to automobile dependency appeared in the Bay Area.

For instance, Critical Mass rides, monthly bicycle rides that began in San Francisco in 1992, see thousands of cyclists take over city streets as a monthly reminder of pre-automobile life. Critical Mass rides now take place in 300 cities around the world.

Another example of Bay Area organized chaos is the system of casual carpools—informal carpools that form when drivers pick up passengers, without specific previous arrangement, at designated locations for a ride from the East Bay to San Francisco. Drivers benefit from being able to avoid tolls when crossing the Bay Bridge in the carpool lane, and riders get a free ride to work. Though it is not run by any organization or authority, the Bay Area's casual carpool system has evolved to include over 30 pickup sites with tens of thousands of daily participants. Here, as in other metropolitan areas including Washington, D.C., casual carpooling has worked for several decades in compliance with a few simple social norms that have evolved among drivers and passengers.

Another innovative transportation solution born in San Francisco is City CarShare. Working with the city and the San Francisco Planning and Urban Research Association, Bay Area transit activists in 2001 created the nonprofit City CarShare service, based on European models, allowing members to have access to an automobile while avoiding the high fixed costs of car ownership. The fully automated, pay-as-you-go approach results in less driving and lower costs, as well as fewer cars in the city. The program, which is being replicated across the country, now serves 15,000 members with 350 cars in San Francisco and the East Bay. With car sharing available in nearly every neighborhood in the city, San Francisco's private car ownership rates hover at just 60 percent of the population, lower than all other major

U.S. cities except New York City. Many developers include City CarShare pods as a strategy for attracting tenants.

Even before the regional focus on planning and the capital costs of transit, several cities in the Bay Area were pursuing major TOD projects. San Jose has grown from a small town in the early 20th century to the region's largest city, reaching a population of 1 million in 2008. While much of San Jose has developed in a suburban land use pattern, leaders have made recent significant investments in transit and higher-density TOD, including many new miles of light rail.

Another urbanizing suburb, Hayward in the East Bay, has encouraged development near its BART station since the mid–1990s. New development has helped revitalize a struggling community and increased tax revenues.

The combination of a smart growth movement and regional leadership has resulted in the Bay Area recently spending a larger percentage of its transportation dollars on transit than any other region of the country. While development has long been overwhelmingly low density and automobile oriented, the Bay Area has a history of grassroots movements and policy leadership to draw upon to meet the ecological, economic, and social challenges of the 21st century through transportation innovation and compact land use patterns.

Chapter 49

Mass Transit Systems Are Expanding into the Suburbs

Ellen Dunham-Jones *and* June Williamson

The dearth of good, cheap, undeveloped sites in suburban markets, the escalating number of vacant greyfield properties, and the expansion of mass transit systems into suburban areas are all factoring into a changed American suburban market.

The recession has brought the 50-year expansion of suburban development patterns to a halt. It also is accelerating the trend to retrofit, reinhabit, and "regreen" the rising numbers of dead malls, dying office parks, and other declining suburban properties. While no one likes to see businesses fail, redevelopment of these sites to respond to new suburban demographics, rising transportation costs, and infrastructure investments provides the opportunity to transform the most automobile-dependent landscapes into more sustainable, more urban places. The big development project for the next 50 years likely will be retrofitting suburbia.

Some of the changes will be incremental—a change of use here, a new street or building there, much as one sees in the "incremental urbanism" that characterizes the perception of how the world's great cities evolved over time. However, American suburban development patterns are so highly specialized for single uses that their layouts

are resistant to incremental adaptation. Consequently, the most effective redevelopments will be those that retrofit the streets, blocks, and lots to provide a compact, connected, walkable mix of uses and housing types. Unfortunately, projects at this scale often evoke criticism as "instant cities" or "faux urbanism." The challenge for all involved is to provide settings and buildings that transcend their "instant" status and inspire their communities.

The global urgency of reducing greenhouse gases provides the most time-sensitive imperative for reshaping sprawl development patterns, for converting areas that now foster the largest per-capita carbon footprints into more sustainable, less automobile-dependent places. The transformation of aging and underperforming shopping centers, office parks, garden apartment complexes, and other prototypical large suburban properties into more urban places allows new population growth to be redirected from metropolitan greenfield edges into more central grey-field sites where vehicles-miles traveled (VMT) can be reduced. It also allows for consideration of how redeveloped suburban areas collectively add up to "incremental metropolitanism" at a scale far more capable of confronting the

Originally published as "Retrofitting Suburbia," *Urban Land*, Vol. 68, No. 6 (June 2009), by the Urban Land Institute, Washington, D.C. Copyright, the Urban Land Institute, all rights reserved. Reprinted with permission.

problems of sprawl than is incremental urbanism.

Many of the retrofits produced to date have in fact been incremental and indicative of both gradual demographic shifts and public efforts to induce change. For instance, the original Levittowns have added not only countless additions to individual houses, but also multiunit housing for seniors as inhabitants have aged. A decade after Boulder, Colorado, revised zoning and setback regulations along suburban arterials, new mixed-use buildings with sidewalk cafés appear cheek by jowl with older carpet-supply stores set behind large parking lots.

Similarly, numerous older retail buildings have been adapted for community-serving purposes. More than a dozen Wal-Mart stores have been converted to churches. La Grande Orange in Phoenix is a reborn strip mall containing locally owned restaurants and shops that have become so popular that La Grande Orange has its own T-shirts and is regularly mentioned as a selling point in real estate ads for the neighborhood. An L-shaped mini-mall was made into the award-winning Camino Nuevo Charter Academy elementary school in Los Angeles. The addition of sidewalks and previous public green space figured into the transformation of a grocery store into a public library in Denton, Texas, and conversion of a Super Kmart into a megachurch in Woodstock, Georgia. Many other vacant big-box stores, malls, and shopping centers have been converted to office space, health care facilities, and civic space— including the headquarters for Hormel Foods, which includes the Spam Museum in a former Kmart in Austin, Minnesota, and the revival of Crestwood Court Mall in St. Louis by artist, theater, and dance groups as ArtSpace. Sometimes, the best approach to a dead retail site is to return it to nature, as in the reconstructed wetland that replaced a failed strip shopping center in Phalen Village, Minnesota, or the proposed park on the site

of the Columbus City Center mall in Columbus, Ohio. Countless additional examples of this kind of recycling exist, showing welcome improvements to the physical and social infrastructure.

However, retrofitting's greater potential goes well beyond incremental adaptive use or renovation. Through urbanization of larger suburban properties with a denser, walkable, synergistic mix of uses and housing types, more significant reductions in carbon emissions, gains in social capital and public health, and changes to systemic growth patterns can be achieved.

Mixed-use new urbanist greyfield retrofits routinely achieve projections of 25 to 30 percent internal trip capture rates, and substantially higher performance has been measured in recent studies. Belmar, a dead mall retrofit in Lakewood, Colorado, tripled density on its 100-acre (40-ha) site but did not require a single new traffic signal on surrounding streets. Such capturing of internal trips is dependent on achieving the critical mass associated with instant cities, not with incremental changes to the suburban pattern.

The most dramatic and prevalent retrofits tend to be on dead mall sites— retrofits such as Belmar; Mizner Park in Boca Raton, Florida; and Santana Row in San Jose, California. Each replaced a typical low-rise shopping mall surrounded by parking lots with a more or less interconnected, walkable street grid, lushly planted public spaces, and ground-level retail space topped by two to eight stories of offices and residences. In Denver alone, eight of the region's 13 malls have undergone or announced plans for retrofitting. There are also, however, significant retrofits on the land adjacent to thriving malls. The retrofit of Downtown Kendall/Dadeland outside Miami incorporates a mall (the Dadeland Mall) and new 20-plus-story residential towers, as does Perimeter Place adjacent to Perimeter Center Mall in Atlanta. Both are examples of how 30-year-old edge cities, even bête noire Tysons

Corner, in northern Virginia, outside Washington, D.C., are being repositioned by infilling and urbanizing.

Suburban office and industrial parks are also being retrofitted. The parking lots of an Edward Durell Stone–designed office park of ten-story buildings in Hyattsville, Maryland, have been infilled with a new main street and a mix of uses to become University Town Center. The owners of a low-rise industrial park in Westwood, Massachusetts, are taking advantage of its location on a commuter rail line to redevelop it as Westwood Station, a four- to five-story live/work/shop transit-oriented development (TOD) and the largest suburban development project ever in Massachusetts. Golf courses, car dealerships, park-and-ride lots, garden apartment complexes, residential subdivisions, and entire commercial strip corridors are being retrofitted in ways that integrate rather than isolate uses and regenerate underperforming asphalt into urban neighborhoods.

What has been driving all this? Several factors: shrinking percentages of households with children and a growing market for multi-unit housing in the suburbs, an aging population, continued suburban job growth, regional growth patterns that have given leapfrogged suburban areas a new centrality, higher gasoline prices that have made closer-in living more attractive, and local smart growth policies and transit investments that are limiting sprawl and redirecting growth to existing infrastructure. The dearth of good, cheap, undeveloped sites in suburban markets, the escalating number of vacant greyfield properties, and the expansion of mass transit systems into suburban areas are all factoring into a changed American suburban market.

Collectively, these market forces and policies are enabling implementation of the principal benefit of projects like these: the retrofitting of the underlying layout of the streets, blocks, and lots so as to change unhealthy suburban patterns and behaviors into

more sustainable ones. Incremental infill within as-of-right zoning in most suburban municipalities is simply not a feasible path toward achieving diversification or densification.

The larger, denser, and more urban the redevelopment, the greater the ability of its designers to change the existing development pattern and do the following:

- reduce vehicle-miles traveled and improve public health by creating a transit-served or transit-ready mix of uses in a walkable street pattern connected to adjacent uses;
- reduce land consumption and per-capita costs of public investment by absorbing growth that, without alternatives, would expand in sprawl and edgeless cities;
- increase the feasibility and efficiency of transit;
- increase local interconnectivity;
- add permeable surfaces and green space;
- add public and civic space;
- increase choice in housing type and affordability;
- increase diversification of the tax base; and
- establish an urban node within a polycentric region.

The key design challenge in altering the suburban settlement structure is internal and external integration of the parts over time and over multiple parcels. Research has yet to uncover built examples of connected culs-de-sac—a longstanding holy grail of suburban reform—or other perfectly seamless transitions between properties. But designers are producing innovative adaptations to zoning and subdivision regulations to overcome suburban fragmentation.

For example, Michael Gamble and Jude LeBlanc, professors at the Georgia Institute of Technology, have proposed trading the right to build liner buildings within the front setback along arterials for giving up half the width of a new street on the side setback as a means to gradually establish a finer-grained street and pedestrian network on suburban superblocks. Similarly, Elizabeth Plater-Zyberk, a partner in the Miami-based town planning firm Duany Plater-Zyberk & Co., and Victor Dover and Joseph Kohl, partners in the urban design firm Dover Kohl & Partners in Coral Gables, Florida, have developed a strategy for linking open spaces within a walkable street grid through the superblocks of Downtown Kendall/Dadeland's 324 acres (131 ha). Working for Miami-Dade County on new zoning across numerous parcels, they devised a system of anchor points at the corners of property boundaries to which each owner's mandated 15 percent of open space had to connect. Their suggested, rather than mandated, shapes of public space have been substantially followed by property owners and are far more appropriately sized to the development as a whole than a series of uncoordinated 15 percent bits would have been.

Internal integration of parts is indeed far easier to control on single-parcel sites—especially sites of 30 acres (12 ha) or more. Projects as small as 15 acres (6 ha), such as San Diego's Uptown District on the site of a former Sears store, can transform the character of suburban areas and generate local input concerning further changes. But larger parcels can more easily justify the inclusion of public space, decked parking, and a fine-grained street network on suburban superblocks. Large sites are also more likely than small ones to be able and/or required to include housing for a mix of incomes.

This has not been universally achieved—witness the exclusively high-end residences at Santana Row or exclusively lower-end apartments at CityCenter Englewood in Englewood, Colorado—but projects like Mizner Park, Belmar, and Addison Circle in Addison, Texas, provide a range of housing types, tenures, and costs. While they do not contain the social and physical diversity of incremental cities, the degree of internal integration, diversification, and densification of these instant cities deserves commendation.

Large, single-parcel projects also foster integration external to the property. By forcing municipalities to address rezoning and use tax-increment financing to provide infrastructure upgrades for the new density, larger projects are gradually reforming the regulations and financing practices that otherwise continue to favor sprawl. Large projects in particular increase a municipality's experience with mixed uses, mixed incomes, shared parking, form-based codes, context-sensitive street standards, transfers of development rights, and other regulations that encourage urban development patterns. As a result, one successful retrofit tends to breed another.

At the same time, the financing community is gaining experience with evaluating mixed-use public/private deals. Gradually, the financial performances of large projects are providing the predictable metrics that lenders require to offer the most competitive rates not only to conventional suburban development, but also to urbanizing redevelopment, increasing the feasibility of including affordable housing. Evidence of the magnitude of change in the rules of the game is that big players have now stepped onto the field. Mall owner General Growth Properties added high-end housing to its mall in Natick, Massachusetts, and was retrofitting the Cottonwood Mall outside Salt Lake City to serve as a town center before problems with commercial mortgage-backed securities loans forced it into bankruptcy.

By 2005, recognition of the changed market led many of the country's high-production single-family-home residential builders to start "urban" divisions offering lofts, yoga studios, and billiards lounges. Not surprisingly, these divisions have been the best performers while the rest of the housing market has tanked.

On the one hand, the urban divisions of K. Hovnanian Homes, KB Homes, and Toll

Brothers, along with compact urban retail formats by Wal-Mart, Target, and Home Depot, are a promising indication that even the big guns are recognizing both the market for and the benefits of urbanism. The impact could be enormous if the new divisions perform well enough to shift these companies' focus away from spreading unwalkable, single-use suburban formats across the country. Combining affordability with urbanism in new construction, whether in new developments or redevelopments, has been difficult, and the expertise of these companies in providing affordable products should be welcomed. On the other hand, their highly repetitive and uninspiring "instant architecture"—a problem they are not alone in creating—is less welcome.

One way to enhance the character and diversity of retrofits is to take advantage of the unique opportunities for adaptive use in redevelopment. Although most aging low-rise suburban buildings lack the systems or construction quality to merit restoration, the most distinctive retrofits tend to creatively retain at least some buildings. Surrey Central City outside Vancouver, British Columbia, revived a mall by grafting a new five-story galleria of university classrooms on top. The multistory department store buildings of several dead mall retrofits have been converted to housing, offices, and city halls.

As counters to "instant architecture," these legacies contribute a sense of history, diversity, affordability, and a reduction of waste. The resulting quirks contribute enormously to the creativity and quality of the place making. They can also insert a cool factor to suburban places. Upper Rock in Rockville, Maryland, and Cloud 9 Sky Flats in Minnetonka, Minnesota, incorporates modern loft conversions of suburban office buildings.

Bit by bit, beneath the static image of uniform tract houses, many suburbs are undergoing significant physical, social, and cul-tural change—not all of it positive. For the first time in history, suburban municipalities now house more people living in poverty than central cities do. Maps showing recent mortgage foreclosures concentrated in the newer outermost suburbs indicate the likelihood of further decentralization of poverty and an ever-shifting terrain.

On the physical side, several aging garden apartment complexes have been retrofitted and entire post–World War II subdivisions in suburban Washington, D.C., and Atlanta have been bought up house by house. One subdivision in Atlanta even self-organized and put itself up for sale for redevelopment. New transit systems, infrastructure improvements, programs to fund planning studies, regulations allowing accessory dwelling units, and new overlay zoning district designations are providing further incentives for suburban urbanization.

But all this has not been happening everywhere. It has been happening at specific nodes and along specific corridors, generally where the transportation infrastructure—usually with some improvements—can support it. The outer rings of new exurban expansion continue to be low density overall, but the densified retrofits and countless revitalized small-town main streets are joining the edge cities as increasingly significant suburban activity centers. Arthur C. Nelson of the University of Utah estimates that 2.8 million acres (1.1 million ha) of greyfields will become available in the next 15 years. If only one quarter is redeveloped into mixed-use centers, it has the potential to supply half the housing required by 2030. As a result, the regional pattern emerging and likely to become more prominent is increasingly polycentric.

While development has indeed been decentralizing away from central cities, it also has been recentralizing around new and existing suburban centers—and becoming more sustainable in the process. More bottom up than top down, these new instant cities are demonstrations of an incremental metropolitanism. While it is fair to fault instant cities when their replication of incremental urbanism is unsatisfying, the more relevant issue today is how well each contributes to retrofitting the larger systems of sprawl.

One of the first steps is to recognize the inefficiencies of sprawl development. Most lower-priced houses are at the outer edges, but come with higher transportation costs that increasingly wipe out the savings gained. Jobs and retail space are located along arterials, but typically with little transit access. Thoroughfares designed for high-speed travel between centers have become so lined with uses that they do not work well for either access or mobility. Everything is designed in isolated pods. Even larger retrofits run the risk of becoming stand-alone fragments unless their urban structure integrates them into both local networks and larger sustainable systems. Only as nodes of a polycentric metropolis can they contribute to regional efficiencies in transit and other civil infrastructure, per-capita land and energy conservation, shorter commute distances, lower housing and transportation costs, a jobs/housing balance, and specialized labor agglomeration.

The inclusion of increasingly significant amounts of office space within mixed-use retrofits is particularly important for balancing polycentric growth and reducing VMT. Twinbrook Station in Rockville, Maryland, and Lindbergh City Center in Atlanta are integrating 12- and 14-story corporate office buildings onto the sites of former park-and-ride lots. SkySong in Phoenix and Surrey Central City are building incubator office space for Arizona State University and Simon Fraser University, respectively, on the site of a dead shopping center and a mall's parking lot.

Transit is especially critical in the effort to network nodes into a metropolitan area–wide economy and system. Unfortunately, most potential retrofit sites are not on transit lines. While retrofitting them can still enhance local conditions and reduce automobile dependency, the larger challenge is connecting retrofits to each other to achieve the benefits of a more sustainable metropolis.

There are two principal strategies for "connecting the dots." The first is to extend transit to improve suburban access, encourage even greater differentiation between nodes, and reduce VMT. The planned extension of Metrorail through Tysons Corner is an example of this strategy and reveals the high cost and design difficulties of inserting stations and TODs into an edge city not planned for them.

The hope is that densification of enough retrofitted sites will make suburban transit feasible. However, the track record so far indicates that more often transit in the suburbs is what makes densification feasible. In fact, examination of over 80 retrofits reveals that the arrival of a rail system is one of the strongest triggers for large-scale suburban redevelopment. In addition to Washington, D.C., the availability (or construction) of rail transit in Boston, Dallas, Denver, Los Angeles, and Phoenix has stimulated suburban retrofitting at existing and proposed rail stations.

The second strategy for connecting the dots is to retrofit corridors themselves. The general argument is that if commercial strip corridors are made more attractive to and safer for pedestrians, they can better attract redevelopment. Cathedral City, California, converted four blocks of what had become a commercial strip corridor back into its downtown by retrofitting it into a multiway boulevard. Palm-lined medians separate the high-speed traffic from slower local traffic and wide sidewalks. Now serving as the town's main street, the retrofitted corridor has attracted upscale hotels, shops, and housing to join the new city hall on a site that would not previously have been considered attractive.

A more incremental approach for retrofitting corridors is being pursued on Columbia Pike by Arlington County, Virginia. A form-based code with fast permitting and the promise of a streetcar are the incentives for its ongoing redevelopment of low-rise supermarkets and strip malls into six- to ten-story mixed-use buildings.

One of the newest strategies for retrofitting corridors is to expand the network efficiency of the local streets surrounding arterial roads. Virginia's new state law requiring connectivity between subdivisions is intended to allow local roads to handle many more local trips so that the arterials can function more efficiently as the links between metropolitan nodes.

So how well do instant cities and suburban retrofits live up to their sustainable aspirations? Each case is unique and merits consideration of at least the following questions:

• At metropolitan and regional scales, does the project make it easier for people to have access to jobs, affordable housing, and affordable transportation while simultaneously reducing VMT and carbon footprints? Or is it gentrifying an important remnant of an affordable landscape and/or draining an existing downtown?

• Are there tangible means, such as transfer of development rights, to link densification at targeted nodes with equally targeted land conservation elsewhere? Or are developers getting a free ride as local communities get overburdened with traffic and displacement, and the region as a whole benefits little?

• At the local scale, does the settlement have an urban structure that supports interconnectivity, density, transit, and walkability? Has it triggered further redevelopment?

• Will its design and mix of uses improve with age and endure, or will it remain a fragment of drive-to walkable "product" with a life span driven by its retail and limited to the fashionability of its scenography?

• At the building scale, does it offer a variety of housing choices to accommodate a diverse population with varied needs and ideas about public and private space, or are the choices too similar and the expectations of behavior too conformist?

These questions will be at the heart of local and metropolitan politics as people move beyond debates of sprawl versus smart growth and tackle the thorny specifics of implementing real change. In many respects, the even more difficult assessment is determining how well instant cities and suburban retrofits live up to their urban aspirations. It is easy to compare them to "real" cities and find them lacking the culture, excitement, diversity, conflict, grit, and suffering that coexist in core cities. But this misses the point. Instant cities and suburban retrofits are not core cities. They are urban nodes within a new polycentric metropolis that simultaneously complement the core city's downtown and serve a predominantly suburban population. They are hybrids and reflect aspects of both centeredness and decentralization.

This hybrid nature is revealed in many ways, including the following:

• suburban parking ratios and urban streetscapes;

• ambiguous "public" spaces developed in public/ private partnerships and privately owned or leased;

• populations that are more diverse than stereotypical suburbs but less diverse than stereotypical cities;

• new, single-ownership parcels deliberately masked to look old and multiparceled;

• urban qualities delivered at suburban costs;

• transit orientation and automobile dependency; and

• the appearance of local town centers and reliance on larger networks of users, tenants, funders, and designers.

Hybrid network nodes are neither suburban nor urban. As a result, they are prone to critique from the advocates of both better-understood categories. But are cities and suburbs really so different in the polycentric metropolis? The old dichotomy of suburb versus city as the separation of home and work was always oversimplified. Today, it is further complicated by continued metropolitan decentralization, new forces of recentralization, the replication of national retailers throughout, and the extended networks afforded by global communications.

More than 60 percent of U.S. metropolitan office space is now in the suburbs, but many of the same metropolitan regions seeing the most retrofitting in suburban contexts are also seeing population growth in their central cities. Post–World War II suburbs originally built at the edges of the metropolis have been so surpassed by new growth, often losing property value in the process, that they now enjoy relatively central locations. New instant cities exploit those centralities and activate them as metropolitan nodes in a network increasingly reinforced by mass transit. Retrofitting ushers in networked urbanity in which living, working, shopping, and playing are no longer separated—but neither are they entirely conjoined.

The networked urbanity of metropolitanism reinterprets the Aristotelian ideal of the city—living together well—at the larger scale. This bodes well for confronting the challenges of economic and environmental sustainability but is less promising for dealing with entrenched social inequity.

Although instant cities and suburban retrofits are neither as sustainable nor as urban as older established cities, they are more sustainable and more urban than the conditions they have replaced. As such, they have great potential to reshape the metropolis—while encouraging the planting of trees on former parking lots rather than chopping them down at the metropolitan fringes.

Retrofits also face many challenges, including addressing gentrification, producing architecture that lives up to cultural aspirations, and constructing the infrastructure to support the changes. Communities interested in retrofitting should revise their zoning codes and regulations to support mixed uses and higher densities while seeking means to invest in transit boulevards and public parking garages to stimulate private redevelopment. Similarly, those not familiar with the complexities of mixed-use redevelopment need to expand their skill sets—and their imaginations.

As the country looks ahead to recovery from this recession, it is clear that public/private partnerships at a multitude of scales—national, state, and local—will be needed more than ever to collectively take on the challenges and opportunities to retrofit suburbia.

Chapter 50

The Design and Usage of Public Streets Is Changing

Seth Ullman

The needs of our communities evolve over time, and our street design should, too. That's the idea behind "rightsizing streets"—reconfiguring the layout of our streets to better serve the people who use them, whether they're commuters driving, shoppers walking, or children bicycling. Across the country, communities large and small are achieving impressive safety, mobility, and community outcomes by implementing such reconfigurations. Project for Public Spaces created this rightsizing resource to highlight the accomplishments of these communities and share best practices. Our transportation staff can advise stakeholders and decision-makers, skillfully facilitate a rightsizing process, and adeptly produce right sized designs for agencies and community groups.

What is "Rightsizing" a Street?

Rightsizing is the process of reallocating a street's space to better serve its full range of users. Picture a four-lane road that was built thirty years ago in an undeveloped area, but that now has housing, shops, and an elementary school in close vicinity. The needs of the community surrounding that road have changed over three decades—and the design of that road may need to change to meet those needs as well. It may need sidewalks or a median to help people cross safely, or on-street parking for folks who want to frequent local shops, or other safety features to prevent injuries. Rightsizing a road can encompass a broad array of redesign measures, and should always be sensitive to context and the vision of the local community, but often involves some or all of the following goals and strategies:

Typical Goals—

- Increasing safety and access for all users
- Encouraging walking, biking, and transit use
- Supporting businesses and the local economy
- Creating places that foster community livability

Typical Strategies—

- Converting vehicle travel lanes to other uses
- Narrowing vehicle lanes
- Adding bike lanes
- Improving pedestrian infrastructure
- Changing parking configurations
- Adding roundabouts and medians

Originally published as "Rightsizing Streets," *Resources/References—Rightsizing* (December 2013), by the Project for Public Spaces, New York, New York. Reprinted with permission of the publisher.

Street rightsizing projects are sometimes called "road diets," or "Complete Streets," but rightsizing also describes street redesigns that might be considered outside of those frameworks.

Communities and transportation departments around the country are successfully implementing street rightsizing projects, with impressive results. Collecting before-and-after data about key issues like safety, mode splits, and mobility is crucial to ensuring that these projects meet their communities' needs and stated goals. Each case study in this resource includes before-and-after results.

Rightsizing: Transforming a Street to a Place

Rightsizing a street is often a prerequisite to the street becoming a place where people want to be, instead of just a corridor to pass through. Rightsizing reconfigures a street to best serve the people who need to use it, whether they're drivers, pedestrians, or bicyclists. By improving safety, especially for people walking or biking, and by increasing space devoted to people, rightsizing projects cause vehicles to slow down and people to spend more time outside on the street. This is great for people who live in the street's vicinity, businesses that line it, and those who travel through it.

The most common type of street rightsizing converts a two-way four-lane street to a three lane street. Removing one of the vehicle lanes can free up space to add or expand pedestrian, bicycle infrastructure, and on-street parking, or other uses. A right-sized three-lane street commonly has one traffic lane and one bicycle lane in each direction, with a shared two-way left hand turn lane in the center that allows cars in both directions to make a left. These changes help make a street better for the range of people using it, typically without restricting vehicle volumes or lengthening travel times.

However, many other street changes could compose a rightsizing project. For instance, on Prospect Park West, in Brooklyn, a one-way three-lane street was converted to a two lane street with a protected bike lane, and The Porch in Philadelphia converted unnecessary parking to a successful public space.

Rightsizing works. Our case studies highlight these projects' positive impacts, and significant academic research confirms that vehicle lanes can be converted to other purposes to achieve safety goals without negative transportation impacts. Rightsizing enables mobility for all users, increases safety for all users, and can contribute to the vitality of communities. The Strategies Glossary includes research describing the positive effects of many of the most common rightsizing strategies.

Rightsizing facilitates street safety. Traffic calming improves safety by reducing dangerous driving speeds and movements. Speeding vehicles are exponentially more dangerous than vehicles traveling at appropriate speeds. Over 80 percent of pedestrians hit by vehicles traveling 40 miles per hour die, compared to less than 10 percent that are hit at vehicles traveling 20 miles per hour. Dedicated pedestrian and bicycle infrastructure also improves street safety.

Rightsizing improves street access for pedestrians by increasing safety and appeal. All transportation trips at least start and end as pedestrian trips, regardless of the intermediate mode. Making these trips safer and more enjoyable for people is crucial for communities' physical health, the cultivation of public spaces, and the success of street-fronted businesses. Not all transportation modes are created equal. Each has its own advantages in terms of safety, cost, efficiency, speed, and inclusivity. When redesigning a street, it is vital to prioritize designs that enable safe mobility for particularly vulnerable users, such as children and elderly pedestrians.

Project for Public Spaces often encourages rightsizing to enable community-driven placemaking, and created this resource to encourage best practices and to raise awareness of rightsizing's benefits for communities and for cities' most common public space—the street.

EDITORS' NOTE

The Project for Public Spaces' website (http://www.pps.org/) has additional information concerning the best practices for placemaking being used to improve neighborhoods in cities throughout the world.

The following information is provided about this chapter to facilitate future research on this timely and important topic.

For more information about the rightsizing of public streets, including commonly acceptable methods of measurement, please check-out their website noted above. The glossary of rightsizing strategies on this website includes a comprehensive list of definitions and appropriate background internet links.

For further reading on rightsizing from national and international professional associations, please check-out their website. The appropriate links to these organizations are noted for future reference.

This article also listed an acknowledgment at the end, noting the following information.

Special thanks to the Anne T. & Robert M. Bass Foundation for their support as well as the Congress for the New Urbanism, Daniel Gallagher of Charlotte, Jeffery Arms of Orlando, Brian Dougherty of Seattle, and many more for their expertise and consultation. If you have a case study or other input to improve our resources on rightsizing streets, please email transportation@pps.org with "rightsizing" in the subject line.

Chapter 51

New Ways of Measuring Streets

Polly Trottenberg

New York City's streets are constantly called on to the meet new and varied needs of a growing, dynamic, 21st Century city—and to do this in a complex environment where there is little opportunity to expand the existing footprint. How do city leaders address these challenges and measure their success? This report discusses key approaches to street design projects, and how results can be measured against goals for safety, serving all users and creating great public spaces while also maintaining the flow of traffic. Using a cross-section of recent NYCDOT street design projects, this report details the metrics NYCDOT uses to evaluate street projects, and illustrates how measuring results can show progress toward safe, sustainable, livable and economically competitive streets. (NYCDOT means New York City Department of Transportation)

Cities need to set new goals for their streets if they are to meet the needs of a dynamic and growing city and address the problems of vehicle crashes, traffic congestion, poor-performing bus and bike networks, and environments that are inhospitable for pedestrians. New York has been able to transform our streets by blending new technologies with time-tested tools to create 21st Century Streets for all users.

The projects described in this report demonstrate this approach. The metrics shown here track the success of these projects, inform the design of future projects and are vital to building public support for world-class streets.

Designing for Safer Streets

(Safe and attractive options for all users)

The City's streets are unique because of the mix of people using the same space. Planning for safety, which is at the heart of every DOT initiative, means helping pedestrians, motorists, bus riders, and cyclists coexist safely. Here our focus has been on organizing the different streams of traffic—by simplifying intersections; by creating dedicated lanes for turning drivers and for cyclists; and by setting aside signal time and safe space for crossing pedestrians.

Building Great Public Places

(Economic value and neighborhood vitality)

New York's streets serve more functions than simply moving people and goods. In such a densely populated city, the streets and sidewalks are places to congregate, relax, and enjoy being out in public.

We have focused on creating great pub-

Originally published as *Measuring the Street: New Metrics for 21st Century Streets* (2012), by the Department of Public Transportation, City of New York, New York. Reprinted with permission of the publisher.

lic spaces that serve individuals and groups large and small. Local organizations that maintain and program our public spaces help us ensure that these spaces will remain functional and useful for all users.

Improving Bus Service

(Rapid transit beyond the subway)

Even though most New Yorkers use mass transit every day, the city's buses are the slowest in North America. In partnership with MTA New York City Transit, DOT has introduced a new level of bus service, Select Bus Service (SBS), to some of the city's busiest corridors. SBS includes off-board fare payment, three-door boarding to reduce boarding time; red bus lanes and Transit Signal Priority (TSP) to keep buses moving; and new shelters, buses, and bus bulbs to improve the passenger experience. SBS projects also include features to enhance pedestrian, cyclist, and traffic flow and safety.

Reducing Delay and Speeding

(Faster, safer travel)

Streets that work for traffic have less congestion and more reliable travel times. Improving traffic flow need not come at the expense of safety, however. Organizing traffic, simplifying complicated intersections, and optimizing signals can reduce peak congestion, but also prevent speeding at other times. We have combined roadway markings, geometric changes, and signal timing to manage traffic safely—reducing congestion but also controlling excessive speeds.

Efficiency in Parking and Loading

(Improving access to businesses and neighborhoods)

Curb frontage is a scarce resource in New York. At the curb, drivers need to park, buses and taxis need to drop-off and pickup passengers, truckers need to load and unload freight, all without interfering with safe pedestrian, bicycle, and traffic flow. When curbs are congested, streets become congested. When curb space is available, the street works better for all users. We have used parking regulations and pricing (through our PARK Smart and commercial paid parking programs) to reduce the amount of time vehicles park, stand, or stop at the curb, so that space turns over for new users, and double parking is minimized. Reducing parking duration by 10–20 percent can have the same effect as creating hundreds of new parking spaces in a neighborhood, while improving traffic flow.

Street Redesign Inventory

Designing Safer Streets

Key Treatments
- Simplified intersections
- Dedicated left, right, and through lanes
- Pedestrian safety islands
- Protected bike lanes
- Leading pedestrian intervals and split phasing

Also Helpful
- Turn bans
- Mixing zones for bicycles and left-turning vehicles
- Medians
- Wide parking lanes
- Speed humps and slow zones

Building Great Public Spaces

Key Treatments
- Create new pedestrian plazas—first using temporary materials, later as capital projects
- Street furniture

- Seasonal seating platform in curbside lane
- Striping and planters
- Maintenance agreements with local organizations
- Programmed events

Also Helpful
- Simplified intersections

Improving Bus Service

Key Treatments
- Offset bus lanes
- Transit Signal Priority
- Bus bulbs
- Bus lane enforcement cameras

Also Helpful
- Pedestrian safety islands
- Turn lanes and turn bans
- Delivery windows

Reducing Delay and Speeding

Key Treatments
- Adaptive signal control
- Signal optimization

- Dedicated left, right, and through lanes
- Simplified intersections
- Neighborhood Slow Zones

Also Helpful
- Protected bicycle lanes
- Pedestrian safety islands
- Wide parking lanes

Efficiency in Parking and Loading

Key Treatments
- PARK Smart
- Commercial Paid Parking Delivery Windows
- Muni meters

Also Helpful
- Offset bus lanes

Chapter 52

Financial Options to Pay for the Public Infrastructure

Jonathan D. Miller

Funding U.S. infrastructure will cost big bucks—money for which federal, state, and local governments have not yet adequately planned or budgeted. So where will they find it? There is a list of familiar revenue sources: income, sales, and property taxes; user fees such as tolls, subway fares, and water bills; developer impact fees; bond issues funded by user fees and general tax revenues; and various forms of public/private partnerships (PPPs) financed by all of the above. But no matter the structure or method, taxpayers, users, and businesses will pay the way and assessments will increase, in some cases substantially. The payback should devolve to future generations, including improved economic productivity and enhanced lifestyles as the country accommodates tens of millions of new residents.

Sound vision and integrated planning will be necessary to help find efficiencies and solutions. Increasingly, economists, academics, and planners argue that those who use infrastructure should pay for it as a way to help orient consumers to the most cost-effective and sound lifestyle and business practices. Bond issues remain politically palatable since costs get pushed into the future, arguably paid for over time by people who are getting the benefits. General revenue taxes hold some favor among

politicians looking to spread the pain and limit fallout from large segments of aggrieved users, but that may mean cutbacks in favored categories like schools and police as well as some other tough policy calculations.

Privatization Wave

Gaining traction as of late, U.S. state and local governments are examining using private investors to build, manage, and/or operate infrastructure assets, particularly toll roads, bridges, and tunnels. "Privatization models can strengthen city or state balance sheets in the short run, redeploy equity locked in assets, access private sector skill sets, and often better management practices." Depending on transaction structures and stipulations, governments gain cash infusions and/or share in future revenues. In addition, they can transfer project and operating risks over to private entities, which are incentivized to manage facilities cost effectively within strictures designed for meeting the public good. If cost overruns hit the tunnel project or new school construction, for example, the private companies and/or investors—rather than taxpayers—pick up the tab. They also must maintain the facility to a certain standard over the life of the contract. "The major benefit for governments is risk transfer and that can be huge."

Private concession operations also tout their incentives to improve service and increase public use, thereby driving up their returns—these efficiencies save money for everyone. "We're in the service business," says a toll road investment manager. "We are in the business of saving time and making roads run better so more people will use them and benefit. The public sector is shackled—workers get no upside bonuses for changing practices, they stick with the status quo, and so the public doesn't gain improvements."

Privatizing infrastructure in the United States is nothing new—railroads, mass transit, telecommunications, and power systems traditionally have been developed and operated by publicly regulated private companies. Over the past two decades, a handful of toll roads has also been privatized, with about $25 billion worth of projects proposed or under development. More recently, a small group of airports has entered into retail management contracts with private operators, and increasing numbers of publicly owned water and wastewater systems are contracting with private providers for system operations and maintenance. But the United States trails other regions of the world, especially in transport-related privatization. In Europe, for instance, public/private partnerships have been building and operating toll roads since the 1970s. More recently, private companies have taken over airports and ports as well as school and hospital management. Public/private infrastructure transactions have been adopted widely in Australia, Canada, India, Asia, and South America.

Investment Funds Proliferate

New to the game is a raft of investment funds, sponsored by global investment banks, private equity firms, and institutional money managers, looking to place money from pension funds, insurance company general accounts, and high-net-worth clients into infrastructure investments. During the mid–1990s, Australian investment firms established the first of these funds, looking for new assets invest in after tapping out on local real estate, stocks, and bonds. The rise of private infrastructure investing in Australia notably coincided with reduced government spending (from 7.2 percent of gross domestic product [GOP] in 1970 to about 3.6 percent in 2006). In 2007, more than $30 billion of Australian infrastructure assets are held in publicly traded or listed entities. Various new global infrastructure funds have raised about $100 billion to invest in infrastructure assets with an initial focus on Europe, where public/private partnerships have been well established in many countries whose governments have sought alternative financing sources.

Fund marketers tout infrastructure as a "new asset class" offering secure, long-term cash flows, inflation protection, and opportunities for reducing overall portfolio volatility and risk. Funds tend to be highly diversified—"a broad basket of things" investing in economic infrastructure like toll roads, parking lots, power plants, water treatment facilities, and airports as well as social infrastructure, including hospitals, schools, and affordable housing. Portfolio managers may balance the known and predictable cash flows of existing infrastructure investments with investments in higher-risk/higher-return greenfield construction projects.

Attractive Returns

Mature infrastructure assets compare to core real estate, offering mid- to high-single-digit annualized returns, often from government-backed income on existing facilities. Pension funds and insurance companies gravitate to core-friendly, long-term lease terms with stable returns from toll roads or government contracts for managing schools and hospitals. These income flows can match up well to actuarial liabilities for retirees and life policies. Core-oriented portfolio managers have felt more confortable operating in western Europe, Canada, and Australia, where political stability, transparent regulatory environments, and rule of law are entrenched. But many of these markets "have been picked over," says a consultant. "It's hard to find deals for mature, core assets in Europe" and all the competition "has brought returns down."

Greenfield investments, meanwhile, match opportunistic real estate on the risk/return spectrum, potentially throwing off annualized gains in the high teens or above from redevelopment or development-style transactions. Investment banks tend to dominate the greenfield arena. Their typical game plans follow a private equity/initial public offering (IPO) model: leverage up equity investments, refinance the assets through bond issues or securitizations, and either sell stabilized assets as soon as possible to core funds and other investors or take the entities public. Transaction fees, leverage, and early sales can translate into big internal rates of return if projects work out, and refinancing strategies can reduce risk for equity investors, if deals sour. China, India, Russia, and other parts of eastern Europe start to draw more opportunistic players, who chance problematic political and regulatory landscapes with histories of corruption. But new highway construction in North America fits squarely in greenfield parameters.

Sandwiched between core and opportunistic categories, core-plus investments favor existing assets, which can be enhanced through operation improvements to produce more income—adding new toll lanes, reconfiguring airport concessions, etc. Private equity firms actively engage in these investments,

looking to provide a value-add through active management, and sharing in investment gains with investor and government partners.

Capturing U.S. Opportunities

Now, the global investment pipeline, flush with cash, eagerly and hopefully shifts some flows to the United States as Americans begin to realize the scope of future infrastructure requirements and size of funding shortfalls. "The best opportunities for mature assets are in North America" and "the [United States] has to do something—they have a need and there is a capital demand." U.S. legal transparency and political stability also attract portfolio managers and investors. In fact, U.S. markets seem receptive—28 of the 50 states have passed legislation enabling private market investment in infrastructure, but the floodgates have not opened yet.

"There's more dialogue with states and governments," says an investment banker looking to score deals. "You see some vibrancy in the market, lots of smoke, needs are great, but few bold strokes of action. So far there have been just five or six recent transport deals in the whole country and it's a big country." Grouses a frustrated investor: "There have been more deals done in Greece in the past five years than in the United States."

Proponents and Critics

Two recent highway concessions transactions on exiting toll roads—the sale of long-term leases for the Chicago Skyway and Indiana East-West Tollway—have attracted attention and elicited mixed reactions. Both deals scored large onetime payments to governments, raising questions about judicious appropriation of the proceeds. "The only reason to do PPP stuff should be to improve road quality and lower the cost of operations, not to get a pile of money. Done well, it could be a boon." Critics express discomfort over private entities having a monopoly on public thoroughfares with the right to raise tolls outside traditional public regulatory channels during lengthy lease terms (75 to 99 years). "Our studies show that the public is generally more comfortable with government controlling infrastructure assets," admits a fund manager.

Governors in Pennsylvania and New Jersey dither over whether to sell outright turnpike concessions to private operators given conflicted reactions to the Chicago and Indiana models. But observers expect that most new highway construction in many states will be funded by private managers gaining long-term toll concessions. To temper opposition, contracts will be structured to give states greater control over toll increases and allow revenue sharing in the event of windfall gains. States look at compensating private concessionaires through "availability payments" based on performance standards, including traffic volumes. "Part of the education process with the public will be to show that the government still has control to ensure that the asset is operated for the public good" and, most important, has retained some discretion over toll rates.

Sharks versus Bureaucrats

Political adversaries also raise fears over Wall Street hotshots taking government bureaucrats to the cleaners in structuring public/private partnerships. "Wall Street's best and brightest make deals happen and collect huge fees, but who can go toe to toe to protect the public's interest? Counters an investment manager: "Governments can call on outside advisers and consultants to deal with financial structuring and best practices."

Both sides struggle with how to struc-

ture deals. The early-on Dulles Greenway (in suburban northern Virginia) toll road transaction, completed in 1995, did not protect the concession operator from new road competition. When alternative free roads were constructed, toll road traffic volumes slowed well below operator profit targets. "You need to protect against competition in concession contracts," says a portfolio manager. But such covenants could preclude integrated regional transport strategies. Private operators have trouble anticipating traffic volumes on new roads without track records. Some deals can sour quickly if debt service targets are not met. Valuing assets and future cash flows can be problematic, and crystal balls cloud up when anticipating technological changes that could make concessions obsolete. Toll road operators roll the dice over the potential introduction of Jetsons-style space cars over the course of 75-year lease terms. "Gas prices could to the moon, too."

Governments, on the other hand, may undersell assets or make mistakes in concession agreements that saddle future administrations with losses. "But that happens all the time with public oversight—what about the Big Dig?" In the U.K. private finance initiative (PFI) process, the private sector "got knockdown prices in early transactions, but the public sector became more savvy and learned, negotiating clawback provisions and revenue sharing." France has courts to reopen contracts and modify terms, based on changed circumstances.

Need for Standards

Negotiating procurement and concession agreements can result in a tortured process. Private bidders complain about the lack of standardized forms and procedures across jurisdictions, which escalates cost in filing proposals and creates delays. In the U.K., the average tendering period for a PFI project is almost three years According to a National Audit Office (U.K.) audit, government departments underestimate the costs for legal and consultant services by an average of 75 percent. "Negotiating transactions is a work in progress. Everyone is learning lessons. The technology and practices are improving, but it's not perfect."

No Magic Solution

Investors emphasize that privatization "is not a panacea to the infrastructure crisis," rather "it's a financing tool." In reality, the nut of the road privatization discussion comes down to the need for increased user fees to pay infrastructure costs. Privatization does not create free money—the public still ends up with the bill. Sums up an investment manager: "The public needs new infrastructure for economic sustainability, the feds won't pay, locals don't want to raise taxes, bond issues are not as attractive, so the best alternative is toll roads and shifting risk by privatizing."

For politicians, privatizing roads provides some cover for instituting tolls or raising them. "They transfer the dirty work." Most tolls run by public authorities are "low-balled" for fear of voter retribution, and private operators can take the heat better for increases. "Private concessions seek to find the maximizing point" for expanding volumes at the highest possible tolls, figuring in congestion pricing mechanisms. "The dumbest thing you can do is raise tolls too high, become a political piñata, and lose volumes." Most concession agreements place caps on increases, but private operators want significant latitude to increase tolls beyond the typical comfort levels of governors and legislators. "The price of our inability to raise taxes or user fees for new infrastructure is turning responsibility over to the private sector." The good news is the pricing system will provide "truer costs for infrastructure" with prices "the market will bear,

not at prices where politicians think will help them win votes."

Blind Eye to the Big Picture

Not surprisingly, the wave of infrastructure fund managers and investment bankers focuses on finding and negotiating their next deals, working through encyclopedic agreements with their government counterparts. Integrated transport and land use policy remains safely off their radar screens, unless something might affect a noncompete clause. Some interviewees from the investment side react quizzically to the topic of intermodal planning and regional infrastructure master plans. "Government must remain in the driver's seat setting policy—that's not our job." But government leaders do not necessarily connect privatization to broader infrastructure planning either, seeking money instead for one-off projects or to fill budget gaps. "It's discouraging to see dollars pushed around Wall Street, handing out highway assets to private companies without looking at how these roads integrate with mass transit and future needs, redesigning development around interchanges, and building more high-rise, pedestrian-friendly communities," says a planning consultant.

"The privatization process should be wrapped up in smart growth initiatives. To make it work for more responsible land use, funds should be allocated to various integrated transportation projects. Otherwise, privatization just means more money for more roads for more cars." "The jury is out on privatization benefits. Clearly, private owners are interest in increasing volumes and profits from their assets—they are not focused on integrated solutions or land use issues." Government must fill that gap intelligently, devoting resources to extensive regional, multimodal planning incorporating land use and housing.

Narrowed Scope

Public/private partnerships may also have limited application in helping finance overall infrastructure needs. "In Europe, governments have had naïve expectations about what can be privatized successfully. Railways, waterways, and urban transport lines have less success in finding private partners" than airports, motorways, hospitals, schools, and ports. Private operators want to "cherry pick" the prime high-trafficked intercity turnpikes and city/suburban connectors. Secondary and suburban roads fall off wish lists. They obviously do not want to manage vast sections of light traveled rural highways either—"better a New York tunnel than a prairie road." "Private investors look for assets with proven demand and relative monopoly positions that are capacity constrained and where raising tolls will have limited impact on volumes." In the United States, "privatization will amount to a small piece, a maximum 5 percent of roads." Another expert suggest "10 percent."

More Tolls

The long-term finance trends for major highways arterials, whether managed by private operators or public authorities, seem clear, expecially for those around most gridlocked metropolitan areas. Governments eventually will impose tolls on increasing numbers of these roads to raise money for improvements and maintenance as well as control traffic flows through congestion pricing schemes. They may start with new congesting pricing lanes, but will expand from there. Entire regional road systems ultimately will collect tolls through transponder technologies, calibrated to traffic flows and rush-hour conditions. Despite initial public distress and outrage, drivers will swallow electronic tolling and get used to monthly bills in return for functioning highways. New private toll concessions will ease the initiation process, helping "depoliticize tolling and move rates closer to real costs." Reality sets in—there won't be any other viable way to pay for these roads. "Every urban interstate could make a case for two additional lanes and each could be tolled."

Separately tolled, truck-only lanes and corridors will become more common to relieve congestion for commuters and help move freight traffic. But truck corridors will require significant construction funding and impose engineering challenges, especially related to adding lanes in built-out suburban areas and through urban environments. Some 24-hour cities may choose to impose congestion pricing cordons like London's.

Higher Taxes

Washington, D.C., will run slam-bang into whether to increase the federal gas tax (currently 18.4 cents per gallon) in order to maintain solvency of the Highway Trust Fund. Like the federal government, states will swallow hard before raising fuel taxes. But when push comes to shove, the feds and states may have no choice: $50 billion is needed immediately to fill the gap for basic maintenance of roads and transit systems in the United States, with an additional $50 billion required for necessary improvements. People gradually will come to grips with the reality of higher driving costs to pay for infrastructure, including tolls and high fuel taxes.

Global positioning technologies eventually could supersede pump-exacted fuel taxes and tolling by charging fees based on vehicle miles traveled over specific road networks. These tracking systems also could impose surcharges for congestion pricing, car weight, and vehicle emissions–all designed to help traffic flows and orient behaviors around efficient vehicle use. In addition, parking fees and assessments will become more common in cities as well as many suburban areas. Transit fares will steadily climb, too.

Other primary infrastructure funding sources will continue to derive from state income and sales taxes and local property taxes, including special tax districts for improvements and upkeep of community streets and water/sewer systems. Six large states (California, New York, Pennsylvania, Virginia, Massachusetts, and Indiana) dedicate a portion of sales taxes to transit and other states earmark sales taxes for highway expenditures. Nearly 30 states have enacted legislation allowing impact fees charged to developers for funding streets and water/sewer infrastructure associated with projects. These costs ultimately get passed on to tenants and buyers through higher rents and sales prices.

States and cities will continue to use bonding authority to raise funding through securitizations, which can offer investors attractive tax-free returns.

Equitable Cost Burdens

Regions may need to rethink how to pay for the benefits of their established 24-hour cores and integrated infrastructures, which make surrounding suburbs cheaper and more viable. "Many people have moved out of the center city, because of high taxes and living costs, but still work there because of opportunities. Commuters get bargains—they use the urban core, the transit, the sewers, the sidewalks, but don't pay the full costs, which fall on city taxpayers." Various forms of commuter taxes would make the costs and benefits more equitable for taxpayers across regions and help "avoid a free lunch for discounted use of infrastructure." New York State recently forced New York City to drop its commuter tax in a gesture to suburban residents. But the infrastructure discussion and higher driving related costs may force changes in how people value housing, location, roads, and transit ... eventually.

Chapter 53

Creating Successful Citizen Places
Out of Routine Public Spaces

Project for Public Spaces

Great public spaces are where celebrations are held, social and economic exchanges take place, friends run into each other, and cultures mix. They are the "front porches" of our public institutions—libraries, field houses, neighborhood schools—where we interact with each other and government. When the spaces work well, they serve as a stage for our public lives.

What makes some places succeed while others fail?

In evaluating thousands of public spaces around the world, PPS has found that successful ones have four key qualities: they are **accessible**; people are engaged in **activities** there; the space is **comfortable** and has a good image; and finally, it is a **sociable** place: one where people meet each other and take people when they come to visit. PPS developed **The Place Diagram** as a tool to help people in judging any place, good or bad:

Imagine that the center circle on the diagram is a specific place that you know: a street corner, a playground, or a plaza outside a building. You can evaluate that place according to four criteria in the next ring. In the ring outside these main criteria are a number of **intuitive or qualitative** aspects by which to judge a place; the next outer ring shows the **quantitative aspects** that can be measured by statistics or research.

Access & Linkages

You can judge the accessibility of a place by its connections to its surroundings, both visual and physical. A successful public space is easy to get to and get through; it is visible both from a distance and up close. The edges of a space are important as well: For instance, a row of shops along a street is more interesting and generally safer to walk by than a blank wall or empty lot. Accessible spaces have a high parking turnover and, ideally, are convenient to public transit.

Questions to Consider on Access & Linkages:

• Can you see the space from a distance? Is its interior visible from the outside?

• Is there a good connection between the space and the adjacent buildings, or is it surrounded by blank walls? Do occupants of adjacent buildings use the space?

• Can people easily walk to the place? For example, do they have to dart between moving cars to get to the place?

Originally published as "What Makes a Successful Place?," *Great Place Features, References* (July 2013), by the Project for Public Places, New York, New York. Reprinted with permission of the publisher.

• Do sidewalks lead to and from the adjacent areas?

• Does the space function for people with special needs?

• Do the roads and paths through the space take people where they actually want to go?

• Can people use a variety of transportation options—bus, train, car, bicycle, etc.—to reach the place?

• Are transit stops conveniently located next to destinations such as libraries, post offices, park entrances, etc.?

Comfort & Image

Whether a space is comfortable and presents itself well—has a good image—is key to its success. Comfort includes perceptions about safety, cleanliness, and the availability of places to sit—the importance of giving people the choice to sit where they want is generally underestimated. Women in particular are good judges on comfort and image, because they tend to be more discriminating about the public spaces they use.

Questions to Consider on Comfort & Image:

• Does the place make a good first impression?

• Are there more women than men?

• Are there enough places to sit? Are seats conveniently located? Do people have a choice of places to sit, either in the sun or shade?

• Are spaces clean and free of litter? Who is responsible for maintenance? What do they do? When?

• Does the area feel safe? Is there a security presence? If so, what do these people do? When are they on duty?

• Are people taking pictures? Are there many photo opportunities available?

• Do vehicles dominate pedestrian use of the space, or prevent them from easily getting to the space?

Uses & Activities

Activities are the basic building blocks of a place. Having something to do gives people a reason to come to a place—and return. When there is nothing to do, a space will be empty and that generally means that something is wrong.

Principles to Keep in Mind in Evaluating the Uses and Activities of a Place:

• The more activities that are going and that people have an opportunity to participate in, the better.

• There is a good balance between men and women (women are more particular about the spaces that they use).

• People of different ages are using the space (retired people and people with young children can use a space during the day when others are working).

• The space is used throughout the day.

• A space that is used by both singles and people in groups is better than one that is just used by people alone because it means that there are places for people to sit with friends, there is more socializing, and it is more fun.

• The ultimate success of a space is how well it is managed.

Questions to Consider on Uses & Activities:

• Are people using the space or is it empty?

• Is it used by people of different ages?

• Are people in groups?

• How many different types of activities are occurring—people walking, eating, playing baseball, chess, relaxing, reading?

• Which parts of the space are used and which are not?

• Are there choices of things to do?

• Is there a management presence, or can you identify anyone is in charge of the space?

Sociability

This is a difficult quality for a place to achieve, but once attained it becomes an unmistakable feature. When people see friends, meet and greet their neighbors, and feel comfortable interacting with strangers, they tend to feel a stronger sense of place or attachment to their community—and to the place that fosters these types of social activities.

Questions to Consider on Sociability:
• Is this a place where you would choose to meet your friends? Are others meeting friends here or running into them?
• Are people in groups? Are they talking with one another?

• Do people seem to know each other by face or by name?
• Do people bring their friends and relatives to see the place or do they point to one of its features with pride?
• Are people smiling? Do people make eye contact with each other?
• Do people use the place regularly and by choice?
• Does a mix of ages and ethnic groups that generally reflect the community at large?
• Do people tend to pick up litter when they see it?

EDITORS' NOTE

The Project for Public Spaces' website (http://www.pps.org/) has additional information concerning the best practices for placemaking being used to improve neighorhoods in cities throughout the world.

Chapter 54

The Future Design of Vehicles and the Improved Use of Our Roadways

Ronald Adams *and* Terry Brewer

Just as steam engines replaced the water wheel and electric trains took the place of horse trains, so the twentieth-century car-and-highway transportation system is due to be replaced by something dramatically different in the twenty-first century.

Since the halcyon days of its introduction, the automobile has produced half the world's carbon dioxide and hollowed out cities in the United States, and it is now doing the same in cities all over the developing world as their inhabitants rush to embrace industrialization and its mistakes. The car-and-highway system has proved to be a disastrously inefficient land-use choice for high-density urban transport in the United States.

Henry Ford's common-man cars and highways to support them were achievements of the last century. However, the ability of ordinary Americans simply to go where they need to is being vitiated by the sheer volume of vehicles in the system. We can't build enough highways where they're needed to accommodate the traffic that's already there, much less provide for what's coming.

We've reached a stage of almost constant traffic jams in urbanized areas. In a megalopolis, popular destinations add more and more traffic to the system. We simply have no more room for new roads or highways within the present system's architecture. To survive the onslaught of more and more cars, our system must *double* the capacity of urban roadways, and do so without taking up any new real estate.

Dangers of Mixed-Use Highways

One irrational feature of today's jerry-built highway system is the unholy mix of vehicles crowding onto roads and highways—from oversized cars to huge trucks mixed in with buses and vans. Today's Commuter Joe feels he must drive the biggest SUV and duke it out with monster double-bottom trucks on the trip to work. But an 18-wheeler can still squash even the biggest SUV when a truck driver pulls one shift too many and dozes at the wheel.

Since England first ran massive steam-powered trains, we have known that dinky horse-drawn vehicles could not safely share the same right-of-way with them. Mammoths shouldn't mix with mice on the road. But the U.S. highway system has us locked into this unsafe condition.

While traffic balloons beyond the sys-

Originally published as "Changing Lanes: Watch What's Coming on Tomorrow's Roads," *The Futurist*, Vol. 36, No. 4 (July–August 2002), by the World Future Society, Bethesda, Maryland. Reprinted with permission of the publisher.

tem's ability to cope, oil-consuming nations can no longer rely on a free-flowing supply. Now is the time to redirect energy policy away from oil and toward clean, *electrified* transportation using a different, more-sophisticated roadway system.

Super-Productive Lanes

The only way to increase *capacity* in urbanized areas is to maximize vehicle payload and roadway productivity.

A correct mix of Intelligent Vehicle Highway Systems (IVHS) elements and the more arcane dual mode guideways—two new transportation architectures—plus wayside electric power can produce cost-effective, safe, high-density rights-of-way. And it can be done without using additional urban space by allowing certain kinds of vehicles to run in super-productive rights-of-way shoehorned into existing roadways or even above them.

By making vehicles and highways more efficient in terms of both transporting people and cargo and consuming energy, we can move toward a more secure future. Reducing petroleum imports as we phase out the carbon-fuel economy in favor of electricity means slowing global warming as we build a new post-petroleum civilization.

Why Intelligent Systems Aren't Smart Enough

In Intelligent Vehicle Highway Systems (IVHS), the road and the car work together to do the driving. Touted by the professional highway community since the 1980s, IVHS has important features for new roadway system architectures.

Unfortunately, industry pushed a bit too aggressively into the arena of IVHS, hoping to supply a huge assortment of high-tech systems for existing vehicles and an aging

American highway system without addressing the system's critical problems.

Original supporters of guideway systems were shoved aside in the hustle and bustle of IVHS development in favor of keeping the old U.S. interstate highway system as is. Motorola and Detroit's smart-vehicle products stole the show from guideway innovators whose more mechanical, architectural solutions offered higher highway capacities and greater right-of-way productivity.

For example, the highway technology establishment is still prepared to spend big bucks solving "non-recurring" delays like warning drivers of an overturned truck ahead. But that information is available on the car radio or with on-board software—and is much cheaper.

Today's real problems are *recurring* delays at "chokepoints" in urban areas. These delays are as predictable as sunrise, occurring at bridges, tunnels, and merge points along everyone's daily route every day as narrated by local news anchors in every city, morning and evening.

Another highly touted advantage of smart car/smart highway systems is the promise of hands-free driving, allowing commuters to read or munch donuts. But you can do that on the 7:10 a.m. train to Grand Central and save the state billions of dollars.

The most appealing aspect of IVHS is "close-interval operations." This allows vehicles to follow one another on an automated highway with only a hair's breath of space between them—and thus can increase lane capacity by an order of magnitude.

Robotic Trucks Deliver The Goods

One attractive application for IVHS is robotic-trucks operations on guideways eventually moving in close-interval mode. This novel use for robotic trucks provides an exclusive lane—width and height appropriately reduced—between guiderails for driverless "trucks." With fully computerized controls, a standard 20-foot shipping container placed on a wheeled carriage or with bogies attached can roll goods night and day. The achievement of close-interval mode within an IVHS environment will dramatically improve city-to-city trucking.

Robotic trucks will run adjacent to and pick up power from contact rail on the highway's median barrier. When the robo-unit leaves the contact rail, it switches to its own on-board battery power. The robo-unit exits to a designated overpass using an ascending off-ramp and maneuvers itself into an exclusive queue on the elevated crossing roadway. There it waits, out of traffic and with no engine noise or pollution, for an assigned human trucker to board and drive the unit to its final destination. The driver steers and brakes as in an ordinary truck. The "robotic transporter" is driven along ordinary streets to a nearby loading dock. There, after a quick turnaround to empty and reload, the wheeled container is ready to run another hard day's night without a drink, a shave, or a nap.

Two Proposed Systems for Right-of-Way Use

It has been said that insufficient right-of-way space is endemic to older American cities and other cities all over the world because they were designed to accommodate nineteen-century carriages, not modern vehicular traffic. Therefore, common wisdom says enough space can never be found in the present system for today's magnitude of human and goods movement.

With two proposed systems—Metropolitan Personal Transporters Systems (MPTS) and Occupancy-Rated Vehicle Architecture (ORVA)—both the existing highway system and any ordinary urban street or rear prop-

erty zone can be exploited to offer virtually inexhaustible right-of-way space for significantly increased productivity.

The key to increasing commuter traffic flow is to maximize the numbers of people moving in and through the system—that is, passengers per square foot of right-of-way per unit of time. Replacing the Long Island (commuter) Railroad, for example, would require an estimated 40 lanes of interstate highway. The challenge is to achieve this level of right-of-way productivity while maintaining the mobility we associate with private passenger cars.

The typical street—the basic capillary of transportation circulation—has changed little since Iron Age and Graeco-Roman cities were first built and traffic proceeded on foot, by ox, or by two-wheeled horse-drawn chariot. The space allocated for vehicles today is based on two standing and two moving vehicles, or four "lanes."

Ancient and medieval roadways were suitable for cumbersome, horse-drawn carriages or omnibuses, but there were few of them on the road. In Europe, one-lane roads connecting towns and cities were the rule for centuries. By the last half of the twentieth century, America's limited access highways offered multiple lanes in each direction with on/off ramps to facilitate armies of traffic moving in two directions.

But the inherent problem of the loner in a touring car occupying as much street space as a truck has constrained the productivity of the multilane highway system enough to produce virtual megalopolitan gridlock.

The Metropolitan Personal Transporter System

We can launch a Metropolitan Personal Transporter System simply by designating the smallest conventional vehicle widely available in the United States, the subcompact econobox, as our system-compatible vehicle. Using the econobox, which is driven almost universally in Europe and other environmental conscious places, means significantly lower fuel requirements.

Once the econobox vehicles are modified (at low cost), they will operate in new and revolutionary "guidelanes" that exploit existing rights-of-way on modern highways *above* conventional traffic. At present, to prevent large vehicles from striking and rolling over the median barrier, buses and trucks are prohibited from using ordinary inside lanes that are exclusively reserved for passenger cars. Constructing an elevated guidelane above these lanes exploits air space and adds an additional lane in each direction without taking up new real estate. This proposal will also significantly reduce the small car's vulnerability to accidents with larger vehicles.

Furthermore, with a metered on-ramp, there will be no need to a big engine under the hood of our econobox since there will be no need to outrun oncoming 18-wheelers to enter on the highway. The MPTS transformation only requires modest adaption of available products and equipment. There will be no need to break concrete, invent new passenger cars, or reroute traffic.

The innovative MPTS guidelane facility provides an aerial lane within a 5-foot by 6-foot right-of-way—as compared with the 12-foot by 14-foot space of the conventional highway lane. Since only a single class of vehicle is allowed to operate in the guidelane, there is no weight disparity to jeopardize the safety of the occupants of the econobox on its guidelane, as there is on today's open road.

Introducing Metropolitan Personal Transporter System on a six-lane highway increases the total facility's capacity by 25 percent. The number of cars per hour moving on the guidelane would be about the same as an ordinary car lane, about 2,000 vehicles per hour. Adding incremental capacity to existing facilities and adding different guideway

modes will increase productivity while substantially reducing accidents.

Accepting the econobox with its (preferably hybrid) internal combustion engine as our original equipment is likely to speed public acceptance and investor interest, as well as reduce costs and system start-up time. Later, of course, with the installation of wayside power in the right-of-way, gasoline engines will be replaced completely as vehicles are retrofit for electric propulsion.

Occupancy-Rated Vehicle Architecture

An even smaller vehicle than the econobox can achieve urban right-of-way productivity on a par with rapid transit. Occupancy-Rated Vehicle Architecture is a proposed vehicle/system architecture for *solo* travelers in a guidelane high above and safe from street traffic. At its heart is an individual driving (or even pedaling) to work in an authentic micro-car, commuter capsule, or "bubble vehicle" roughly one-fourth the size of an econobox and weighing just a few hundred pounds.

The space that a driver actually uses is but a fraction of the area the typical car or SUV occupies as it moves along street and highway. Likewise, parking ties up available street space, often all day. This means a conventional vehicle's payload simply does not correlate efficiently with its size or with the amount of highway and street area used, and represents an astonishing misappropriation of high-value urban space. To understand the futility of current traffic capacity measurement and associated "traffic correctives," we must realize that these conventional means and measurements will not solve the basic inefficiency of our car-highway system.

The problem today is the ridiculously low lane productivity as seen by comparing the payload (number of occupants—sometimes only one—delivered to a destination) to the cross-sectional area taken up by the vehicle. The conventional highway lane delivers 10 solo drivers per square foot of right-of-way per hour, while MPTS delivers 100 solo drivers and ORVA delivers 200 solo drivers.

Once the benefits of putting econoboxes on these proposed mini-highway guidelane systems are clear, investors and users should be convinced there are ready alternatives. These are far superior to what is being offered by conventional highway planners and automakers, particularly as commuters face the prospect of tens of thousands more cars crowding the ultimately limited traditional highway networks.

Where the Metropolitan Personal Transporter System would deliver a six-fold improvement—up to 60 passengers per square foot per hour, Occupancy-Rated Vehicle Architecture would deliver as much as 15-fold improvement—100 to 150 commuters per square foot per hour. These astounding upgrades in right-of-way productivity would be accompanied by even more compelling fuel economies and emissions reduction than MPTS.

All of these systems—robotic trucks, personal transporters, and individual microvehicles—could be combined in a commuter dualmode system. While robotic trucks would be automated, the others would operate manually and at lower cost.

Personal Transport Goes to Extremes

On the lighter side, there can be a transporter in which the commuter's individual transportation space is only a third of the size of the tiny ORVA transporter. Right-of-way use would be so efficient that it would substantially reduce the need for large rights-of-way as in multilane highways. We can travel through right-of-way facilities that resemble

the structure of today's industrial air conditioning and ventilation ducts using a "MAG-Luge."

In this mode, commuters travel feet first, head raised, body supine. The human/vehicle is buoyed by magnetic levitation, propelled by electric linear induction motors, and protected and augmented by pneumatic pressure management within the tube type construction.

Of course, people who are less physically fit may not be attracted to the MAG-Luge mode of travel. But former skateboarders, rock-and-roll Harley bikers, fitness buffs, and sportsters will be happy to use it.

Message from the Future

Even if these hypothetical architectures became commonplace in North America, global carbon dioxide levels and temperatures will continue to rise for a half century more *after* we put our house in order. Therefore, according to current climate science, we can expect our grandchildren to witness the flooding of coastal zones and the disappearance of the world's islands as glacial deposits melt and anthropogenic warming continues.

Stuck in a car-and-highway system unfriendly to alteration or update, we can still apply innovative thinking and accomplish a (quiet) revolution to save our cities and our planet and break the impasse created by obsolescent infrastructure and old ideas.

The impact of the car-and-highway mode on human society and the biosphere makes it mandatory that the system be transformed to fit the new epoch. Ideally, a new era will allow us to cut ties to global corporations concerned with the bottom line and government institutions mired in fixed paradigms and political pork. Instead, unaffiliated inventors and innovators should rethink the architecture of land transport in the tradition of trailblazing innovation.

Chapter 55

Urban Planning Principles and Practices Are Changing

Center for New Urbanism

The principles of urbanism can be applied increasingly to projects at the full range of scales from a single building to an entire community.

The ten (10) major principles of urbanism are highlighted below, and explained in greater detail in the following paragraphs.

- Walkability
- Connectivity
- Mixed-Use and Diversity
- Mixed Housing
- Quality Architecture and Urban Design
- Traditional Neighborhood Structure
- Increased Density
- Green Transportation
- Sustainability
- Quality of Life

WALKABILITY

- Most things within a 10-minute walk of home and work
- Pedestrian friendly street design (buildings close to street; porches, windows & doors; tree-lined streets; on street parking; hidden parking lots; garages in rear lane; narrow, slow speed streets)
- Pedestrian streets free of cars in special cases

CONNECTIVITY

- Interconnected street grid network disperses traffic & eases walking
- A hierarchy of narrow streets, boulevards, and alleys
- High quality pedestrian network and public realm makes walking pleasurable

MIXED-USE & DIVERSITY

- A mix of shops, offices, apartments, and homes on site. Mixed-use within neighborhoods, within blocks, and within buildings
- Diversity of people—of ages, income levels, cultures, and races

MIXED HOUSING

A range of types, sizes and prices in closer proximity

QUALITY ARCHITECTURE & URBAN DESIGN

Emphasis on beauty, aesthetics, human comfort, and creating a sense of place; Special placement of civic uses and sites within community. Human scale architecture & beautiful surroundings nourish the human spirit.

Originally published as "Principles of Urbanism," *Creating Livable Sustainable Communities* (December 2013), by the Center for New Urbanism, Alexandria, Virginia. Reprinted with permission of the publisher.

TRADITIONAL NEIGHBORHOOD STRUCTURE

- Discernable center and edge
- Public space at center
- Importance of quality public realm; public open space designed as civic art
- Contains a range of uses and densities within 10-minute walk
- Transect planning: Highest densities at town center; progressively less dense towards the edge. The transect is an analytical system that conceptualizes mutually reinforcing elements, creating a series of specific natural habitats and/or urban lifestyle settings. The Transect integrates environmental methodology for habitat assessment with zoning methodology for community design. The professional boundary between the natural and man-made disappears, enabling environmentalists to assess the design of the human habitat and the urbanists to support the viability of nature. This urban-to-rural transect hierarchy has appropriate building and street types for each area along the continuum.

INCREASED DENSITY

- More buildings, residences, shops, and services closer together for ease of walking, to enable a more efficient use of services and resources, and to create a more convenient, enjoyable place to live.
- New Urbanism design principles are applied at the full range of densities from small towns, to large cities.

GREEN TRANSPORTATION

- A network of high quality trains connecting cities, towns, and neighborhoods together
- Pedestrian-friendly design that encourages a greater use of bicycles, rollerblades, scooters, and walking as daily transportation

SUSTAINABILITY

- Minimal environmental impact of development and its operations
- Eco-friendly technologies, respect for ecology and value of natural systems
- Energy efficiency
- Less use of finite fuels
- More local production
- More walking, less driving

QUALITY OF LIFE

Taken together these add up to a high quality of life well worth living, and create places that enrich, uplift, and inspire the human spirit.

Benefits of Urbanism

The four (4) primary benefits of urbanism are highlighted below, and explained in greater detail in the following paragraphs.

- Benefits to Residence
- Benefits to Businesses
- Benefits to Developers
- Benefits to Municipalities

BENEFITS TO RESIDENTS

Higher quality of life; Better places to live, work, & play; Higher, more stable property values; Less traffic congestion & less driving; Healthier lifestyle with more walking, and less stress; Close proximity to main street retail & services; Close proximity to bike trails, parks, and nature; Pedestrian friendly communities offer more opportunities to get to know others in the neighborhood and town, resulting in meaningful relationships with more people, and a friendlier town; More freedom and independence to children, elderly, and the poor in being able to get to jobs, recreation, and services without the need for a car or someone to drive them; Great savings to residents and school boards in reduced busing costs from children being able to walk or bicycle to neighborhood schools; More diversity and smaller, unique shops and services with local owners who are involved in community; Big savings by driving less, and owning less cars; Less ugly, congested sprawl to deal with daily; Better sense of place and community identity with more unique architecture; More open space to enjoy that will remain open space; More efficient use of tax money with less spent on spread out utilities and roads

BENEFITS TO BUSINESSES

Increased sales due to more foot traffic & people spending less on cars and gas; More profits due to spending less on advertising and large signs; Better lifestyle by living above shop in live-work units—saves the stressful & costly commute; Economies of scale in marketing due to close proximity and cooperation with other local businesses; Smaller spaces promote small local business incubation; Lower rents due to smaller spaces & smaller parking lots; Healthier lifestyle due to more walking and being near healthier restaurants; More community involvement from being part of community and knowing residents

BENEFITS TO DEVELOPERS

More income potential from higher density mixed-use projects due to more leasable square footage, more sales per square foot, and higher property values and selling prices; Faster approvals in communities that have adopted smart growth principles resulting in cost/time savings; Cost savings in parking facilities in mixed-use properties due to sharing of spaces throughout the day and night, resulting in less duplication in providing parking; Less need for parking facilities due to mix of residences and commercial uses within walking distance of each other; Less impact on roads/traffic, which can result in lower impact fees; Lower cost of utilities due to compact nature of New Urbanist design; Greater acceptance by the public and less resistance from NIMBYS; Faster sell out due to greater

acceptance by consumers from a wider product range resulting in wider market share

BENEFITS TO MUNICIPALITIES

Stable, appreciating tax base; Less spent per capita on infrastructure and utilities than typical suburban development due to compact, high-density nature of projects; Increased tax base due to more buildings packed into a tighter area; Less traffic congestion due to walkability of design; Less crime and less spent on policing due to the presence of more people day and night; Less resistance from community; Better overall community image and sense of place; Less incentive to sprawl when urban core area is desirable; Easy to install transit where it's not, and improve it where it is; Greater civic involvement of population leads to better governance

Ways to Implement New Urbanism

The most effective way to implement New Urbanism is to plan for it, and write it into zoning and development codes. This directs all future development into this form.

New Urbanism is best planned at all levels of development:

- The single building
- Groups of buildings
- The urban block
- The neighborhood
- Networks of neighborhoods
- Towns
- Cities
- Regions

Increasingly, regional planning techniques are being used to control and shape growth into compact, high-density, mixed-use neighborhoods, villages, towns, and cities.

Planning new train systems (instead of more roads) delivers the best results when designed in harmony with regional land planning—known as Transit Oriented Development (TOD). At the same time, the revitalization of urban areas directs and encourages infill development back into city centers.

Planning for compact growth, rather than letting it sprawl out, has the potential to greatly increase the quality of the environment. It also prevents congestion problems and the environmental degradation normally associated with growth.

Obstacles to Overcome

The most important obstacle to overcome is the restrictive and incorrect zoning codes currently in force in most municipalities. Current codes do not allow New Urbanism to be built, but do allow sprawl. Adopting a TND ordinance and/or a system of "smart codes" allows New Urbanism to be built easily without having to rewrite existing codes.

An equally important obstacle is the continuous road building and expansion taking place in every community across America. This encourages more driving and more sprawl which has a domino effect increasing traffic congestion across the region. Halting road projects and building new train systems helps reverse this problematic trend.

EDITORS' NOTE

The Center for New Urbanism's website (http://newurbanism.org/) has additional information on international transportation initiatives being undertaken in cities throughout the world.

Chapter 56

Planning, Transportation, the Environment, and the Future

Roger L. Kemp *and* Carl J. Stephani

Local governments everywhere are seeking ways to save money, enhance their downtowns, improve their transportation systems, and diminish their carbon footprints—some for ideological and philosophical reasons, some just to save money. The result: We're all better off when it's done, and the arguments about who is right seems to be less and less important, since everyone achieves their goals.

Whatever their reasons, the result is innovation-creativity that has not been seen for many decades. And it's not good enough to simply retrofit some buildings with double- or triple-paned windows and extra caulking. Localities are now inventing applications that wouldn't have been imaginable a mere decade or two ago. These include new regulations and requirements for vehicles, public transit, and our roadways. Citizen expectations have also increased relative to how their neighborhoods are designed, making public roadways pedestrian friendly, and reducing the level of pollution.

What are some of these innovations? They include green roofs, green walls, green parking lots, green buildings, transit oriented development, the redesign of our walkways and roadways, and different types of transportation options! There are several major changes taking place throughout the world,

as well as across our country, and they relate to everything from the management of transportation technology to the design of our public roadways, and new movements such as sustainability, new urbanism, transit oriented development, and going green.

Sustainability and New Urbanism— This involves new planning and development standards that focus on a green environment, reduced energy consumption, using smaller roadways, and more pedestrian oriented walkways; and focuses primarily on walkways, hiking trails, and bicycle lanes in our public roadways. Citizens everywhere wish to enhance the quality of their life by improving their environment. They increasingly vote for public officials to help them achieve these goals.

Data center and server consolidation— Michigan has consolidated some 4,000 servers scattered around the state into just three data centers. Saving the state $19 million so far and freeing up 30,000 square feet of office space. And, the State of Indiana has reduced its seven data centers down to one! Check out this innovative data center consolidation at The Data Cave website listed under "Notes" at the end of this chapter.

Green rooftops—These vegetative cool spots reduce rooftop reflectivity and heat island generation. Chicago is becoming the green-roof capital of the country while it works to enhance the beauty, health, and welfare of its residents and their neighborhoods. Check out these rooftop garden vegetative innovations at the Green Initiatives—Roofs website at the Art Institute of Chicago. Read even more about green-roof topics without having to use any paper at the Greenroofs. com, LLC website, which is listed below.

Green walls—These beauties can reduce interior building temperatures, absorb carbon dioxide, and provide visual diversity to the urban landscape. They demonstrate appreciation of the urban environment and can enhance the affection of city dwellers for "their place." There's also much to read about the new subject of vertical, not horizontal, gardens at the Vertical Garden Institute's website, which is listed below.

Roadway design. Streets can be designed to be safer, more convenient, more efficient, and even more encouraging to pedestrians and cyclists. Instead of the traditional grid street system pattern that was designed foremost for the movement of vehicles, fused-grid street systems that link pedestrian areas together with fewer street crossings can encourage significant increases in home-based non-vehicular trips.

See more information and case studies on these innovative roadway design programs at the Fused Grid website, under Urban Pattern Associates, below. Intersections can be designed as roundabouts to reduce carbon monoxide emissions by more than 25 percent. Read more about these contemporary state-of-the-art roadway design practices from the Department of Transportation, State of New York. Their website is listed below under the Department of Transportation.

Green streets—Streets designed with landscaped curb extensions, swales, planter strips, pervious pavement, and street trees can greatly enhance the interception and infiltration of stormwater into the groundwater system. The City of Portland, Oregon, has taken huge strides toward the husbandry and management of its stormwater. There is a wealth of information on how to do it at the Green Streets Initiative's website, which is listed below under "Notes." We need to further encourage designing our streets for people, who live in our cities, rather than just for their vehicles that are parked there!

Vehicle preferences—The international trend throughout the world is for public transportation, especially light-rail and bicycle stations, smaller vehicles, and making the first-ever transition to less gasoline and oil consumption through the use of smaller vehicles, the greater use of electric vehicles, and the increased use of motorized two wheeled vehicles. These trends are being created by citizens throughout the world, and being followed-up upon by their respective public officials—at all levels of government—in all countries throughout the world.

The exciting thing about many of these innovations is that, because they accomplish such a wide variety of wholesome civic objectives—aesthetics, environmental preservation, economics, reduced energy consumption, and improved safety and security—they do not need to create ideological, philosophical, or political conflict. Almost everyone can identify a personal value that is satisfied by helping to *green* America's communities.

Communities are also ripe for the redesign and redevelopment of many of their fundamental structures to make them even better and more sustainable, beautiful, and health sustaining. Those who are engaged in that process have much to gain by sharing their experiences and advertising their success stories to the citizens whom we serve as we make continued progress in the greening of our communities, and their neighborhoods.

The planning and development practices facilitated by these downtown revitalization, preservation, and development trends increasingly can be applied to projects of all sizes—from single buildings, to full blocks, to whole neighborhoods, and even to entire communities, as well as their parks, roadways, walkways, and other forms that facilitate pedestrian transportation.

The state-of-the-art planning and development practices that achieve these goals have been conceived and implemented with greater frequency in recent years, throughout the entire world. The various diseconomies associated with past planning and development practices, which have served to deteriorate the natural aspects of our environment, have facilitated the positive going-green innovative applications described in this volume.

Many cities, in countries throughout the world, have advanced planning, preservation, and development practices unique to their respective environments, both public and private. But the problems that public officials throughout the world encounter are common, and so are the solutions that can be used to improve the quality of our environment— on our blocks, in our neighborhoods, in our cities, in our states and territories, as well as throughout our respective nations.

This volume highlights the best start-of-the-art planning, preservation, and development practices being used in local governments (e.g., cities, towns, boroughs, townships, and communities) throughout the world to improve their respective transportation systems—both vehicular and pedestrian.

Generally, public officials respond to increasing citizen demands to improve their environment, reduce their energy costs by making their respective community a more positive place to live. Public officials and planners in the United States, as well as in other countries throughout the world, can gain significant insight from the important codification of knowledge in this dynamic and evolving field.

Notes

The organizational websites referred to above are listed below, in the order in which they were mentioned above, to facilitate future research on these timely topics.

The Data Cave
Website: http://www.thedatacave.com/

Art Institute of Chicago
Green Initiatives—Roofs
Website: http://www.artic.edu/webspaces/green initiatives/greenroofs/main.htm/

Greenroofs.com, LLC
Website: http://www.greenroofs.com/

Vertical Garden Institute
Website: http://verticalgardeninstitute.org/

Urban Pattern Associates
The Fused Grid: A Contemporary Urban Pattern
Website: http://www.fusedgrid.ca/

Department of Transportation
State of New York
Website: http://www.nysdot.gov/main/roundabouts/

Green Streets Initiative
Website: http://www.gogreenstreets.org/

Appendices

Containing: *A. Periodicals Bibliography*, *B. Glossary*, *C. Acronyms and Abbreviations*, *D. State Municipal League Directory*, *E. National Planning and Development Resource Directory*, *F. International Planning and Development Resource Directory*, *G. International Local Government Resource Directory*, *H. State Library Resource Directory*

A. Periodicals Bibliography

ITE Journal—Washington, D.C.: Institute of Transportation Engineers. Monthly. Abstracts available online at: http://www.ite.org/itejournal/index.asp

Traffic and transportation engineering with and emphasis on U.S. urban and suburban environments.

Journal of Advanced Transportation—Calgary, Alberta: Institute for Transportation. Three issues per year. Abstracts available online at: http://www.advanced-transport.com/

State of the art developments in mass transportation technologies and operational innovations.

Journal of Public Transportation—Tampa: University of South Florida, Center for Urban Transportation Research. Electronic resource access available at: http://www.nctr.usf.edu/jpt/journal.htm

This quarterly, international journal presents original research and case studies relating to public transportation and policy issues. There is a special emphasis on innovative solutions to transportation problems. Many full-text issues are freely available online.

Journal of Transportation Engineering—New York: American Society of Civil Engineers. Bi-monthly. Abstracts available online at: http://scitation.aip.org/teo/

Includes technical and professional papers of the ASCE Urban Transportation Division.

Journal of Urban Planning and Development—New York: American Society of Civil Engineers. Bi-monthly. Abstracts available online at: http://scitation.aip.org/upo/

Application of civil engineering to area-wide transportation, urban development, and planning of public works and utilities.

Public Transportation Fact Book—American Public Transportation Association, Washington, D.C. Annual.

Provides aggregate data for the United States and Canada on transit finances and operating statistics by mode, transit vehicle characteristics, and deliveries, as well as legislative and industry historical information.

Urban Transportation Monitor—Fairfax Station, VA: Lawley Publications. Available online through subscription at: http://www.urban-transportation-monitor.com/

This bi-weekly publication presents current news on all modes of urban transportation and includes regular readership surveys, and a section on new publications.

Source: Bureau of Transportation Statistics, *National Transportation Library* (virtual library). Published by the Research and Innovative Technology Administration, U.S. Department of Transportation, Washington, D.C. (Website: http://ntl.bts.gov/)

B. Glossary

Aerial Tramway—Unpowered passenger vehicle suspended from a system of aerial cables and propelled by separate cables attached to the vehicle suspension system. The cable system is powered by engines or motors at a central location, not on board the vehicle.

Automated Guideway Transit—Guided transit vehicle operating singly or multi-car trains with a fully automated system (no crew on transit units). Service may be on a fixed schedule or in response to a passenger-activated call button. Automated guideway transit includes personal rapid transit, group rapid transit and peoplemover systems.

Bus—Rubber-tired vehicle operating on fixed routes and schedules on roadways. Buses are powered by diesel, gasoline, battery or alternative fuel engines contained within the vehicle.

Commuter Rail—Urban passenger train service for local short-distance travel operating between a central city and adjacent suburbs. Service must be operated on a regular basis by or under contract with a transit operation for the purpose of transporting passengers within urbanized areas, or between urbanized areas and outlying areas. Such rail service, using either locomotive-hauled or self-propelled railroad passenger cars, is generally characterized by multi-trip tickets, specific station-to-station fares, railroad employment practices and usually only one or two stations in the central business district. It does not include heavy rail rapid transit or light rail/street car transit service. Intercity rail service is excluded, except for that portion of such service that is operated by or under contract with a public transit agency for predominately commuter services. Predominately commuter services means that for any given trip segment (i.e., distance between any two stations), over 50 percent of the average daily ridership travels on the train at least three times a week. Only the predominately commuter service portion of the intercity route is eligible for inclusion when determining commuter rail route miles.

Ferryboat—Vessel carrying passengers and/or vehicles over a body of water. The vessel is generally a steam or diesel-powered conventional ferry vessel.

Heavy Rail—High-speed, passenger rail cars operating singly or in trains of two or more cars on fixed rails in separate rights-of-way from which all other vehicular and foot traffic are excluded.

Inclined Plane—Special tramway type of vehicle operating up and down slopes on rails via a cable mechanism so that passenger seats remain horizontal while the undercarriage (truck) is angled parallel to the slope.

Light Rail—Lightweight passenger rail cars operating singly) or in short, usually two-car, trains) on fixed rails in right-of-way that is not separated from other traffic for much of the way. Light rail vehicles are driven electrically with power being drawn from an overhead electric line via a trolley or a pantograph.

Monorail—Guided transit vehicle operating on or suspended from a single rail, beam, or tube. Monorail vehicles usually operate in trains.

Source: Federal Transit Administration, *Glossary of Transit Terms*. Published by the U.S. Department of Transportation, Washington, D.C. (Website: http://www.fta.dot.gov/)

C. Acronyms and Abbreviations

The following list represents common acronyms used in the field of transportation. Many of these acronyms relate to federal laws and policies that focus on many aspects of public transportation.

AADT—Annual Average Daily Traffic

AASHTO—American Association of State Highway and Transportation Officials

ACOE—Army Corps of Engineers

AM—Peak Traffic volumes in the morning usually 2 hours in duration

ANSI—American National Standards Institute

ATR—Automatic Traffic Recorder for counting vehicles

B/C—Benefit over Cost ratio

BMP—Best Management Practices-effective and practical methods to protect water quality

CAA—Federal Clean Air Act

CAD—Computer Aided Design

CCTV—Closed-Circuit Television

C-D—Road Collector-Distributor Road

CE—Categorical Exclusion under NEPA regulations

CFR—Code of Federal Regulations

CO—Carbon Monoxide

CORSIM—Corridor Simulation—a microscopic traffic simulation model

CTPS—Central Transportation Planning Staff

CWA—Federal Clean Water Act

CZMA—Coastal Zone Management Act

DMS—Dynamic Message Signs

EA—Environmental Assessment under NEPA (Federal) regulations

EB—Eastbound

EIR—Environmental Impact Report

EIS—Environmental Impact Statement

EJ—Environmental Justice

EO—Executive Order

EPA—Federal Environmental Protection Agency

ESA—Federal Endangered Species Act

FHWA—Federal Highway Administration

FONSI—Finding of No Significant Impact under NEPA regulations

GHG—Greenhouse Gas

GIS—Geographic Information System

HCM—Highway Capacity Manual

HCS—Highway Capacity Software to analyze operational performance of highway systems

HEP—Habitat Evaluation Procedure

ITS—Intelligent Transportation Systems

ITE—Institute of Transportation Engineers

ITS—Intelligent Transportation Systems

LEDPA—Least Environmentally Damaging Practicable Alternative under ACOE permitting procedures

LOS—Level of Service usually performed for roadway segments or turning movements at intersections

MEV—Million Entering Vehicles (used in computing crash rates at intersections)

MTM—Manual Turning Movement Counts for counting vehicle turns at intersections

MPO—Metropolitan Planning Organization

MVM—Million Vehicle Miles (used in computing crash rates on highways)

NAAQS—National Ambient Air Quality Standards

NAC—Noise Abatement Criteria

NB—Northbound

NEPA—National Environmental Policy Act

NIST—National Institute of Standards and Technology

NPDES—National Pollutant Discharge Elimination System surface water discharge permitting program

NOx—Oxides of nitrogen

O-D survey—Origin-Destination survey

PDO—Property Damage Only (crash type)

PL—Public Law

PM—Peak Traffic volumes in the late afternoon/evening usually over a 2 hour period

QA/QC—Quality Assurance and Quality Control

RCNM—Roadway Construction Noise Model

ROW—Right-of-Way

RTA—Regional Transit Authority

SB—South Bound

SIP—State Implementation Plan

SPUI—Single Point Urban Interchange

SYNCHRO—Software package for performing traffic engineering calculations

TDM—Transportation Demand Management

TIP—Transportation Improvement Program

TMA—Transportation Management Area

TSM—Transportation Systems Management

V/C—Volume-to-Capacity ratio

VHT—Vehicle-hours Traveled

VMS—Variable Message Signs

VMT—Vehicle-miles Traveled

VOC's—Volatile Organic Compounds

VISSIM—Visual microscopic traffic simulation to graphically show traffic conditions in near realistic modeling

WB—Westbound

Source: *Department of Transportation, State of Massachusetts*, July, 2013. Published by the Department of Transportation, State of Massachusetts, Boston, MA (Website: http://www.massdot.ma.us/)

D. State Municipal League Directory

Most states have a municipal league, which serves as a valuable source of information about city government innovations and programs. Additional information on city and school practices is available from the various state municipal league websites, which are shown below in alphabetical order by state name (not all organization names start with the state name).

Alabama League of Municipalities
(http://www.alalm.org/)

Alaska Municipal League
(http://www.akml.org/)

League of Arizona Cities and Towns
(http://www.azleague.org/)

Arkansas Municipal League
(http://www.arml.org/)

League of California Cities
(http://www.cacities.org/)

Colorado Municipal League
(http://www.cml.org/)

Connecticut Conference of Municipalities
(http://www.ccm-ct.org/)

Delaware League of Local Governments
(http://www.ipa.udel.edu/localgovt/dllg/)

Florida League of Cities
(http://www.flcities.com/)

Georgia Municipal Association
(http://www.gmanet.com/)

Association of Idaho Cities
(http://www.idahocities.org/)

Illinois Municipal League
(http://www.iml.org/)

Indiana Association of Cities and Towns
(http://www.citiesandtowns.org/)

Iowa League of Cities
(http://www.iowaleague.org/)

League of Kansas Municipalities
(http://www.lkm.org/)

Kentucky League of Cities
(http://www.klc.org/)

Louisiana Municipal Association
(http://www.lamunis.org/)

Maine Municipal Association
(http://www.memum.org/)

Maryland Municipal League
(http://www.mdmunicipal.org/)

Massachusetts Municipal Association
(http://www.mma.org/)

Michigan Municipal League
(http://www.mml.org/)

League of Minnesota Cities
(http://www.lmnc.org/)

Mississippi Municipal League
(http://www.mmlonline.com/)

Missouri Municipal League
(http://www.mocities.com/)

Montana League of Cities
(http://www.mlct.org/)

League of Nebraska Municipalities
(http://www.lonm.org/)

Nevada League of Cities and Municipalities
(http://www.nvleague.org/)

New Hampshire Local Government Center
(http://www.nhmunicipal.org/)

New Jersey State League of Municipalities
(http://www.njslom.com/)

New Mexico Municipal League
(http://www.nmml.org/)

New York Conference of Mayors and
Municipal Officials
(http://www.nycom.org/)

North Carolina League of Municipalities
(http://www.nclm.org/)

North Dakota League of Cities
(http://www.ndlc.org/)

Ohio Municipal League
(http://www.omunileague.org/)

Oklahoma Municipal League
(http://www.oml.org/)

League of Oregon Cities
(http://www.orcities.org/)

Pennsylvania League of Cities and
Municipalities
(http://www.plcm.org/)

Rhode Island League of Cities and Towns
(http://www.rileague.org/)

Municipal Association of South Carolina
(http://www.masc.sc/)

South Dakota Municipal League
(http://www.sdmunicipalleague.org/)

Tennessee Municipal League
(http://www.tml.org/)

Texas Municipal League
(http://www.tml.org/)

Utah League of Cities and Towns
(http://www.ulct.org/)

Vermont League of Cities and Towns
(http://www.vlct.org/)

Virginia Municipal League
(http://www.vml.org/)

Association of Washington Cities
(http://www.awcnet.org/)

West Virginia Municipal League
(http://www.wvml.org/)

League of Wisconsin Municipalities
(http://www.lwm-info.org/)

Wyoming Association of Municipalities
(http://www.wyomuni.org/)

Source: Alphabetical listing, *State League Programs*, National League of Cities, Washington, D.C. (Website: http://www.nlc.org/).

E. National Planning and Development Resource Directory

Major national professional associations, foundations, and research organizations serving all levels of government, as well as environmentally concerned professionals and citizens, are listed here.

American Association for State Highway and Transportation Officials
Website: http://transportation.org/
American Planning Association
Website: http://www.planning.org/
American Public Transportation Association
Website: http://www.apta.com/
American Public Works Association
Website: http://www.apwa.net/
American Society of Civil Engineers
Website: http://www.asce.org/
Association for Commuter Transportation
Website: http://tmi.cob.fsu.edu/act/
Association of Metropolitan Planning Organizations
Website: http://www.ampo.org/
Center for Design Excellence
Website: http://www.UrbanDesign.org
Center for New Urbanism
Website: http://www.NewUrbanism.org
Center for Transportation Excellence
Website: http://www.cfte.org/
Community Transportation Association of America
Website: http://www.ctaa.org/
Department of Transportation
(See U.S. Department of Transportation)
Federal Highway Administration
Website: http://ops.fhwa.dot.gov/
Federal Transit Administration
Website: http://www.fta.dot.gov/
Institute of Transportation Planners
Website: http://www.ite.org/

Intelligent Transportation Society of America
Website: http://www.itsa.org/
Main Street Project
Website: http://www.mainstreetproject.org/
National Alliance of Public Transportation Advocates
Website: http://www.publictransportation.org/napta/
National Association of City Transportation Officials
Website: http://www.nacto.org/
National Community Development Association
Website: http://www.ncdaonline.org/
National Complete Streets Coalition
Website: http://www.completestreets.org/
National Main Street Center
Website: http://www.nthp.org/
Partnership for Walkable Communities
Website: http://www.walkableamerica.org/
Project for Public Spaces
Website: http://www.pps.org
Rails-to-Trails Conservancy
Website: http://www.railstotrails.org/
Reconnecting America
Website: http://www.reconnectingamerica.org/
Sierra Club
Website: http://www.sierraclub.org/
Smart Growth America
Website: http://www.smartgrowthamerica.org/
The National Center for Bicycling and Walking
Website: http://www.bikewalk.org/
The Urban Institute
Website: http://www.urban.org/
Urban Resources Group
Website: http://www.UrbanResourcesGroup.com
U. S. Department of Transportation
Website: http://www.dot.com/

F. International Planning and Development Resources Directory

Major international professional associations, foundations, and research organizations serving all levels of government, as well as environmentally concerned professionals and citizens, are listed here.

Alliance for Biking and Walking
Website: http://www.peoplepowermovement.org/
Congress for the New Urbanism
Website: http://www.cnu.org/
EcoMobility Alliance
Website: http://www.ecomobility.org/
International Association of Public Transport
Website: http://www.uitp.org/
International Association of Transportation Regulators
Website: http://www.iatr.org/
International City/County Management Association
Website: http://www.icma.org/
International Conference of Building Officials
Website: http://www.icbo.org/
International Council for Local Environmental Initiatives
Website: http://icle.org/
International Downtown Association
Website: http://ida-downtown.org/
International Making Cities Livable
Website: http://www.livablecities.org/
International Society of City and Regional Planners
Website: http://www.isocarp.org/
International Transportation Economics Association
Website: http://www.iteaweb.org/
International Transportation Management Association
Website: http://www.itmahouston.org/
International Transportation Safety
Website: http://www.itsasafety.org/
International Union of Local Authorities
Website: http://www.iula.org/
International Urban Planning and Environment Association
Website: http://www.iupea.net/
New Urbanism
Website: http://www.newurbanism.org/
Partners for Livable Communities
Website: http://www.livable.com/

Projects for Public Spaces
Website: http://www.pps.org/
Sustainable Cities Collective
Website: http://sustainablecitiescollective.com/
United Cities and Local Governments
Website: http://www.uclg.org/
United Nations—Habitat
Website: http://www.unhabitat.org/
United Nations—Sustainable Communities
Website: http://www.sustainabledevelopment.un.org/
Urban Land Institute
Website: http://www.uli.org/
Walkable Communities
Website: http://www.walkable.org/
World Carfree Network
Website: http://www.worldcarfree.net/
World Future Society
Website: http://www.wfs.org/

G. International Local Government Resources Directory

Most nations have national professional associations that serve those public officials that work in their local governments. Local laws and policies, as well as model practices, are available from these organizations.

Association of Cities of Vietnam
Website: http://www.acvn.vn/
Association of Indonesian Municipalities
Website: http://www.apeksi.or.id/
Canadian Association of Municipal Administrators
Website: http://www.camacam.ca/
City Managers' Association of Gujarat, India
Website: http://www.cmag-india.com/
City Managers' Association of Karnataka, India
Website: http://www.cmakarnataka.com/
City Managers' Association of Orissa, India
Website: http://www.cmao.nic.in/
Dutch City Managers Association
Website: http://www.gemeentesecretaris.nl/

Federation of Sri Lankan Local Government Authorities
Website: http://www.fslga.lk/

Indonesian Regencies Cooperation Agency
Website: http://www.apkas.or.id/

Institute for Local Government Management of South Africa
Website: http://www.ilgm.co.za/

International City/County Management Association
Website: http://www.icma.org/

Korean Urban Management Association
Website: http://www.kruma.org/

Local Government Managers Australia
Website: http://www.lgma.org.au/

Mexican Association of Municipalities
Website: http://www.ammac.org.mx/

Municipal Association of Nepal
Website: http://www.muannepal.org.np/

Municipal Service Providers' Association of Georgia
Website: http://www.mspa.ge/

National Association of Chief Executives in Danish Municipalities
Website: http://www.komdir.dk/

New Zealand Society of Local Government Managers
Website: http://www.solgm.org.nz/

Russian National Congress of Municipalities
Website: http://www.rncm.ru/

Slovak City Managers' Association
Website: http://www.apums.sk/

Society of Local Authority Chief Executives in the United Kingdom
Website: http://www.solace.org.uk/

Union of Local Authorities in Israel
Website: http://www.masham.org.il/

H. State Library Directory

Most state libraries have copies of state information relating to transportation laws and policies adopted in the local governments in their state.

Alabama
(http://www.apls.state.la.us/)
Alaska
(http://www.library.state.ak.us/)

Arizona
(http://www.lib.az.us/)
Arkansas
(http://www.asl.lib.ar.us/)
California
(http://www.library.ca.gov/)
Colorado
(http://www.cde.state.co.us/)
Connecticut
(http://www.cslib.org/)
Delaware
(http://www.state.lib.de.us/)
District of Columbia
(http://delibrary.org/)
Florida
(http://dlis.dos.state.fl.us/)
Georgia
(http://www.georgialibraries.org/)
Hawaii
(http://www.librarieshawaii.org/)
Idaho
(http://www.lili.org/)
Illinois
(http://www.cyberdriveillinois.com/departments/library/)
Indiana
(http://www.statelib.lib.in.us/)
Iowa
(http://www.silo.lib.ia.us/)
Kansas
(http://www.skyways.org/KSL/)
Kentucky
(http://www.kdla.ky.gov/)
Louisiana
(http://www.state.lib.la.us/)
Maine
(http://www.state.me.us/msl/)
Maryland
(http://www.sailor.lib.md.us/)
Massachusetts
(http://www.mass.gov/mblc/)
Michigan
(http://www.michigan.gov/hal/)
Minnesota
(http://www.state.mn.us/libraries/)
Mississippi
(http://www.mlc.lib.ms.us/)
Missouri
(http://www.sos.mo.gov/library/)

Montana
(http://msl.state.mt.us/)
Nebraska
(http://www.nlc.state.ne.us/)
Nevada
(http://dmla.clan.lib.nv.us/)
New Hampshire
(http://www.state.nh.us/nhls/)
New Jersey
(http://www.njstatelib.org/)
New Mexico
(http://www.stlib.state.mn.us/)
New York
(http://www.nysl.nysed.gov/)
North Carolina
(http://statelibrary.dcr.state.nc.us/)
North Dakota
(http://ndsl.lib.state.nd.us/)
Ohio
(http://winslo.state.oh.us/)
Oklahoma
(http://www.odl.state.ok.us/)
Oregon
(http://oregon.gov/OSL/)
Pennsylvania
(http://www.statelibrary.state.pa.us/libraries/)

Rhode Island
(http://www.olis.ri.gov/)
South Carolina
(http://www.statelibrary.sc.gov/)
South Dakota
(http://www.sdstatelibrary.com/)
Tennessee
(http://www.tennessee.gov/tsla/)
Texas
(http://www.tsl.state.tx.us/)
Utah
(http://library.ut.gov/index.html/)
Vermont
(http://dol.state.vt.us/)
Virginia
(http://www.lva.lib.va.us/)
Washington
(http://www.secstate.was.gov/library/)
West Virginia
(http://librarycommission/lib.wv.us/)
Wisconsin
(http://www.dpi.state.wi.us/dltcl/pld/)
Wyoming
(http://www-wsl.state.wy.us/)

About the Editors and Contributors

The affiliations of the editors and contributors are as of the time the articles were written.

Ronald **Adams**, technology assessment consultant, New York, New York.

Ben **Adler**, urban leaders fellow, Next American City, Inc., Philadelphia, Pennsylvania.

Brian **Baker**, freelance journalist, Glasgow, Scotland.

Tom **Brandes**, freelance writer, Plymouth, Minnesota.

Terry **Brewer**, freelance writer and independent management consultant, New York, New York.

Dan **Burden**, co-founder and director of innovation and inspiration, Walkable and Livable Communities Institute, Port Townsend, Washington.

Cleto **Carlini**, manager, Mobility Department, City of Bologna, Emilia-Romagna Region, Italy.

Center for Design Excellence is based in Alexandria, Virginia.

Center for New Urbanism is based in Alexandria, Virginia.

Ryan **Chin**, managing director and research scientist, City Science Initiative, Media Lab, Massachusetts Institute of Technology, Cambridge, Massachusetts.

Joan **Clos**, executive director, Urban Transport Section and Policy Analysis Branch, UN-Habitat, Nairoba, Kenya.

Committee on Intelligent Transport, World Road Association (PIARC) is based in Paris, France.

Bertrand **Delanoe**, mayor, City of Paris, France.

Ellen **Dunham-Jones**, professor of architecture and urban design, School of Architecture, Georgia Institute of Technology, Atlanta, Georgia.

Faisal **Durrani**, analyst, Landmark Advisory Co., Inc., Dubai, Emirate of Dubai, United Arab Emirates.

EcoMobility Alliance, ICLEI—Local Governments for Sustainability is based in Oakland, California.

Luuk **Eickmans**, associate member, African Bicycle Network, Kisumu, Kenya, Africa.

Yasser **Elsheshtawy**, associate professor, Department of Architecture, College of Engineering, University of Abu Dhabi, United Arab Emirates.

Michael **Glotz-Richter**, sustainable mobility expert, City of Bremen, State of Bremen, Germany.

Kenneth W. **Harris**, chairman, The Consilience Group, LLC, Memphis, Tennessee.

Michael **Horn**, aerospace scientist (retired), Corporate Research Center, Northrop Grumman Corporation, Falls Church, Virginia.

Lawrence (Larry) **Houstoun**, partner, BID Experts, Philadelphia, Pennsylvania.

Guenter **Karl**, acting chief, Partners and Youth Branch, UN-Habitat, United Nations, Nairobi, Kenya, Africa.

Roger L. **Kemp**, Ph.D., ICMA-CM, city manager, distinguished adjunct professor, practitioner in residence, and lecturer, in cities and at universities on both coasts of the United

States—California, Connecticut, and New Jersey, for more than 25 years.

Santhosh **Kodukula,** EcoMobility officer, EcoMobility Alliance, ICLEI—Local Governments for Sustainability, Bonn, North Rhine-Westphalia, Germany.

Paul **Lukez,** founder and president, Paul Lukez Architecture, Sommerville, Massachusetts.

Silvia **Marchesi**, project assistant, EcoMobility Alliance, ICLEI—Local Governments for Sustainability, Bonn, North Rhine-Westphalia, Germany.

Thomas **Melin**, coordinator, Human Settlements Program, Global Division, United Nations, Nairobi, Nairobi County, Kenya.

Jonathan D. **Miller**, partner, Miller and Ryan, LLC, New York, New York.

Dae-Hong **Minn**, principal, DeStefano & Partners, Ltd., Chicago, Illinois.

Felipe **Morales**, project manager, Urban Development Institute, Bogotá, Colombia.

Jim **Motavalli**, freelance journalist, author, and speaker, Bridgeport, Connecticut.

Imelda **Nasei**, associate member, African Bicycle Network, Nairobi, Kenya, Africa.

Carlos Felipe **Pardo**, technical advisor, Urban Development Institute, Bogotá, Colombia.

Seong Jae **Park**, climate data assistant, Seoul Metropolitan Government, Seoul, Gyeonggi Province, South Korea.

Hana **Peters**, EcoMobility assistant, EcoMobility Alliance, ICLEI—Local Governments for Sustainability, Bonn, North Rhine-Westphalia, Germany.

Sarah Jo **Peterson**, senior research associate, Urban Land Institute/Curtis Regional Infrastructure Project, Urban Land Institute, Washington, D.C.

Tommy **Poulsen**, chief executive, Municipality of Allerod, Zealand, Denmark.

Project for Public Spaces is based in New York, New York.

Troy **Russ**, principal and director, Urban Design and Transportation Service Group, Glatting Jackson Kercher Anglin Inc., Orlando, Florida.

Christian **Ryden**, director, Department of Transport Planning, City of Lund, Sweden.

Brad **Scheib**, community planner and vice president, Hoisington Koegler Group Inc., Minneapolis, Minnesota.

Angie **Schmitt**, manager, Street Blog Network, Streetblog Capitol Hill, OpenPlans, Washington, D.C.

Daniel **Seleanu**, research writer, Landmark Advisory Co., Inc., Dubai, Emirate of Dubai, United Arab Emirates.

Michael **Shiffer**, vice president, Planning and Policy, TransLink (South Coast British Columbia Transportation Authority), New Westminster, British Columbia, Canada.

Tanya **Snyder**, editor, Street Blog Network, Streetblog Capitol Hill, OpenPlans, Washington, D.C.

Jeffrey **Spivak**, senior research analyst, HNTB Corporation, Kansas City, Missouri.

Carl J. **Stephani**, MRP, ICMA-CM, has worked for cities, counties, and regional governments in New York, New Mexico, California, Oregon, Colorado, and Connecticut, during his distinguished public service career.

Todd **Litman**, founder and director, Victoria Transport Policy Institute, Vancouver, British Columbia, Canada.

Gary **Toth**, senior director, Transportation Initiatives, Project for Public Spaces, New York, New York.

Polly **Trottenberg**, commissioner, Department of Transportation, City of New York, New York, New York.

Seth **Ullman,** transportation associate, Project for Public Spaces, New York, New York.

Kate **White**, executive director, Urban Land Institute, San Francisco, California.

June **Williamson**, associate professor, School of Architecture, The City College of New York, New York, New York.

Lars **Wilms**, chief executive, Municipality of Egedal, Etenlose, Denmark.

Index

www.ingramcontent.com/pod-product-compliance
Lightning Source LLC
Chambersburg PA
CBHW080551270326
41929CB00019B/3264